Praise for Julie Morgenstern and
Never Check E-mail in the Morning

"As someone who is always one stack of papers or one missed meeting away from being on top of things, I found *Never Check E-mail in the Morning* invaluable."

—Macus Buckingham, coauthor of *First, Break All the Rules* and *Now , Discover Your Strengths*

"Morgenstern is a house whisperer and able to tame the most tangled mess, all the while calming and enchanting the person trapped beneath its crushing weight."

—Lisa Kogan, O, *The Oprah Magazine*

"This book is brimming with great ideas for making our working lives better. And when work is working for us, that's when we can serve ourselves and others best."

—Ken Blanchard, coauthor of *The One Minute Manager*® and *The On-Time, On-Target Manager*

"I have experienced the magic and mystery of Julie firsthand. Magic because she makes the complex so simple. Mystery because she makes it look easy. And it is! These tips and strategies can help you be more productive and efficient—immediately."

—Cathie Black, president of Hearst Magazines

"Wow! What a great book. Here in one place you learn how to get organized and get more done, faster than you ever thought possible. This is a handbook for personal success."

—Brian Tracy, author of *Time Power*

"Put this book in the hands of your friends, colleagues, and employees and you will give them the gift of more time, efficiency, and work smarts. You cannot afford to be without this book."

—Barbara Corcoran, founder, the Corcoran Group

"If you're like me, you're probably sick and tired of the Dilbert-eye view of the world of work. The good news is, there's an alternative. Work can be meaningful, productive, worthwhile, even fun. Want to know how? Read this book! Real help is inside these covers."

—Alan M. Webber, founding editor, *Fast Company*

"Julie Morgenstern has created another island of sanity in an increasingly chaotic sea of physical and informational clutter. Her advice is grounding, cheering, and subtly life-changing."
— Martha Beck, author of *Finding Your Own North Star: Claiming the Life You Were Meant to Live*

"Julie Morgenstern is one smart woman, and this is one smart book you won't want to do without. Julie has the indelible ability to break things down into concrete, achievable steps. She makes the work of work clear and puts you at the helm of your ship—at the top of your game—in-step, balanced and alive!"
— Laura Berman Fortgang, author of *Now What? 90 Days to a New Life Direction* and *Living Your Best Life*

"Apply the information in *Never Check E-mail in the Morning* to catapult your efficiency to unprecedented heights. If you want to see a dramatic improvement in your performance, this is your book."
— Rosalene Glickman, Ph.D., author of *Optimal Thinking: How to Be Your Best Self*

"Having counseled thousands of business people over the last twenty-six years for the U.S. Small Business Administration, I can assure you that Julie Morgenstern's book *Never Check E-mail in the Morning* is a must-read for everyone facing the pressures of the modern work world."
— Harry Lowenstein, former New York State SCORE district director, United States Small Business Administration

"A brilliant and original insight into work's essential survival skills. Julie Morgenstern makes work work for you."
— Dr. Judith Sills, author of *The Comfort Trap*

"Achieving success on the work and home fronts does not come easily—it takes a carefully designed plan. *Never Check E-mail in the Morning* helps readers develop that plan and stick to it. This is required reading for those who want to get and stay ahead in a challenging environment."
— Subha Barry, first vice president and head, Merrill Lynch Multicultural and Diversified Business Development Group

ALSO BY JULIE MORGENSTERN

Organizing from the Inside Out

Time Management from the Inside Out

The Teenager's Guide to Getting Organized

Never Check E-mail in the Morning

*and Other Unexpected Strategies for
Making Your Work Life Work*

JULIE MORGENSTERN

Featuring 34 Grab-and-Go Strategies for the New World of Work

A FIRESIDE BOOK
Published by Simon & Schuster
New York   London   Toronto   Sydney

Originally published as *Making Work Work*

FIRESIDE
Rockefeller Center
1230 Avenue of the Americas
New York, NY 10020

This Fireside Edition 2005

FIRESIDE and colophon are registered trademarks
of Simon & Schuster, Inc.

For information about special discounts for bulk purchases,
please contact Simon & Schuster Special Sales at 1-800-456-6798
or business@simonandschuster.com.

Designed by Katy Riegel

Manufactured in the United States of America

20 19 18 17 16 15 14 13 12

The Library of Congress has cataloged the hardcover edition as follows:
Morgenstern, Julie.
    Making work work : new strategies for surviving and thriving at the office /
Julie Morgenstern.
        p. cm.
    "A Fireside Book."
    1. Paperwork (Office practice)—Management. 2. Time management.
3. Office management. I. Title.
HF5547.15.M67 2004
650.1—dc22   2004042901

ISBN-13: 978-0-7432-5087-0
ISBN-10:   0-7432-5087-7
ISBN-13: 978-0-7432-5088-7 (pbk)
ISBN-10:   0-7432-5088-5 (pbk)

To Joni Evans,
who saw the power in this book long ago
and lovingly cleared the path for its creation

Acknowledgments

WRITING THIS BOOK was an extraordinary and rewarding journey. The translation of an intuitive one-on-one process into a format accessible to readers took several years, the encouragement of many people, and the devotion of a talented team. It is my honor to express my appreciation to the people who played a vital role along the way.

First and foremost, my deepest gratitude goes to my clients, who continuously grant me the privilege of working with them. Thank you for letting me into your work lives, and for trusting me to share your dreams, struggles, and successes.

Early on, the following people generously provided lengthy interviews on their creative approaches to make work work. A world of thanks to Parry Aftab, Paul Argenti, Barbara Comforti, Hal Denton, Jim Eikner, Lisa Lee Freeman, Robin Gillespie, Faith Hallem, Sonia Kiman, Lisa and John LaVecchia, Susan Merry, Jean Francois Pilon, Ellen Shankman, Dawn Sharp, and Maureen Starr for sharing your very inspiring experiences.

My agent, Joni Evans, shepherded this book into existence, so much so that I dedicated the book to her. Thank you for believing in me, advising me so wisely every step of the way, and for inspiring my very best work.

Tremendous gratitude to my editor, Doris Cooper, at Simon and Schuster for her steadfast devotion to this project. I am so grateful for your skillful editorial direction, and for giving me the time to bring this book to its full development.

One couldn't ask for a more committed, skillful team than the wonderful people at Simon & Schuster, who embraced this project with gusto from the beginning. Thank you to Mark Gompertz, Trish Todd, Chris Lloreda, Carolyn Reidy, Marcia Burch, and London King for your tremendous support. And to Cherlynne Li, Brian Blatz, Nancy Inglis, and Sara Schapiro for producing such a wonderful book.

Deep gratitude to my assistant, Cloe Axelson, who worked side by side with me making sure every page said exactly what I wanted. Thank you for bringing out the best in me, and inspiring me to trust my truth.

For his structural wizardry as I neared the finish line, I thank John McCarty, a master of moving mountains with remarkable speed. And to Ellen Dreisen, who deftly provided research assistance, along with her friendship and a loving shot in the arm when I needed it most.

Thank you to my readers: Roland Axelson, Anna Sutherland, Eliot Kaplan, Ellen Kosloff, Lisa LaVecchia, JJ Miller, David Morgenstern, Gordon Rothman, Sara Scrymser, and Charlotte Sturtz for so generously sharing your time, unique points of view, and invaluable feedback on the manuscript. You each helped make this a better book.

A universe of appreciation to my staff at Julie Morgenstern, Inc.: Anna Hicks, Ellen Kosloff, and Diana Petrushevskaya, who kept the business going so that I was free to spend the majority of my time writing. To Ross McLean and Miron Dion-Arivas of EasyComp, for keeping the computers humming. And to Carol Crespo and Lee Harris of HarrisMedia for the greatest of friendships and most extraordinary of Web site service.

Immeasurable gratitude to Oprah, for your loving embrace and for setting the bar with such grace. To the Rolls-Royce of editors, writers, and staff at *O, The Oprah Magazine;* the remarkably talented Amy Gross, Gayle King, Sudie Redmond, Valerie Monroe, Pat Towers, Lisa Kogan, Liz Brody, and Susan Chumsky. Thank you for teaching me to be a better writer. An extra special thank you to Dawn Kopfel, my editor at *O Magazine,* along with Adam Glassman, Carla Frank, and Kim Guggenheim in the art department, for your tremendous support and flexibility while I was on book deadline.

For their very special contributions: Linda Jacobs, for helping me find and embrace my voice. Susan Moldow, for allowing me to share our process. Urban Mulvehill, for providing me with sage advice and calm support. Alex Linden, for being there, when it really counts. Mercedes Carlton, Sara Brant, and Connie Arroyo, for so brilliantly translating my work to the Web. To Harry Lowenstein of SCORE, for his tremendous support. And to the memory of my SCORE mentor Irwin Coplin—suddenly lost and whom I still miss.

Great appreciation and much love to my amazing circle of friends and family for keeping me laughing, loved, encouraged, and in balance as I do my work.

And above all to my daughter, Jessi, who graduated from high school and launched her dance career during the time span in which I wrote this book. As you get older, you continue to enrich my life in ways beyond description. I feel so privileged to be your mom—you are a constant source of joy, love, laughter, and pride.

Contents

Competency Four
Create the Time to Get Things Done
95

Competency Five
Control the Nibblers
115

Competency Six
Organize at the Speed of Change
141

Competency Seven
Master Delegation
167

Competency Eight
Work Well with Others
191

Competency Nine
Leverage Your Value
215

Index
241

Never Check E-mail in the

Morning

Introduction

WELCOME TO THE
NEW WORLD OF WORK

Rita is hearty and tenacious, with a powerful presence and an air of resolve. A brilliant strategic thinker with years of experience and an eye for details, she takes tremendous pride in her work. Upon starting her job as vice president of strategic marketing at a premier ad agency, she was exuberant. Her fresh perspective helped her make a visible contribution right away: within six months of her coming on board, the agency broke into a whole new market, landed four huge accounts, and created major buzz in the industry. By the end of her first year, the company had won two prestigious awards and was beginning to attract the brightest designers and salespeople in the business.

Rita loved her job and was great at it. Her coworkers and boss appreciated her efforts, and Rita felt confident and in control. Her daily activities provided an outlet to showcase her talents—and getting the work done left her with feelings of satisfaction, fulfillment, and accomplishment. In a phrase: *Work was working*. Sounds great, doesn't it?

At some point, she can't remember when, Rita began to drown. Her to-do list got longer and longer, as did her days. Her family would call, sometimes at ten at night, to find her still toiling at her desk. Rita was snared in all breeds of daily details and drudgery—solving tedious production problems and assembling complicated advertising reports. Meetings devoured her day. Sorting through her in-box required a Herculean effort. Her office became a Hoover Dam—piles of work so literally congested her space that what went in might never come out.

No matter how long or how hard Rita worked, she could never get to the bottom of her mile-long to-do list. Rita felt sidetracked by work that didn't draw on her talents and strengths. By the time she called me in for help, her confidence had waned, her performance had plummeted, her brain was fried. Overwhelmed and pulled in a million directions at once, she asked, what more could she possibly do? In the hustle and bustle of the modern-day workplace, she felt stuck, unproductive, and hopeless. Frustrated and discouraged, Rita quietly wondered, "Is it me, or is it them?"

I am in the business of untangling messes. When a client calls me in to help sort out his work life, his head is usually swimming; he feels wound in a big knot. Like Rita, he feels a sense of responsibility but is unsure where he leaves off and where his company or coworkers come in. When work isn't working, the perplexing and commanding puzzle we are all faced with is, *Is it me or is it them?* Who, or what, is causing the meltdown? We wonder whether we're the ones who've somehow changed and are slipping, or if the work itself really has become impossible. Is there something we can do to correct the situation, or is it truly beyond our control?

It's not easy to succeed, much less thrive, in today's world of work. That's everyone's challenge. Change and speed are the orders of the day. The workplace is leaner, more competitive, and less secure. You may feel lucky just to have a job, let alone have time for a personal life. Workloads inflate to absurd proportions, a situation that is neither rewarding nor enjoyable nor puts you in your best light. It's easy to be gradually pulled into tasks that don't match your job description, make use of your particular expertise, or coincide with your goals. You long for the days when you could spend quality time with your family, get to the gym, feel relaxed during your time off. Like Rita, you may feel downtrodden and burned out. Work has become anything but fulfilling.

When Work Is Working

No matter what the industry or economic climate, there is a universal definition of when work *is* working.

Happiness at work involves liking what you're doing and being good at it—feeling appreciated, in control, successful, and in balance. When you get your work done, or at least conquer your most important tasks, you finish your day with a victorious sense of accomplishment. When you leave the office on time, and not three hours into your family's evening, or after breaking plans to go out with friends, you feel in control.

Does that seem like an impossibility?

It's not.

There are new skills and techniques needed to excel in the new world of work, and this book is dedicated to teaching them to you. My goal is to help you learn these techniques from the inside out—so that they become a part of you and the way you approach your work.

The Nine Competencies

During my seventeen years as a professional organizer, I've helped clients take control of their work lives in every industry and environment imaginable: publishing, law, government agencies, manufacturing, newsrooms, sports teams, and hospitals. I've consulted with executives and their assistants, salespeople and their managers, professors, librarians, graphic designers, and financial planners.

What I've found through my work with clients, and through careful observation of people on the job, is that the ability to thrive in the new world of work encompasses a very consistent set of skills. Together, mastering these "competencies" offer the key to surviving—*and thriving*—in the new work environment.

These skills will enable you to achieve the seemingly impossible—to boost your value and increase your job security, while *still* having time to have a personal life.

Recognizing the importance of these aptitudes, understanding their implications, and mastering the strategies behind each one will help you to excel in the tough new world of work, whether it's "you" or "them."

In unstable times, these competencies will ensure that you are, at the very least, the last man (or woman) standing. In flush times, they will help you seek, capture, and retain the perfect opportunity:

Competency 1   Embrace Your Work/Life Balance
Competency 2   Develop an Entrepreneurial Mindset
Competency 3   Choose the Most Important Tasks
Competency 4   Create the Time to Get Things Done
Competency 5   Control the Nibblers
Competency 6   Organize at the Speed of Change
Competency 7   Master Delegation
Competency 8   Work Well with Others
Competency 9   Leverage Your Value

The skills seem straightforward, but can be hard to implement. There are many obstacles—some are internal (you) and some are external (them). But whether the problem is you or them, you'll come to learn that the solution always lies within you.

At its core, this book is about your relationship to your work, combining psychology and practical techniques to help you take control, accomplish more, and be happy. People at every stage of their career can benefit from every one of the competencies, not just a few. It's a book that can be read, learned from, and then referred back to every time you get thrown off balance. This is a book that should be carried with you for the rest of your working life—no matter what position, industry, or circumstance you find yourself in.

How to Use This Book

SELF-ASSESSMENT

This brief quiz and diagnostic tool is essential reading for everyone. In less than thirty minutes, you'll get a benchmark score for measuring your progress as you work your way through the book. In addition, you'll begin to diagnose the obstacles to your performance (Is it *you*, or is it *them?*), zero in on problem areas, and identify which chapters in the book you may want to start with, or focus on.

COMPETENCIES

Each competency is a world unto itself—meant to be studied, mulled over, and plucked from. Each time you read a chapter, you are likely to find something new and practical, and in many cases life-changing. Mastering the competencies is an inside-out process. Small changes in your thinking or behavior can drastically alter the timbre of any situation. The adoption of even one technique, within any one competency, will make a huge impact on your work life.

The order of the competencies mirrors the individual consulting services I provide, starting on the inside, at the most basic, personal level, and moving on to the more complex issues of work relationships and the job itself. Organizing yourself is always the starting point, because by boosting your own productivity and abilities first, you gain the confidence and leverage to tackle more difficult issues.

You can choose to march through the competencies in the order I've presented them, or skip around, zeroing in on what you need at any given moment. But once you have read a competency, give yourself ample time to sit with, practice, and integrate the lessons.

REAL-LIFE ANECDOTES

Rita is the first of several characters we're going to follow as they wind their way through the sticky wicket of the modern workplace. Each character represents a client I've worked with (although the details have been fictionalized to spare their identities), and illustrates the real challenges we've faced and triumphed over together. As you read each competency, think about which characters you identify with and how their breakthroughs may inspire you.

YES, But . . . BOXES

Scattered throughout the book are classic obstacles to implementing the skills—individual situations, or ways of thinking, that will make it difficult for you to take action. I've included the most common points of resistance, and a diagnosis of whether the barrier is internal (it's YOU) or external (it's THEM). Practical solutions are provided to overcoming the hurdles in both cases.

SIDEBARS TO MANAGERS

Though the focus of this book is on what the individual can do to improve his own work situation, many of the techniques can be adopted to become departmental policies and practices. Managers are in a position to change systems and support their teams. Scattered throughout the book are sidebars with ideas on how to convert these individual principles into departmental or company-wide policies to help your entire staff work more efficiently.

Unraveling the Knots

When I began working with Rita, she was tied in such a tight knot that it was all I could do to loosen the strings a little in our first consultation. She felt as if she was in an impossible, desperate situation—stuck with no recourse but to grin and bear it. As Rita and I worked to rescue her from the deluge and identify the true source of the problem, we discovered (as is common) that the answer was a little bit of both—it was her, *and* it was them. Over the two years she'd been at her job, Rita's industry had changed. Advertising dollars had shrunk, clients demanded more with no guarantees of loyalty, and vendors were dropping like flies. Rita's old work habits, which had served her well in the past, were no longer quite as effective or relevant. By applying the nine competencies presented in this book (with her kicking and screaming at points along the way), she broke patterns that had been with her for years—and entered the new world of work with an upgraded skill set that made her feel productive. Work became meaningful again.

Working from the inside out with the reliable, methodical process taught in this book will help you feel less trapped and more in charge—you'll able to make a bad situation better, restore a formerly good situation to balance, or confidently search for a job that's a better fit for who you are. No matter what, if you read and follow even a third of the advice in this book, you will boost your clarity, confidence, and performance, and find a way to make work work.

That is my promise to you.

SELF-ASSESSMENT

Is It You . . . or Is It Them?

The Three Tiers

Several years ago, while flying home to New York from a business trip, I found myself sitting next to a trim, silver-haired man who emanated a striking sense of calm contentment. In his interactions with the flight attendants and other passengers, he was gracious and kind. There was a sparkle in his eye; he was quick to smile and dapper in his dress—the kind of guy who seemed to have figured out some of the secrets of life.

We got to talking, and I learned he owned a food-packaging company. Not a glamorous-sounding business, but one that he had made extremely successful. Seventy percent of the frozen foods you and I eat come in boxes manufactured by his company. He radiated quiet pride as he described how he built his company from the ground up, starting twenty years ago with two employees and now boasting a workforce of four hundred.

As I was in the midst of growing my own small company, I seized the opportunity to ask this successful man what he'd learned over the years about the problems, challenges, and rewards of managing others. How do you get the best performance out of each employee? How do you retain good people? What do you do if someone is not performing up to snuff?

He shared his approach. Employees fell into three tiers, he explained, and each group should be managed a little differently:

- **Top tier (20 percent).** These are the star performers and high achievers, who can appear in any position in the company. They are totally tuned in to the company's mission and make it flourish. Do everything you can to keep them happy and motivated, he advised me. They deserve all the extra attention and recognition you can afford.
- **Middle tier (60 percent).** Most employees, he explained, do a reliable, respectable, straightforward job. They aren't perfect, they make mistakes, but they are generally on target and aim to please. He told me they should be treated fairly and respectfully, and rewarded in normal, regular increments.
- **Bottom tier (20 percent).** These are the underperformers who rarely pull their weight, drag everyone else down, and don't care about their work. They're a bad match for your company, he explained. If you can't replace them right away, move them into low-stakes jobs until you can. Don't waste your efforts trying to fix them.

I've since learned that many bosses and managers follow a similar rule of thumb, with a few variations. Some speak of a 10:80:10 ratio, others divide it as 20:70:10. Regardless of the numbers, all tend to think in terms of a tiered system, which guides the time and resources they invest in their employees.

Of course, the only true security at work comes from being solidly in the top tier. But it's not as easy as it used to be to clamber up to the top. Fierce competition poses a great challenge, but what also makes it tricky is that the rules can change on you. If your industry changes focus, your old skills may not be so useful anymore. During tough times, what an employer can afford to provide even to top-tier employees may not be much, which can send a confusing message, making you wonder where you really stand.

WHAT MAKES FOR THE TOP TIER?

Placement on the tiered system results from a combination of performance and productivity, talent and efficiency. A supremely talented person who is unable to complete his work can't get into the top tier. (Competency 4 features someone with this issue.) On the other hand, a highly organized and efficient individual without the necessary talent or skills has limited value to her employer.

As both an employer and a consultant, I've observed that most top-tier employees share a few common traits.

They not only understand but truly believe in the company mission. They are able to connect their daily tasks to that vision to consistently deliver measurable results. They're in positions that bring out their best talents and skills, are confident about their own abilities, and are ready, willing, and able to go the extra mile. But they also keep their lives in balance, as we'll learn in Competency 1, so that they can replenish their energy and recharge their perspective for their work.

The good news is that what works for you, works for your employer. Understanding your role, making a significant contribution, and delivering measurable results is exactly what provides value to your company, and at the same time makes your job meaningful and satisfying.

WHERE DO YOU STAND?

Where do you think you fall right now—the top 20 percent, the middle 60 percent, or the bottom 20 percent? Where would you like to be?

To get a sense of where you might fall, answer the following quiz about your performance and relationship to your job. Your score provides a benchmark for evaluating your progress as you improve your work situation, and will help tell you where in this book to seek solutions.

Rate yourself from 5 (always true) to 1 (never true) on each of the fourteen questions, circling the answer that most closely represents your current reality. Don't belabor your answers. This quick assessment shouldn't take you more than ten minutes to complete.

Respond from your gut, and be honest! No one else has to see what you write but you. The key is to get the truth out—not necessarily to your peers or to your boss, but to yourself. There's great re-

---

REALITY CHECK

A skewed view of your performance at work puts you at a disadvantage. Sometimes we deny our flaws; other times we're so hard on ourselves, we can't see our own strengths. If you're feeling courageous and want a really honest snapshot of your performance at work, ask a trusted coworker or boss to fill out this assessment about you. Compare your answers to see how your views line up.

lief in facing the truth. Denial just eats you alive. Rest assured that whatever imbalance you are feeling, once we know what the problems are, this book will help you find the solution. Once we have a realistic gauge on your work performance, we'll delve deeper to diagnose that looming question ringing in your ears—"Is it me, or is it them?"

Before any of that can happen, though, you need to be brutally honest with yourself . . . NOW.

1. When overloaded, are you easily able to prioritize and focus in on the most critical tasks?

1	2	3	4	5
Never	Rarely	Sometimes	Usually	Always

2. Do you turn work around quickly, rather than letting it get backed up on your desk?

1	2	3	4	5
Never	Rarely	Sometimes	Usually	Always

3. Do you have a good way of tracking your to-dos?

1	2	3	4	5
Never	Rarely	Sometimes	Usually	Always

4. Do you have a general structure to your day or week that enables you to feel in control of when you do things?

1	2	3	4	5
Never	Rarely	Sometimes	Usually	Always

5. Are you physically organized, keeping papers, computer documents, contact information, and work materials in order and at your fingertips?

1	2	3	4	5
Never	Rarely	Sometimes	Usually	Always

6. Do you have productive, efficient working relationships with your coworkers, assistant, direct reports, boss?

1	2	3	4	5
Never	Rarely	Sometimes	Usually	Always

7. Are you generally pleased with your work/life balance?

1	2	3	4	5
Never	Rarely	Sometimes	Usually	Always

8. Can you clearly identify the core responsibilities of your job?

1	2	3	4	5
Never	Rarely	Sometimes	Usually	Always

9. Do you feel secure in your ability to perform in each area of your key responsibilities?

1	2	3	4	5
Never	Rarely	Sometimes	Usually	Always

10. Can you easily let go of low-priority items, without guilt?

1	2	3	4	5
Never	Rarely	Sometimes	Usually	Always

11. Do you understand and believe in the mission of your company?

1	2	3	4	5
Never	Rarely	Sometimes	Usually	Always

12. Do you know what your most valuable contribution is? What makes you unique?

1	2	3	4	5
Never	Rarely	Sometimes	Usually	Always

13. Is your most valuable contribution what your employer wants?

1	2	3	4	5
Never	Rarely	Sometimes	Usually	Always

14. Do you keep yourself current in the expertise required by your job?

1	2	3	4	5
Never	Rarely	Sometimes	Usually	Always

SCORE YOURSELF

Okay, take a breath, then total your answers for a grand total starting score, which serves as your benchmark for beginning this book. You can take this same performance assessment at periodic intervals throughout the book, to check your progress. Here is what your score means:

- **14–30 points:** Drowning. Hang on. You are struggling to keep your head above water, and barely making it. You're not getting much done, and are probably frustrating yourself and your coworkers, boss, family, and friends. You feel terribly out of alignment, your morale is low, and you may be on the verge of losing your job (or quitting!) before you've found a better fit. STOP—turn immediately to Competencies 1 and 4 for a rescue mission, and then explore the rest of the book in the following order: Competencies 3, 6, 5, 2, 7, 8, 9.

- **31–50 points:** Treading water. You're mostly holding it together, but it's a constant struggle. You get your most critical tasks done, but beyond that, many items (including your personal life) don't get the attention they deserve. You feel under constant pressure and stress, and are often filled with self-doubt. Follow the competencies in order (1, 2, 3, etc.), as they will provide relief in the way you are most likely to need it.
- **51–70 points:** Doing the breast stroke. Good for you. You have excellent organizing and time-management skills, and people can count on you to deliver. You feel pretty much in alignment with your job, appreciated, and confident in your abilities. Of course, you're always looking for ways to become more efficient, and seeking new strategies to stay on top of your game. Jump ahead to Competency 9, and then dip in and out of the competencies in any order that feels appropriate to you—to reinforce, refine, and expand your existing skills.

Moving up the Tiers

So what does it take to increase your score? Do you have to sign your life away in blood? Must you move into the office and leave your personal life behind? Absolutely not. The good news is, we are looking at a win-win. The very same abilities that improve your value to your company offer the freedom to enjoy your work AND have a personal life. And it all boils down to the nine competencies in this book.

Whether it's you or them, the other good news is that you are in control. If it's you, you can change and improve your habits and approaches to your job. If it's them, you need to stop fighting the reality, and find your way around it. It's important to determine whether it's you or them, so that you can pinpoint the problem and zoom in on a quick, decisive solution.

Half of the assessment questions assessed the strength of your organizational systems and productivity. The other seven questions focus on your relationship to your job—how much ownership, clarity, and alignment you feel, how in tune you are with the company's mission, the strength of your working relationships, and your satisfaction with your work/life balance.

Improving Your Own Productivity

If you scored low on questions 1, 2, 3, 4, 5, 10, or 14, you are struggling with your productivity. In the bottom-line world of work, productivity is king. For institutions large and small, nonprofit and commercial, it's all about getting things done. But let's face it, your productivity doesn't only please your employer; getting things done makes you happy too. It feels terrible to have large backlogs of work. Nothing feels better than being on top of your work.

Do you spend too much time on e-mail or going to unimportant meetings? Mopping up other people's mistakes or filling out cumbersome paperwork? Is your time consumed by overly chatty coworkers, fixing computer problems (or spending hours on hold with the tech department), or searching for misplaced paperwork or phone numbers?

What do you wish you were able to take care of more often? What do you feel guilty about neglecting?

For example, maybe you spend more time drumming up new business than managing your staff. Or maybe you get to all your urgent tasks, but never get around to long-term projects. What piles up while you are busy tending to crises or other "stuff"?

Given the fact that modern-day workloads frequently exceed our capacity to produce, it's important to determine if the things you are ignoring are nice but not necessary—or really have an impact on the company's bottom line and your ability to produce a very high work product.

What's standing in your way? Is it you or is it them?

It Could Be *YOU* If:

- You don't plan well.
- You lack confidence on some tasks.
- You are unable to prioritize.
- You're a perfectionist.
- You feel guilty saying no.
- You gravitate toward quick, easy tasks.
- You're poor at estimating how long things take.

- You're physically disorganized.
- You start many things, finish none.

It Could Be *THEM* If:

- Your boss, customers, or coworkers are always in crisis mode.
- Your boss is a perfectionist.
- The corporate culture is driven by fear.
- The company is understaffed, requiring you to pick up slack.
- Coworkers are not pulling their own weight.
- Meetings are poorly run.
- You are lacking materials or direction from leadership.
- You have an unrealistic workload.
- You work in an interruption-rich environment.

RECOMMENDED COMPETENCIES

Competency 3, "Choose the Most Important Tasks"
Competency 4, "Create the Time to Get Things Done"
Competency 5, "Control the Nibblers"
Competency 6, "Organize at the Speed of Change"

Improving Your Relationship to Your Job

If you scored low on questions 6, 7, 8, 9, 11, 12, or 13, your relationship to your job is askew.

Are you aware of your most valuable contribution on the job? Everyone brings different talents, knowledge, experience, people skills, and work style to a job. Can you identify what distinguishes you from your coworkers? Why did your employer hire you? Do you possess a particular technical knowledge? Do you have a unique level of experience? Is it your willingness to work flexible hours? What would the company lose if you were gone? In other words, what makes you *you*?

Is your best contribution what your employer is actually asking from you? This is a tough yet very important question to address. I don't mean what you *think* she wants from you (or should want), but what she *does* want. There's a big difference. And you will know it immediately if you keep trying to get recognition for some accomplishment but are consistently ignored, or even argued with.

How honest are you about your weaknesses on the job? Are you investing the time to improve and expand your skill set? Maybe you're good with people but terrible at numbers; or great at brainstorming but awful at following through. Has your supervisor mentioned that you need to improve, or are your weaknesses your own little secret? Be honest with yourself here. As difficult and painful as that can be at first, knowing and facing the facts can provide relief— and position you to do something about them, which may involve reaching out for help or support, or delegating a task to someone who is better at it than you. But ignoring or denying or trying to hide your weaknesses can make you unsafe and insecure in your job.

Most important, are you able to clearly define the core responsibilities of your job, and divide your work into three to five broad categories? For example, a salesperson *pursues leads, prepares contracts, monitors clients, submits reports;* an administrative assistant *coordinates travel, keeps daily schedules, drafts letters, screens phone calls.*

Keep in mind that there is a difference between core responsibilities and tasks. Phone calls, e-mail, and attending meetings are *not* core responsibilities—those are simply tasks, each of which can be subsumed into an area of responsibility.

The more clear and in alignment you are on your job, your value, your expertise, and your balance, the happier you will be.

What's holding you back? Is it you or is it them?

It Could Be *YOU* If:

- You lack the ability to see the big picture.
- You're caught in the daily details.
- You don't like your role.
- You feel like a victim.
- You have a fear of tooting your own horn.
- You lack confidence.
- You are not the best judge of your own abilities.
- You took the wrong job.
- You have poor people skills.
- You feel guilty breaking away from work.

It Could Be *THEM* If:

- Your job description keeps changing.
- The company is in transition.
- Your industry is rapidly changing.
- Your boss forgets what he's asked you to do.

- Your boss is inexpressive and short on feedback.
- There is a lack of honesty in performance reviews.
- The boss or culture is hypercritical.
- The company has different values from yours.
- There's a change in management.
- Your company makes unrealistic demands.
- The culture is cutthroat.
- There's a pressure for face time.
- The organization is disorganized.

RECOMMENDED COMPETENCIES

Competency 1, "Embrace Your Work/Life Balance"
Competency 2, "Develop an Entrepreneurial Mindset"
Competency 7, "Master Delegation"
Competency 8, "Work Well with Others"
Competency 9, "Leverage Your Value"

By simply following the program in this book, you will be able to monitor the improvement in your score, so that you will move yourself up the tiers, be able to rally for that promotion, improve upon your working relationships, reconfigure your work/life balance, and achieve your career goals.

Just like riding a bike, learning a piece of software, or becoming a better presenter, each of these competencies is a learnable skill. They are your gateway to improving your position at work. Mastering them will boost your value to your organization—and, most important, will make you feel much happier and at peace at work.

So, come on, let's move you up the tiers. Let's start changing your

---

TIPS FROM THE MASTERS

When you're a highly motivated and ambitious person, you usually rise to the top and you get used to being a star. Wherever you go, you come out smelling like a rose. But suddenly you get to a certain level and you look around and there are people who are twice as ambitious as you, twice as smart, twice as experienced. And you either can die and shrivel away, or you can say, "Now I have to compete at another level. I'm just going to kick it up a notch."

—Lucy L., TV producer

old approaches to work and those old patterns that have been with you for years, but which are now no longer relevant.

It's time to upgrade your skill set so you can survive, *thrive,* and enjoy yourself in this challenging but exciting new world of work.

Let's get to it.

One

EMBRACE YOUR WORK/
LIFE BALANCE

PICTURE THIS: You're hanging off the side of a cliff by your fingertips. Gravity is pulling, and you are slipping down, down, down. You see a large rock jutting out just above your hand. Your only chance of survival is to let go of the narrow ledge you're sliding off and quickly grab hold of that big rock above. For one split second, you won't be holding on to anything at all—you'll be suspended in midair. What would you do?

RITA

Rita, an overstressed advertising executive, is in this situation. Forever scrambling to keep her head above water, she worked crazily long hours (7:30 A.M.–9 P.M. most nights), often lugging projects home with her on the weekends. Rita had a tremendous work ethic—but she was so caught up in a sense of responsibility to her company and job survival that she felt too guilty to take time off for herself. Yet she never even grazed the bottom of her to-do list.

Rita felt terrible. She'd gained forty pounds, and it was no wonder—she hadn't gotten near the gym in over a year. Every afternoon, with her energy and spirits flagging, she'd keep herself going with sweet snacks and diet soda. Often, she didn't eat dinner until 11 P.M. She suffered from chronic back pain, and her doctor warned that if she didn't begin to lose weight and exercise regularly, her health would be at risk.

Rita kept promising her doctor that she'd start taking better care of herself, just as soon as she got on top of her workload.

For many people, breaking away from the gravitational pull of work is extremely difficult. In fact, it's counterintuitive. You'd think that if you are struggling at work, you should try to fix things on the job first. Certainly, improving your performance at the office will give you more leverage in asking for some work/life balance benefits, like extra time off. So why would I make "Embrace Your Work/Life Balance" the *first* competency rather than the last?

Because in the crazy, sped-up, pressure-cooker world of work, our personal lives are usually the first thing we sacrifice. That puts us in a precarious situation—when our balance is off, our performance suffers, along with our happiness and motivation.

If you are feeling overworked, exhausted, and depleted, the *first* step is to let go at work and take care of yourself. Though it may feel like breaking away from the office could be deadly to your career, embracing your work/life balance, even with something as simple and straightforward as catching up on your sleep, is actually one of the most effective ways to improve your productivity on the job.

NOT JUST NICE, BUT NECESSARY

Mastering your work/life balance is not just a nice idea—it's necessary. The extraordinary stresses of today's workplace *require* you to

DID YOU KNOW?

We are workaholics by nature. According to Harvard economist Juliet Schor, the average American works 163 additional hours, or one month a year, more today than in 1969 ("The Overworked American"). The Employee Benefits Research Institute tells us that Americans work more hours per year than any other industrialized nation—putting in an average of 6.5 weeks longer than the French workforce, and 8 weeks longer than Germany's. Lest we forget, the United States is the only industrialized country without a government mandate on vacation time.

take control of your work/life balance and to make sure that the time off you do have is rewarding, refreshing, and energizing. Creating a vibrant personal life is one of the best investments you can make in your work! If you don't stop to reclaim your work/life balance first, you will never have the energy, creativity, and wherewithal to learn any of the other competencies presented in this book—let alone improve your work performance.

The concept of reclaiming a balance between work and life may strike you as a fantasy, impossible under the stresses of the modern workplace. It's not.

TOP-TIER PERFORMERS ARE COMMITTED TO THEIR WORK/LIFE BALANCE

In every industry I consult in, I've noticed that the top-tier performers are deeply committed to their work/life balance. They may be working long hours, but they are very thoughtful about their leisure, so that they make excellent use of time away from the office. This is a critical skill—*especially* if you're working long hours, because you have fewer hours to play with in the first place.

The most successful workers create a balance that ensures they are energized, refreshed, and renewed every day. Their balancing act isn't perfect, and it requires constant attention—but they are vigilant about maintaining that balance, because they appreciate the continuity between home and rest, work and productivity.

A solid work/life balance will provide you with:

- **Energy.** The more energized you are, the more productive you will actually be. When you are burned out, you move more slowly. You may not realize it because your judgment is off, but simple tasks can take two, three, four times longer.
- **Accuracy.** When you are rested, refreshed, and in balance, you think more clearly, making better, swifter choices. You don't waste time doing work over, or correcting mistakes.
- **Innovation.** The best ideas often come when you step away from your work and stop staring at a problem. A change in environment or activity—going for a drive, visiting a museum, or just taking a shower—often stimulates innovation, enabling you to solve problems in new ways.
- **Patience.** A rewarding, enjoyable life outside work makes it easier to tolerate frustrations at work. It's easy to lose perspective when you are working fourteen-hour days—little problems can become treacherous monsters.

- **Motivation.** Being in balance enhances your overall quality of life, which makes you feel fulfilled and enlivened with a sense of purpose. By creating a life that you enjoy, you can flip the switch—and begin "working to live," instead of "living to work."

ARE *YOU* SLIPPING OFF THE EDGE?

How far off balance are you? Are you hanging on with both hands, your fingers, or just your fingertips? Circle True (T) or False (F) for the following eleven questions and find out how close you are to the edge:

T F I'm constantly feeling sleep-deprived. Artificial stimulants like sugar and caffeine are the primary way I keep myself going.

T F Things take far longer to do than they used to—I'm operating in slow motion. It's hard to make decisions, think clearly, prioritize. Sometimes I'm in a daze.

T F My fuse is very short—I've become cranky and quick to anger over even the smallest annoyances.

T F I've gotten out of shape and/or gained weight because I have no time to exercise or eat properly.

T F I haven't been to the doctor in ages—just too busy at work.

T F Vacation! What's that? I sometimes fantasize about getting sick, just so I can take a break.

T F Many of my friends and family are often hurt or disappointed because I'm never around.

T F I'm putting too much stock in work—it's my only source of recognition and self-worth.

T F I used to love (gardening, painting, listening to music—fill in the blank with your favorite pastime), but I don't have the energy to enjoy it anymore.

T F I'm always too tired to do anything other than collapse at night and weekends. I'm in a constant state of exhaustion.

T F During the workday, I have to steal time for myself—doing personal e-mail, calls, taking a shopping detour after lunch—because I have no time for myself otherwise, what with the twelve- to fourteen-hour days I'm putting in.

SCORING: How many Trues did you circle?

9–11   Danger zone—need rescuing

5–8   Losing your grip

1–4   Good balance—keep it up

Obviously, everyone works hard these days . . . and finding time for a personal life is a challenge we all face. Mastering your work/life balance will give you the incentive to acquire the rest of the competencies in this book, and be a happy and successful top-tier performer.

Grab-and-Go Strategy #1
Let Go and Grab Hold

When you are exhausted and depleted and don't know where you'll find energy to tackle that next project—take a leap into the unknown. Trust that work will survive without you for an hour, an evening, or a weekend. You must embrace the fact that sometimes your best hope for getting to the bottom of your to-do list is to let go and take care of yourself personally.

What constitutes "balance"? Being in balance is about energy management—about spending your time on things that restore and relax you, knowing what springs you back up to eight cylinders when your engine is beginning to cough and choke. It's about identifying when you're close to your breaking point, then making the choice to quit for the day while you're still ahead. If you work so long and so hard that it's all you can do to crawl home and spend the evening on the couch staring out the window at a fire hydrant as reruns of *The Golden Girls* drone on and on, it's no wonder you are feeling burned out.

Everyone's idea of "being in balance" is a little different. Some people are thrilled with a Sunday to themselves once a month, while others can't imagine life with fewer than four weeks of vacation a year. Some people find joy in gardening, while others just want to curl up with a good book every night. For parents, balance may mean time with their kids; for singles, it might constitute time at a spa with friends. The commonality among us is the guilt—no matter how we define balance, most people believe we should be responsible to work before ourselves.

Yet you have everything to gain and nothing to lose from letting go of that ledge and grabbing hold of that rock above.

Two months ago I found myself unexpectedly delayed at the At-lanta airport. I was returning from a demanding three-day busi-ness trip, which involved a TV appearance, a book signing, and research for an upcoming article. It was a Saturday evening, and I was absolutely exhausted. My mind was fried. I was running on empty.

As a result of being out of the office for four days, I had a stack of writing assignments that required my attention. All of those tasks were deadline-driven, all were important, and each required enormous creative thought and focus. Should I push through the exhaustion? I'm a workhorse; I could pull it off. It was tempting.

But the truth was that in my depleted state, I knew it would take me two to four times longer to do any one of those writing jobs than if I were rested. As much as I craved the relief of cross-ing some of those items off my to-do list, I decided to recharge instead—to let go and regrab.

But now I needed to figure out the best choice for the moment—what would refresh, energize, and renew me? What was the most solid rock jutting out above? Was it to stare into space and do nothing? (Nah, not so refreshing.) Take a catnap? (No. Those airport terminal seats are too uncomfortable—plus I'd worry about missing my flight.) Escape into the novel I was reading? (Nope—too tired to concentrate.)

My choice? A snack—nothing sugary, but something physi-cally fortifying and sinful. For the first time in twenty years I in-dulged in the delicious juicy crispness of Popeye's fried chicken. And watched two boys, also delayed, share their toys on the floor. Ahhh . . . a transporting escape. I crept into bed so late on Saturday night that all I did was sleep on Sunday. But by Monday, I was refreshed, and I knocked out three assignments by 1 P.M.!

You may fear that letting go and regrabbing requires drastic mea-sures. You may fantasize about quitting your job, changing careers, moving to a desert island, seeking a more peaceful existence. But if you take care of yourself in little ways on a consistent basis, reclaim-ing your balance does *not* call for radically altering your life. The truth is, even if you do make a huge change, you may not be able to leave your hard-driving impulses behind.

Look at this e-mail sent to me from one of my readers:

Dear Julie:

I'm a classic Type A: total organization/efficiency freak, workaholic. I left working as a litigation lawyer in a big firm and became a Realtor so I could have more of a life. I moved out of New York City (where I had grown up) to a quiet place in the country. But I couldn't leave my workaholism behind despite my dreams of having time to garden, play electric bass more, and travel more. Bottom line: I need your advice BADLY!!

Embracing your work/life balance is an internal process. It is very subtle—small changes can yield big results, and even the tiniest shift can give you a whole new perspective.

When I first begin working with my clients, many feel light-years from a healthy lifestyle and assume it will take forever to regroup and restore. But the solutions are actually quick and easy, and the payoffs for making the investment come fast and furious.

Start nice and easy, with one activity at a time. Think of three things that refresh you, that you wish you had more time to do. Now, let go and regrab, by planning to do one of them today.

Grab-and-Go Strategy #2
Balance Your Balance with PEP

People often make the mistake of dividing their lives into just two parts—work and home. That's misleading—there are multiple elements to your life outside work, and it's important to balance your time between all of them.

"Balancing your balance" is the real secret to being in control. You need to balance three categories of your personal life to give yourself true energy:

- Physical health
- Escape
- People

Together, these three categories form the acronym PEP, which is exactly what they will give you. Let's look at them one at a time.

PHYSICAL HEALTH

Lack of sleep and poor nutrition can be compensated for with caffeine, sugar, power bars, or the pure will to concentrate, but nothing substitutes for genuine physical health. Sleep, exercise, a proper diet, and regular checkups maintain your physical body. This is a basic, essential priority, which provides the well of energy from which you draw the strength to accomplish everything else you need to do. Some people, like Rita, neglect their own physical health for so long that they forget what it feels like to be healthy and rested. Making the commitment to your physical health will have an immediately visible effect on your productivity.

- **Monitor how much sleep you currently get, then increase your sleep time in half-hour increments.** Studies show that getting the same amount of sleep every night is healthier for your body than trying to run on five hours a night during the week, then sleeping ten hours on the weekends to catch up.
- **Choose bedtime reading material carefully.** Try reading only fiction or poetry before sleep; nonfiction, self-help, business books, and the newspaper tend to rile you up rather then settle your brain.
- **Discover a form of exercise you love.** Try Pilates, yoga, aerobics classes, rowing, softball—anything that you enjoy and that takes your mind off the torture of exercise! Start small and don't be overambitious. Exercising three times a week is just fine.
- **Listen to business tapes while on the treadmill or out for a walk.** Combining the two makes you feel your exercise time is *for* your work, not a break from it.
- **Buy a pedometer—and walk everywhere, instead of taking the elevator or the car.** Keeping track of how many miles you trek a week, month, or year can motivate you to keep on truckin'.
- **Find a great multivitamin and start taking it.** You'll be surprised what a difference it makes. Replace your afternoon energy booster with something more organic than sugar or caffeine—an energy bar, juice, jumping jacks, a walk in the fresh air.

YES, But . . .   **It's YOU!**
I hate to exercise!

Change your motivation to exercise. Exercising for vanity's sake doesn't work for many people. One woman told me she loved exercise because it connected her to her body's muscles. Exercise for energy, longevity, stress relief, for the perspective, and for the great ideas that pop into your head while you're on the treadmill.

- **Establish a personal relationship with each of the doctors on your core team.** Know each of their receptionists—those personal connections are key to swift appointments. Aim for the mornings—doctors fall behind later in the day—so you can get in and out fast. Try to bunch all your yearly checkups at the same time of year—autumn and springtime usually present the fewest scheduling problems.

ESCAPE

Certain activities renew us by providing relaxation, refreshment, or just sheer delight. Think about the activities that instantly transport you to a place of pure joy. It could be reading, gardening, painting, dancing, listening to music, or pampering yourself by taking a long bath or a long weekend. This element of your personal life is what defines you—what makes you YOU. These activities—the no-brainers of joy—are important to build into our everyday lives.

Adding something new and joyful to a crammed schedule actually has the effect of *stretching* the hours and days. You will suddenly feel like you have more time on your hands than ever, because you will be energized as you look forward to your time off, and renewed as you think back on how pleasant that time was. Try starting your evening and weekends with one of these great escapes—it will take you to a higher, more mindful state of relaxation. What takes you away?

- **Remember what you used to enjoy.** It's easier to escape into something that instantly transports you than to learn something new. Listen to music, play an instrument, join a dance class.
- **Get pampered.** Schedule a massage, manicure, pedicure, facial, or haircut, and let someone else take care of you while your mind wanders.
- **Tune in to your senses.** Slow down and pay attention to what's around you. A simple walk home can become an escape if you pay closer attention to the sights, sounds, and smells, and the activities of people. Every day we are surrounded with fascinating scenes and wonderful opportunities to escape; escape from your own head and pay attention to your environment.
- **Get season tickets.** Purchase a series of tickets to the symphony, local jazz ensemble, opera house, or sports team to build several delightful escapes into your schedule in advance. Once you have the performances on your schedule, and have spent the money, you'll be less likely to sacrifice the tickets for work. And

if a real work emergency comes up, you can always give the tickets away—a nice way to build your people connections.

- **If you are a reader,** escaping into a good novel can have the feeling of a vacation each time you open the pages.
- **Listen to music instead of watching TV.** A lot of people just turn on the TV whenever they walk in the door, out of habit, for a sense of company. The danger is, you intend to sit down for ten minutes, and don't get up for two hours. Music sets a mood, transporting you instantly. Get refamiliarized with your CD collection, and choose music to come home to, to cook dinner to, clean the house to, and so on.
- **Do nothing.** After a particularly intense workweek of one deadline after another, a weekend of sleeping in, lazing around, or wandering the neighborhood with no list or schedule is sometimes the perfect tonic. Just make sure you're *choosing* to do nothing, rather than just passively letting time pass out of a habit!
- **Vacation in short bites.** Schedule four long weekends, four days each, throughout the year instead of two solid weeks off. These long weekends can be a quarterly treat to look forward to, refreshing your spirit without breaking your momentum or fueling your guilt.

PEOPLE

With the busyness of everyone's lives, it's very easy to take relationships for granted—you count on the history, the good times, and familial bonds to hold them together. Yet relationships thrive on more than good feelings and memories—actually spending quality, focused time with people lets them know they are important to you. Staying connected to the people you care about isn't only for them, though, it's for you.

There are people in your life who give you a sense of value, love, and connection. Whether they are family, friends, or people in your community, spending time with them is essential to your being. Keeping our relationships strong feeds our spirits, grounds us, reinforces our identities, and brings out our best selves. Rewarding relationships at home can help us to tolerate tensions at work more easily.

Some relationships may be easier and more rewarding than others, so make sure you're spending the greatest amount of time with the people who bring an easy joy to your life. Their support and love will help you get through tough times at work.

YES, But ...   It's YOU!
What about the lost hours?

People frequently ask me how to account for things that don't seem to fall under one of those categories—the miscellaneous obligations like household chores and commuting that eat up time in our schedules. I believe that there are no miscellaneous activities. It's both possible and essential to funnel each activity into one of the three categories outlined above. The trick is to change these have-tos into want-tos by connecting them to one of your bigger goals in life. Flipping that switch in your mind will alter your relationship to the tasks in question, making each one restorative in its own way. A few examples:

CHORES

I categorize chores as "self-renewal"—getting my laundry done brings peace of mind, grocery shopping allows me to explore new and exotic foods and cook healthy meals, while house-cleaning imbues my home with a sense of order and calm. Power-walk to do your errands instead of driving; that contributes to physical health. Team-clean the garage with your family; that's relationship time.

TRAVEL TIME

Whether commuting, shuttling your kids from one after-school activity to the next, or taking a business trip, make a conscious choice about how you want to use that travel time. Travel time should *never* be lost time. Listen to music to escape. Talk to your kids to strengthen your connection to them. Listen to business books on CD to enhance your work. Also, choose the best mode of transportation for whatever you're planning to do. A cross-country car trip is a great way to build relationships; public transportation offers plenty of time to sleep (physical health), read or watch movies (escape), and concentrate (work).

- Say "Hello," instead of asking, "Who made this mess?" when you first get home. Before making note of the chores, plans, and arrangements, take a deep breath when you get home and ask,

"How are you?" This sets the right tone for the evening and improves the quality of the short amount of time you may have with your family.

- **Balance your friendships.** Don't always hang out with the same person (your most needy friend). Each relationship in our lives feeds a different part of our beings. Get together with friends in person, on the phone, via e-mail. But do stay in touch.
- **Find common interests** between you and your family and friends. If you and your son share a love of music, make it your special thing to do together. If your wife loves to garden, offer to go to the annual bulb festival together. Know a friend who loves Indian cuisine as much as you do? Take an Indian cooking class together.
- **Grab commuting and travel time.** When traveling for pleasure or business, enjoy the contact with family, friends, or strangers. Conversations in transit offer a chance to build on relationships or to make new friends.
- **Stay on top of holiday, birthday, and anniversary cards.** Greeting cards that you take the time to write out and mail go a long way. Nothing says friendship like a heartfelt, handwritten card that arrives in the mailbox on time. Buy cards for the entire year, address them, stamp them, and schedule a "date-to-mail" in your planner.
- **Create a routine.** Establish every Friday night as a time to have a drink or dinner with your favorite group of friends, or to rent a movie with your family. Routine takes the guesswork out of planning and frees you of guilt when you are at work.
- **Entertain with pot luck.** It's easier to have people over if gathering a crowd doesn't require too much prep on your part. You clean your house, let your friends do the cooking. Assign parts of the meal to each person—appetizer, salads, main course, vegetable, and dessert. Switch houses each month, and make it a tradition.

WHAT'S GETTING SHORT SHRIFT?

Is your balance out of balance? Has your time off fallen into a rut, where you are always doing the same thing? Do you always just hang out with friends after work, instead of exercising or just taking time for yourself? Do you only work out, leaving no time to spend with your family?

If you want to quantify and measure your actual balance, study

---

TIPS FROM THE MASTERS

Kate White, editor in chief of *Cosmo* and author of the Bailey Weggins murder mystery series, manages to go away to the country every weekend with her family, a four-hour drive in each direction. She trained herself to read without getting carsick by forcing herself to read for one minute, then two minutes, then five minutes, then ten, then thirty. Once she reached the thirty-minute mark, the nausea went away. Now she is able to read manuscript pages for four hours in each direction while her husband drives. They get the weekends in the country, and she gets a full day's work done. How could you make this work for you?

---

yourself. Track yourself for a week or two (two weeks is best to get the average). Write down how much time you spend on each element of your personal life—the hours you sleep, time with friends or family, errands, and so on. Make a little check mark for each hour or half-hour increment. Alternatively, color-code your planner. Use a different color of highlighter for each category—e.g., work, blue; health, green; self-renewal, yellow; relationships, pink—so you have an instant visual picture of the balance you are creating. The idea is to get a good read on where you are spending your time off, so that you can determine if it's enough, and what would be the ideal.

Once you see the patterns of your time off, set some goals for yourself. What will it take to rebalance your balance? Which of the three elements of PEP are feeling the most depleted? What are you not doing now that would have a powerful and positive impact on your energy?

Drawing from all three categories of PEP, you can create your own à la carte menu. Dream up combination activities—you can run with a friend (relationships and physical health), or read your book on the bike (physical health and escape!). Customize your menu. Mix it up. Have fun with it. Ask yourself, What would make me happy?

If you're already feeling overloaded and can't imagine finding time for all three categories, don't panic; it isn't necessary to catch up all at once. Just start with one or two. Everybody needs a variety of activities, and we all benefit from a different mix at different times. Keeping your life in balance is a fluid, ongoing process; find the right mix for the time in your life.

Reach for the three biggest, most solid rocks—you'll notice an improvement in your work/life balance, even if you *only* make time for these three things.

Grab-and-Go Strategy #3
Break Through Your Resistance

Reclaiming your work/life balance sounds great, doesn't it? With all the tangible and intangible benefits to "getting a life," why can I already feel you digging in your heels? There's some hesitation on your part, a tape running round in your mind saying, "Yes, but that won't work for me. Balance is a pipe dream . . . there's no way I can pull it off."

What makes you linger at the office? You keep saying you're leaving by 6:30 P.M., but as six o'clock rolls around, you start a new project, make an extra call, start puttering . . . and before you know it, it's eight-thirty. What keeps you at the office after hours? What could be standing in your way? Is it you, or is it them?

WORK AS ESCAPE

Many people are happier and more at ease when they're consumed by work. The practical, measurable results offered by work are more immediately gratifying than the effects of a personal life. Getting the report done, landing the contract, and running a successful meeting are tangible accomplishments, with concrete results. The payoffs of a personal life—a feeling of fulfillment, energy, and love—are more ambiguous, and much harder to measure, define, and access.

Sometimes work is a form of escapism—from loneliness, unhappy marriages, oppressive family life, disturbing emotions that arise when the mind is not occupied with work. You need to ask yourself honestly, are your long work hours the result of passion or avoidance?

SARA

Thirty-five and single, Sara had never led a balanced life. A highly accomplished political director, she was notorious among friends and family for abandoning plans at the last minute because of work conflicts. En route to a brunch at her sister's one Sunday, she stopped by the office to check e-mail and never got back out the door. She'd joined a supper club to meet new people but had attended only one event all year, because of office emergencies. Her annual New Year's resolution to create more balance never lasted. In fact, Sara spent last New Year's Eve at the office instead of one of the three parties she was invited to. And the truth was, she was happier there.

During our initial consultation, she confessed, "I give the appearance of having an incredibly demanding job, but the truth is, I often use work as an excuse for getting out of social engagements." I asked her why. She pondered the question for a moment and explained, "I get maxed out at work, taking care of my staff and clients. All my smiling and interacting with people is done. Many of my friends are very, very needy. In every relationship, I end up in the role of the caretaker, therapist, friend, boss, mother." Are all of your relationships like that? I asked. Yes. Do you have any relationships that give to you? No, she couldn't think of one. No wonder she avoided going out—it was too much *work*.

I asked Sara what she was hoping to gain from getting balance back in her life. She looked at me silently, stumped. The idea of doing anything for herself was so foreign, she couldn't fathom the concept. Sara couldn't imagine being in a situation focused on anything other than how she could help people.

We had to find a way to make taking time for herself more palatable. Sara and I put our heads together and uncovered a couple of activities she could do that would not require giving to others. When she was younger, she'd always enjoyed hiking and antiquing. We planned her next few Sundays as days purely for herself. She enjoyed herself, but the time alone got her to thinking. She read me a passage from her journal:

I don't think I have anything to offer except my help. When I look at a situation and ask, "What's in it for me?" it feels selfish and bad. If I let go of this caretaker role, is there anything else? Am I anyone else?

Our next hurdle was to find a way to make socializing restorative rather than burdensome. Changing patterns is always easier to do with new relationships than old ones. I suggested she attend the next supper club event—but with a brand-new focus. To keep her from jumping into her caretaker role, we came up with a rule. If someone described a problem, she could not offer a solution. Instead, she was to say, "I know just what you mean"—and relate a similar problem of her own.

Sara and I spoke the day of the supper club dinner, and I could hear she was terrified. It's hard to let go of old roles. I suggested that the caretaker role is not a *bad* thing. It's a great quality, and Sara shouldn't feel obliged to give it up. So I revised her assignment. Instead of leaving this role behind, she went to the dinner as herself, ready to offer suggestions and advice to anyone with a problem—*but she was also to ask for help on a matter of her own.* Her assignment: She had to ask a minimum of three people, "How do you find time for a social life?" It was a subtle difference, but it ended up giving Sara the courage she needed to attend.

That evening was a huge success. Sara found the balance between giving and taking extremely comfortable. No one thought she was sucking them dry by asking advice—the entire group was captivated by the topic. Sara was also shocked to discover that many people are as obsessive about their personal lives as they are about their work lives. Skipping after-work exercise classes simply wasn't an option for one woman—they made her happy and more effective at work. Perhaps Sara's biggest revelation of all had been that these were nice, normal people—no one had horns or a tail!

A few subtle shifts gave Sara the perspective she needed to make a profound transformation: She didn't need to give up her life, or change her personality, to find a better balance. She recently took a trip to Spain with her sister. Coworkers and staff have commented on how happy and productive she's become. It seems, in learning how to take care of herself, Sara got even better at taking care of others.

If you work superhuman hours, be honest about your motivation. Is this merely a vital stage in your life, when work serves as the healthiest outlet for your energy? Or are there relationship problems, or other deep-seated issues, that you should address? Do you truly love your work, or do you fear the alternatives?

YES, But . . .   It's YOU!
I like work best!

An environmental scientist I met once was so passionate about his work that he'd show up at the airport five hours before his flight left, simply to observe the patterns of travelers moving through the terminal (studying flow, he told me, helped him solve problems with environmental spills). In the midst of working on a heavy-duty project, he'd often disappear for days. This was a guy who would get so absorbed in his work, fourteen-hour days would fly by without his even noticing. For him work was truly a place of pure joy. If work is less an escape and more a joy, be sure to periodically plan time with family and friends to keep those relationships going.

Tips for People Who Are More Comfortable at Work Than at Leisure

People who thrive on the tangible nature of work can apply some of the same principles to their personal life. To get a grip:

- **Think of creating a personal life as an investment in your work.** If you are refreshed and balanced, you will have more energy and be more productive. If you feel uncomfortable taking time for yourself, do it for your clients, boss, and colleagues.
- **Ask yourself if work is a comfortable refuge.** Identify what you are using work to avoid, and find alternate, more palatable ways to spend your time off. If you are avoiding a difficult relationship, use your weekends to paint or exercise. If you hate to be alone, make plans in advance to make sure your evenings and weekends are filled with company.
- **Keep a fun/leisure log to track your activities,** how long you spent, whether you enjoyed yourself or not. You may need to discover what you find enjoyable, if it's been a while.
- **Measure your doses.** Make subtle, gradual changes in your life. You may fear that if you take a break from work, you'll lose your momentum and never get it back. It may seem scary at first, but do it. Start by reintegrating the easiest, most comfortable area of your life. As your tolerance builds, slowly increase your time off—e.g., begin with a weekend away, then a week, then two weeks.

- **Carve out one weekly oasis from work.** Do something you absolutely love, that you can look forward to all week. It'll completely transport you every time you do it: gardening, dancing, cooking, a movie.
- **Picture success.** Visualize yourself aglow in the peak of fitness, or involved in a warm, loving relationship. Imagine how good you'll feel performing community service, or taking up a hobby and sticking with it. Set specific goals and timelines for each category you choose.

WORK AS DUTY

For some, workaholism comes from a deeply ingrained work ethic, a powerful sense of duty and loyalty to your job. People with a strong work ethic feel obligated to their jobs—there's always a crisis, emergency, or issue, and people are depending on them. Do you feel guilty when you aren't working? A lot of workaholics don't believe they're entitled to a week at the beach or five days wandering the Tuscan hills.

Consider why you may feel guilty. Is your own self-worth tied up entirely in your job? Do you relish the feeling that you are the office workhorse, the perennial go-to person, with the biggest work ethic and unsurpassed loyalty? Do you have a fantasy of indispensability? Or do you fear that self-replenishment is just another way of saying "self-indulgent"? Did you grow up learning that work is good, leisure is wasteful?

RITA

Rita, the workhorse advertising executive we began this chapter with, confessed a genuine, paralyzing fear that the whole company would fall apart if she turned her back. As she heard herself speak those words, she laughed self-consciously, realizing she must sound very egocentric—but it was a genuine fear, coming from a place of integrity, more than ego.

I couldn't get Rita to let go of the workday right away. We had to work up to it. On the job, I wanted her to see that she could let go of some tasks, and the company would still stand strong. We started by eliminating the most peripheral tasks in her workday. That was scary but manageable. She was surprised—nothing crumbled.

Next, we moved on to something of slightly more importance. Rita would follow up every staff meeting by typing up a long, thorough summary report. It often took her a full day to prepare this summary, because she felt it must be perfect. The truth was, most of the staff didn't ever read it.

I suggested that Rita delegate the task of typing the summary to someone else on staff, allowing them to create a one-page bulleted list of decisions and next actions. Rita was worried about letting this go, thinking it might not be complete enough—yet she happily discovered that the briefer report was actually more useful to everyone. Still, as we pulled things off Rita's task list to make time for her personal life, it was like a hole in the sand, where each time you dig, more sand and water floods in to fill the hole. Rita was still busy working long hours. I had to pull out the big force.

I asked Rita to plan on leaving early one Friday afternoon to enjoy a long weekend with her husband in the country. Even if the work isn't finished? she gasped. Yes, no matter what was left undone, Rita was to leave at 3 P.M. The work is never done. Rita was racked with guilt but willing to give it a try. We engaged her assistant to help her out the door, and had Rita let her boss and key colleagues know she'd be leaving by three in case they had anything they needed done that day. She was nervous, but managed to leave by three-thirty. Once she was on the train, Rita was delighted. And she was rewarded with a glorious weekend of sunshine—a wink from the universe, I told her.

The following week, Rita planned a dinner after work with a friend, attended a movie screening, and even began actually taking lunch out of the office. Her guilt at taking time for herself subsided as she saw that the office continued to function just fine, her colleagues were able to solve a few problems without her, and her own energy began to return. Most important, Rita began to glow—her sense of fun and energy returned.

If Your Sense of Duty Is in Overdrive

- **Consider the idea that your perceptions may be off.** Working longer and harder than anyone else doesn't necessarily mean you're operating at peak productivity. There are certain points of diminishing returns when the wisest, most productive thing you can do for yourself (and for your colleagues and company) is to STOP WORKING—recognize your limits and call it a day *before* you reach the omega wipeout zone.

- **Let other people solve problems too.** People with a very strong work ethic often automatically think that they have to solve every problem. Learn to delegate. This way you can get as much done as the job requires, and still have a life for yourself. See Competency 7 for more strategies on delegation.
- **Try neglecting one small task.** You'd be surprised how much your colleagues can fill in for you, if you'd only leave them a little work. You may be hogging all the responsibility because you like the role of martyr.
- **Get a buddy at work who will leave with you.** You'll motivate each other to get out on time. If that buddy happens to have as big a sense of duty as you do, all the better.
- **Tend to your own crisis over the office's, sometimes.** Caring for others is a choice. If you are the company's in-house rescue service, when an issue comes up at the end of your day, if you have personal plans, choose your own emergency instead of the office's. Your "crisis" may be your health, or your family life, or your personal relationships. It's counter to your impulse, but you must turn left instead of right.

POOR PLANNING

Maybe you're not a workaholic, but you just get so busy at work that you neglect to prepare for your time off. A failure to plan can put the kibosh on your work/life balance in several ways.

If your workday is disorganized due to procrastination or failure to look ahead, you can easily get stuck at the end of your day, or up against the weekend with a huge unfinished project (or more). Everyone has one customer, colleague, or boss who always comes in with a project at the last minute. You need to know what those possible obstacles are, and be prepared to preempt them so you aren't taken by surprise every time. Many times, you can let them know that you'll be gone by a certain time—giving the last-minute Charlies a chance to get the work to you early enough in the day to get out on time.

A less obvious way that poor planning makes for late nights at the office is a laissez-faire approach to organizing your personal life. Many people put all their effort into planning their workday and then neglect to think about what they will do with their time off. No planning, or a plan you're not comfortable with, can make for lingering.

Who wants to rush home to yet another night or weekend of star-

ROB

Rob, an urban-planning consultant, hired me for time-management and organizing coaching. For as long as he could remember, he stayed too late at the office every night and had no time for a personal life. We organized his desk so that he wasted no time searching for contracts. We tightened his time-management skills, prioritizing his day, streamlining his paper-work, batching his appointments, and creating shortcuts for the preparation of bids. Yet after three months, he found he was still hanging around the office after everyone had started to go home. One day he cocked his head to the side and confessed to me quietly, "You know, Julie, I could leave early like everyone else. But I don't think I want to. There's nothing really fun to leave for."

Rob hadn't had a personal life in so long, he didn't know how to spend his time off. What would be fun? He'd lost touch with who he was. So he was more likely to stay late at the office, where his identity was clear, than wander home to veg out in front of the TV.

He needed to replace his after-work plans with things he'd truly enjoy—going to movies with friends, taking a sculpture class, riding his bike. Once we changed his plans and activities to things Rob could really get excited about, he used his time-management skills to leave the office at a normal hour and re-claim the life he had (almost) forgotten he could have.

ing at the television, or just staring at the piles of clutter that have ac-cumulated while you were at the office? No, better to stay at the of-fice, where any request that comes across your desk will seem more compelling that what you'd planned for the evening.

If you get to your evenings and weekend without a plan, if you are too laissez-faire about your time off, it tends to slip away. The effect is that you aren't refreshed, you lose energy and momentum, and lethargy sets in.

Tips for Poor Planners

- **Start your evening and weekends with a self-renewal activity.**
  Listening to transporting music, playing an instrument, or get-

ting a manicure or massage immediately after work will speed the transition from work to relaxation mode, changing the entire feeling of your evening and weekend.

- **Plan something time-sensitive immediately after work.** Take a class, meet a friend for dinner, have a particular train or carpool to meet. A nonnegotiable deadline will get you out the door on time.

- **Fill in the toughest blanks first.** If you're starting from scratch, make definite plans for immediately after work, and/or Saturday or Sunday nights. In other words, pick the times you're most likely to be stuck with nothing to do.

- **Prepare the people you work with.** If everyone is accustomed to your being there till all hours of the night, you need to prepare them to adjust to an earlier dismissal. Let them know in the morning what time you'll be leaving that day. If you are worried that your coworkers, boss, and assistant might come to you with last-minute requests, e-mail them a reminder, letting them know that you'll be leaving in a couple of hours, and if they have any urgent matters that need addressing today, they should bring them to you immediately.

- **Set a two-hour wrap-up alarm on your computer, beeper, or cell phone.** This will help you focus on your upcoming exit time, and will force you to finish up what you are doing without starting one more big project or call.

- **Be prepared.** If you work unusual hours, think through what is possible to do with your time off. One producer who worked the overnight shift had to plan social events way in advance to make sure he was rested. A police detective whose shift constantly changed kept a personal list of the best barbers in the city, places to shop, and good restaurants, so that whenever he found himself with a few hours between shifts, he could get something personal done.

JANE

Jane is an accomplished attorney and mother of four. Her firm had a fairly conservative culture that lauded face time as one of the primary factors in evaluating its employees. The attorneys that put in long hours—in some cases over eighty hours per week—were praised for their hard work and dedication to the firm.

With four children at home, and ten years at the firm under her belt, putting in eighty-hour weeks wasn't something Jane wanted to do. She proposed a "part-time plan," which had her working twelve-to-fifteen-hour days, three days a week (yes, that's part-time for a lawyer), but also allowed more time for her family.

Because Jane was highly productive and a valuable asset—she held the bar in three states and knew a certain area of case law better than any other attorney in her firm—the managing partners agreed to her proposal.

Those extra two days at home gave her the opportunity to reinvigorate her relationships with her four boys (aged ten to seventeen) while continuing to be a sufficient contributor to her family's income. The plan was giving her the balance she wanted. During her three days at work, she was 100 percent focused on work—no long lunches, no personal errands or phone calls—and convinced that she was as productive in her three days as others were in five, who had to use company time to take care of personal matters. She also kept a log of her accomplishments and made sure coworkers, bosses, and partners knew what and how much she was producing.

When it came time for the annual partnership meeting, Jane was fully expecting to make partner. She was still billing hours at a high rate and had recruited more clients in the past year, working part-time, than she had in any previous year with the company.

Instead, she was forced headlong into battle, required to fiercely defend her part-time schedule from attacks at every pass. Management felt she'd accomplished great work, but outright refused to make her a partner unless she agreed to resume a full-time schedule. In their eyes, her part-time status was a threat to company culture—it would send a bad message to young attorneys if one of the firm's partners was a "part-timer."

One female partner took Jane's schedule personally, as if it was some kind of personal affront to her lifestyle and abilities as a mom!

With firm mores bearing down, Jane stood her ground. She reemphasized her value and made it clear that time was her currency; after all, she'd been flawless on her side of their original bargain. Ultimately, she won her well-deserved partner status and maintained her three-day workweek.

COMPANY PRESSURE

Okay, so maybe you have no problem taking whatever time you need for yourself. You don't fear having a personal life, nor do you worry about letting down your company or your customers.

But what if you operate in a culture (legal work, investment banking) that seems to measure your value by the sheer number of hours you put in rather than by the quality of your output? What if your boss and coworkers keep totally different hours than you? What if they start their day at 11 A.M., not realizing that you began yours at eight? In other words, what if face time is very important where you work?

Tips for the Face-Time Pressured

- **Understand resistance.** Even those who wish you well, such as family and coworkers, have their own agenda; try to weather their resistance with grace and cheer. Your supervisor loves that you work such long hours and is less than delighted when you want to cut back. Your teammates thrive on your daily presence and are thrown when you get the okay to work at home one or two days a week. Colleagues who don't have children may resent you when you are given time off to care for them. It might be based on their own fear, their inconvenience, or their own conscious or unconscious wish to have a different balance for themselves.

- **Stick to your guns.** When you encounter resistance, you need to be flexible, yet strong. *Make accommodations on the route, but not the destination.* If you want to work a four-day week and your boss is skeptical, start by trying it every other week. Be extra energetic and prove that you can get it all done and more in four days. After a trial period, request to switch to the four-day week permanently.

- **Remember your value.** One of the common reasons for resistance from managers is that they're afraid of setting a precedent—if you're permitted to work at home two days a week, suddenly everyone wants this privilege. In these circumstances, you must be clear on your value. Remind the manager of your contributions and your talent, expertise, and efficiency. This is the currency that earns you the accommodations.

- **Focus.** When you're at work, really concentrate; take no calls on family matters unless it's an emergency. And when you're with your kids, let your machine take messages. Compartmentalize, so that whatever you're doing, you're giving it your all.

RITA

Rita's transformation over the course of our work together was striking. Once she got over the guilt, she's consistently made time for her family, friends, and *herself*. Her regular hours dropped from twelve to nine hours per day; she got back to the gym, started going to the theater twice a month with her husband, and often gets together with friends after work and on the weekends.

Once she made a habit of taking better care of herself, Rita began to glow. With each follow-up consultation, I have noticed her wearing more colorful, flattering clothes, coming across relaxed, and actually looking like she was having fun at work. Remarkably, the most important things get done. Why? Because by letting go and regrabbing on a consistent basis, Rita is happier, more energetic, and more clear-minded at work. By getting a new lease on life, Rita has become more productive than ever.

There will be times you have to sacrifice your balance. If your company is in the middle of a merger or some other crisis, everyone in the office may be working triple-time. You may work in a cyclical industry, such as magazine publishing, where there are always two weeks of high intensity to close an issue when everyone works round the clock, followed by two calmer weeks. But even during times like these, you need to periodically let go and regrab, finding some way to restore your energy and recharge your battery so that you can keep on producing.

Remember, there is no magic formula, no one-size-fits-all prescription. Except that *everyone* needs to feed *all* aspects of their being (physical, psychological, and emotional) in order to stay healthy, energized, and ready to roll up their sleeves to produce results.

Once you embrace your work/life balance, a zillion things will try to throw you off. Maintaining your balance is a fluid process. It's your role to protect your balance from the "you" and "them" lions constantly clawing at you, imploring you to stay one more hour, bring one more file home, postpone that vacation, skip that class after work. Trust yourself to let go, reach up, and grab hold of that rock, to break through your resistance, embrace your personal life, and balance your balance with PEP.

Chapter Summary
EMBRACE YOUR WORK/LIFE BALANCE

Which grab-and-go strategies do you plan to use?

- Let go and grab hold.
- Balance your balance with PEP—physical health, escape, and people.
- Break through your resistance.

When do you plan to implement them?

What do you think will be your biggest obstacle in applying the strategies?

How will you overcome that obstacle?

What is your motivation for mastering this competency?

DEVELOP AN ENTREPRENEURIAL MINDSET

LET'S FACE IT, we live in a time when surviving and thriving at work is exceptionally challenging.

Perform. Faster. Better. Prove your value to the company yet again—especially now, when everything is up for grabs. Out there big companies are eating little companies. In here, the obvious place to create savings is to reduce head count. That could mean you. Opportunities arise suddenly, and can disappear just as fast if you aren't prepared to act. Frequent mergers set in motion a new wave of restructuring, of raised expectations, of reshuffled jobs. Not only are you worrying, Am I going to lose my job? you're also wondering, What *is* my job?

In reaction to the increasing volatility of the job market, more people today dream of owning their own business because they crave a sense of security, freedom, and choice. Yet the reality of owning a business, or even freelancing, has also become more challenging. In a high-speed, high-expectation world, client loyalty isn't reliable. For example, in the past, corporations would often stay with the same advertising agency for decades, while now they constantly shop around for the hottest agency in the world. The Internet makes it possible. Many formerly loyal customers have abandoned their favorite specialty stores in favor of discount chains, simply because the prices are better.

In every area, competition is fierce. The new world of work is defined by a sense of fleetingness, interchangeability, and insecurity.

It's easy to operate from a place of fear in this environment. But fear is paralyzing and counterproductive. To live in fear is to be so afraid of losing your job that you no longer enjoy your work; to be so worried about doing something wrong that you defer all thinking and judgment to those who hire you—and the truth is, they may not be so sure either. You were hired and are retained because you offer some sort of value. Now more than ever, it's critical to understand that value, cultivate it, and think far beyond any one boss, job, or even industry that you've ever been involved with. To stay strong, you must retain your sense of self and the power of your individuality.

You must release yourself from the fear that you are a dime a dozen.

Once you get over the shock that nothing's permanent, you can start to see the new world of work as a phenomenal opportunity to learn, grow, and develop new skill sets. You can live powerfully, with deep job satisfaction. Yes, you can be let go anytime, but you are also free to change jobs whenever you want. It is up to you to choose where you want to be and find the work that matches who you are. You can create absolutely any work configuration you desire. All you need is a vision of what you want—and the confidence to make it happen.

This is a bold and brave thing to ask of yourself in the face of today's job-market volatility—but it's necessary. If you seek job security from the outside, you're putting yourself in a dangerous position. The only true job security today comes from the inside out. In the midst of all the external chaos, we must turn inward for order, for control, for clarity. We must become secure in the knowledge that we have valuable qualities and talents to offer, and constantly work to identify and meet the needs of the marketplace. Having to learn new things all the time keeps your mind alive and your brain exercised. If you develop a sense of adventure, you can view the fleetingness of jobs, companies, and industries as an opportunity to develop a unique and amazing set of skills, which can help you adapt and bring value to almost any work configuration.

Whether you have your own business or work for a company, in order to survive and flourish in this new world of work, you must think—and act—like an entrepreneur.

THE ENTREPRENEURIAL MINDSET

Webster's Riverside Dictionary defines an entrepreneur as "one who launches or manages a business venture, often assuming risks." Sure, it's easy to see how that applies to a business owner—but how does it apply to an employee?

Your "business" is your entire career. You are in charge of it. And every employer you have is a client on the long journey of your career. Whether you change jobs annually or stick with one company for five years or longer, whether you work for a small business or a large corporation, you are the owner of a service-based business where you must meet and exceed customer expectations, adapt to the needs of the marketplace, and stay competitive by offering something unique.

Once you realize that *you own your career,* it's easy to stop feeling like a victim. No one and nothing has control over you. It's your career, and you are free to fix it and direct it in any way that you like. You're in the business of developing *yourself* as a commodity, marketing yourself, and finding fulfillment in work. You pick your clients, and work to see if there is a match. You learn to be gracious and solid, because you never want to burn any bridges. If you're not finding fulfillment at work, you have the responsibility and power to find the solution. If you do everything you can to make it work and still find yourself unfulfilled, you may need to look for a different "client" (i.e., employer). But no matter what the problem is, it can be solved once it's identified.

My aim here is not to turn everyone into an independent business owner. Indeed, not everyone has the capacity, or desire, to succeed as an entrepreneur. There are many advantages to working for a company, including the infrastructure support, steady paycheck, benefits, and built-in community. But we all have the aptitude to take control—to invest in ourselves and make decisions based on our own values, interests, and abilities, to the benefit of ourselves and our employers.

Yes, the new world of work is scary, but like a fast-moving ride, it can also be exhilarating and fun—if you embrace it as an opportunity to develop your greatest self. There is the potential for tremendous cross-pollination of skills in the new world of work. A journalist carried over her knowledge of the media to become the public relations director of a school system; the production manager of a plastics factory converted his knowledge of materials and manufacturing into an asset at a scenery design firm; a waitress used her people skills to become an effective human resources counselor. There's no slowing down the new millennium. To survive and thrive in the new world of work, you need to stop being the victim, and start thinking and acting like an entrepreneur.

Grab-and-Go Strategy #4
Embrace Your Choice

It's easy to feel like a victim in the workplace: Customers can be rude, deadlines impossible, bosses unfair, pay too low. There's nothing more demoralizing than feeling trapped in a job, feeling that you are there because you *have* to be, not because you *want* to be.

The victim pays more attention to what is wrong than what is right; to what's impossible than what she can control. The victim feels stuck—that she has no choice—when in fact everyone *does* have a choice.

Entrepreneurs take ownership. When faced with a dilemma, the entrepreneur gets busy fixing the problem, instead of wasting valuable time and energy blaming or complaining. The entrepreneur recognizes that even with an imperfect client, she always has a choice, and is not stuck with anything she doesn't want.

One way not to feel stuck is to reconnect to what you are getting out of the job. Ask yourself: Besides the steady paycheck, why am I there?

We're all driven by different things—money, pride, an opportunity to learn. No situation is perfect, but if you are in a job, I guarantee that you are there for a reason. Your first task is to remember what that reason is and embrace your choice fully.

Understanding and embracing what motivates you will change the entire energy with which you approach your day. It brings dignity to your work, empowering you from the inside out. It creates the difference between feeling helpless and feeling powerful—between seeing your work life as something that was forced on you and seeing it as something that you are choosing.

You can have any reason for staying in your job; you don't have to justify it to anyone. The dignity that accompanies the opportunity to choose can make even the worst situation tolerable. Various studies have proven the patterns of why people stay in their jobs. Do any of these ring true for you?

- **Friendship.** The "workplace community" is a major deciding factor for many employees when they are considering whether to start or stay with an organization, or to commit themselves more to their work. Today, the vast majority of our friends are made in the workplace, and that is one of the major keys to job satisfaction.
- **Autonomy.** The opportunity to complete tasks in an autonomous fashion is a key facet of job satisfaction. A high level

of autonomy gives an employee the opportunity to take control of their jobs and invest in it personally. (*Journal of Social Behavior and Personality,* March 2001)

- **Challenge.** Employees rank having the opportunity for exciting and challenging work as a primary priority. Second on the list is the chance for career growth, learning, and development. They also value working with "great" people and the building of interpersonal relationships. Having supportive management and a "great" boss rounded out the top five priorities. (John S. McClenahen and Jill Jusko, "Pay Is Not Enough," *Industry Week,* April 2003)
- **Meaningful Work.** Focus groups show that most of us crave meaning as well as money in our work, and this engagement is key. A more satisfied employee makes better use of time, shows up for work for more days, has longer tenure, and earns higher performance ratings. (*Gallup Management Journal,* March 15, 2003)
- **Leadership.** What attracts people to an organization is often quite different from what causes them to stay or leave, according to TalentKeepers, an employee retention company in

---

YES, But . . .   **It's THEM!**
Things have changed!

What if the job that once fulfilled your deepest values has become a frustrating environment due to company mergers, marketplace conditions, or a new boss? Or what if your increased responsibility has actually taken you further away from fulfilling your values? You loved working with clients one-on-one, but now you're busy managing staff instead. Or you enjoyed selling and nurturing customers, but now you're overloaded with merchandising.

Solution: Reconnect to your goal, or find a new reason to stay. Take advice from one senior editor in the publishing industry:

"I became an editor because I always loved to read. I wanted to discover and help shape books that would change people's lives. But as the publishing industry changed, I found there was less and less time for the thoughtful editing of meaningful books. My time is consumed by marketing meetings, auctions, sales conferences, all the business and less of the art. I've had to open myself to discovering and enjoying the business side of the industry."

Orlando, Florida. A survey of 4,299 workers revealed that "organization issues" (such as compensation, benefits, and career opportunities), followed closely by "job issues" (i.e., work schedules, opportunities to learn new skills, and challenging work), were most often cited as the reasons people joined their present employer.

Leadership issues (the degree to which a leader/boss makes employees feel valued, and whether the leader is trustworthy, a good motivator and coach, and flexible in solving problems) were a distant third.

But the issues reversed after as little as three months on the job. Leadership issues then became the most powerful contributor to why employees stayed, and also became the primary driver behind what makes them leave.

WHAT KEEPS YOU AT YOUR JOB?

- Salary
- Benefits
- Lifestyle/hours
- Relationships with coworkers, customers, boss
- Recognition
- Opportunity to grow
- Autonomy
- Doing something meaningful
- Chance to be creative
- Other . . . ?

YES, But . . .   **It's YOU!**
There's nothing left to learn.

You're in a boring, dead-end job and have grown tired and cynical. It probably feels like you've mastered everything there is to know about your position already. As you get older and more established in your job, if you thrive on learning new things, you may feel bored.

Solution: Find one new thing to master. After fifteen years in the business, Brendan, a building code inspector, thought, This is it, there's nothing more for me to learn about this job. Yet by expanding his knowledge of codes in neighboring states and developing courses to teach others, he was able to reignite the feeling of learning something new. The truly uninspired should ask for a new project to spice up their workdays, or exercise other skills, so as to build and strengthen their memory through their work.

YES, But . . .   It's YOU!
I am stuck.

You are paralyzed by the need to make money. The only thing about this job is the paycheck! If that's true, then use it. Use that paycheck to enjoy what it earns you, whether it's the chance to save money or feed your family, keep your nice car, or just to provide shelter and security until you find a new job. And P.S.— never, never, never leave one job before you've found another. A jobless person is instantly less appealing to every employer . . . it's like a little mark on your forehead. Even if all you are getting out of your current job is the security that comes from being employed while you look for another job, stay positive. As long as you are getting *something* from your job, you are one up on the situation.

USE YOUR SENSE OF CHOICE TO BE MORE OPTIMISTIC ON THE JOB

Even if there are things about your job you do not like, focusing on the positive will keep you optimistic and fuel success. You can smell people who resent their jobs from a mile away. Think about the clerk in the department store who wishes she were elsewhere—miserable and mean; her nastiness makes you think twice about spending money in the store.

Human resources managers tell me that a negative attitude is the most dangerous characteristic to let loose in a group: one person's constant complaining, bitterness, and water-cooler whining can pull a whole department down. Revealing your ambivalence or dissatisfaction in a victimized way is a huge mistake. No smart entrepreneur would make a client feel bad about using his services. Harboring resentment and projecting dissatisfaction places a huge burden on your employer, who would much rather work with someone with a positive attitude.

You may not love everything about your job, but as long as you feel you are choosing to stay, rather than being forced to, you will feel your power.

Most business owners know never to put all their eggs in one basket; they understand that true choice comes from having options. Every employee should take that lesson to heart. How do you increase your sense of freedom when you work for someone else?

Give yourself options, to prevent being overly dependent on your boss, or job, for any one thing—be it money, recognition/fulfillment, intellectual challenge, or goals. Having options automatically puts you back in the driver's seat.

- **Create a financial cushion.** Save six months' worth of living expenses, no matter how much sacrifice it takes. Having a little cushion (even if you never use it) eliminates the unhealthy panic that if you do one thing wrong at work, you're fired and out on the street. A cushion gives you a sense of freedom and safety, which makes you relax and be able to tolerate more imperfections on the job. You feel less stuck. Save like the dickens; create some alternate revenue streams from investments, or a part-time gig, or freelance projects, until you save at least enough to feel secure.

- **Use current job challenges to enrich your résumé.** Each project you work on and every challenging experience you endure helps you develop a skill set. Sure, you may be working with no budget, but if you can be creative and manage without it, innovation becomes a marketable skill. If your company expects you to meet impossible deadlines, and you mastermind shortcuts and processes at the peak of efficiency, you will be coveted by future employers. Have a tough boss? Developing a thick skin will open up more job options in the future.

TIPS FROM THE MASTERS

Sam Hanson, an assistant economist/research associate at the Federal Reserve Bank of New York, works on a several different research projects a month. Some, he says, are more interesting than others. When Sam's assigned to a project he isn't truly excited about or challenged by, he views it as an opportunity, not an annoyance. He uses the project as a chance to recharge his energy and take a break from the intense, quiet work that usually fills his days. He sets actionable goals that will keep him engaged, even if the work doesn't: e.g., forge a relationship with an upper-level economist, refine data management skills, or learn the basics about a new area of research. How could you use similar thinking?

Change your attitude. Convert challenges into marketable skills. Always think about how a challenging situation will look good on your résumé.

- **Study and develop knowledge.** Take classes, join professional associations, attend conferences. Constantly sharpen yourself. If your job is underutilizing you, and you have spare time on your hands, study. Get a mentor. Learning keeps you energized and engaged, and boosts your overall value. If your company offers continuing education, take full advantage of it. If your employer won't provide these career development services, invest in your own enterprise and do it yourself.

Grab-and-Go Strategy #5
Cultivate Your Value

Every entrepreneur knows that to sustain and grow a business, you must provide a service or product that your clients need. Furthermore, there must be something about what you offer—a level of service, quality of materials, interpersonal relationships, location—that is unique and/or superior to that of your competition. Whatever it is, there must be a reason why customers go to you and not the competition.

The same basic supply-and-demand rules apply to employment. Your job is to determine the needs of your supervisor, other department heads, coworkers, and customers (your clients) and meet or exceed them. As long as you can do that, you have value.

Your *value* constitutes everything you bring to the job: your strengths, knowledge, talent, experience, and expertise. Knowing what makes you valuable keeps you grounded and offers something solid and real to fall back on when work is hard, confusing, or moving so fast that you can't keep up. When you face criticism, competition, and difficult people on the job, connecting to your value gives you the confidence and courage to press forward.

Change is a fact. You must not let these variables throw you, or lead you away from the knowledge that you have a perspective to offer, a contribution to make, and are more than a Johnny-one-note. When you know your value in the bigger context, you can be nimble, adjusting your approach as needed to remain a potent force, and not be outrun by the constant variations.

Cultivating your value restores your confidence in who you are; it imbues you with a sense of trust in yourself to know what's right, what's wrong, and how to solve problems based on your own unique experiences, personality, and point of view. You must believe in your-

AUDREY

Audrey was the brand manager for a cosmetics company. Bright, incredibly innovative, and dedicated to her job, she was at the top of her game. But then her company underwent sweeping management changes, and she started feeling lost. She had a terrible relationship with her new boss, a cold, critical woman who was very skimpy on praise.

When we first started working together, Audrey told me, "When I took this job, I had just gone through a divorce. There I was, thirty-five, no kids, no real hope of meeting the right man. So I decided to have this super career; I planned to put everything into my work. And for the most part, it's paid off. I'm well respected in my industry, have made a very comfortable living, and genuinely enjoy my life. Then a hypercritical woman came in as the CEO. Her criticism is especially hard to take because I'm not getting validation from anywhere outside my job. And I'm certainly not getting it from her. I really began to lose my self-confidence."

I knew immediately that Audrey was in trouble. Demoralized and frustrated, she was too dependent on other people to tell her when she was doing a good job. She'd lost sight of her value and had allowed herself to be defined by others. With one stingy boss, Audrey had lost her way, and lost her identity in the process.

self. If you don't start, no one else will. It's not your boss's job, or the job of anyone else in the workplace, to make you embrace your value. It's yours. You are the one who stands to gain from recognizing your contributions. Easier said than done, right?

EXAMINE THE BIG PICTURE

Typically, most of us focus on just a few of our value characteristics—usually the ones we enjoy most—and don't even realize we bring others to the table. Think back over the course of your working life. What unique talents, skills, experiences, attitudes, and connections do you bring to the table?

Write down the triumphs, recognitions, and successes you've

achieved in your career, no matter how big or small. Have you received any awards? Been promoted? Landed a big raise or bonus? Received a thank-you note from a grateful client or coworker? Completed a new task, or project, you never thought you'd survive with the excellence of a seasoned professional?

Keep your eye on the bigger picture and see yourself separate and apart from any one environment. Taking a big-picture view helps you see change as an opportunity to find a place for more of the skills and services you can provide. Which of your skills are transferable? What knowledge used in one situation is applicable to another? For example:

- I always make the people I work with laugh. I feel like they count on me to tell a joke, make a funny face, or do something goofy to brighten the mood during a stressful situation.
- I am honest—no matter what. People know I'll always tell them the truth.
- Everyone I work with tells me I should be a therapist. I've really excelled in helping to solve personnel problems at the office.
- I'm great in a crunch. I love the adrenaline rush you get from thinking on your feet.
- I'm an excellent problem solver. I stick with the details until I find the solution.

Each of these value characteristics goes wherever you do—because *they are you.* They don't get turned in and left behind like a set of keys when you leave one job for another—unless you let them.

When you are unsure of everything else in your work environment, what are you always clear about when it comes to evaluating yourself? What do you always come back to? Recall past experiences and things former bosses, coworkers, and clients have said to you about yourself as you begin to explore your value with this free-form exercise. Write your responses as they occur to you. Don't edit them. And think in broad strokes.

Your Big-Picture Value Assessment

1. What are your unique skills and talents? Where do you excel?

_____

_____

2. What length and breadth of experience do you offer? _____

_____

3. What industry contacts and connections do you have? _____
_____

4. What is your level of productivity? How much do you get done
   in a day? _____
   _____

5. What is your attitude/work ethic? Are you willing to go above
   and beyond the normal effort? _____
   _____

6. What results have made you especially proud? _____
   _____

Your answers are the beginning of your awareness of who you are
and what you bring to the marketplace. Keep these questions nearby,
and continue to fill them in as more thoughts occur to you. Don't
hesitate to ask friends from work, or people in your family who have
known you for many years. We often forget what we've accomplished, or don't think it's that big a deal, because it came so easily to
us. There are career counseling services with tests that can help you
define your skills and value. The bestselling book *Now, Discover
Your Strengths* (Marcus Buckingham and Donald O. Clifton) is another tremendous resource in better understanding who you are in
the workplace. Getting an outside point of view is often the best way
to get a richer and fuller picture of our assets and value.

EXAMINE THE CURRENT PICTURE

Just as important as determining your big-picture value is determining your current value to one client in particular—your present employer. What makes you particularly valuable to your employer *now*?
Where are you making your greatest contribution currently?

Your most valuable contribution can be any combination of
"hard" or "soft" skills. "Hard" skills tend to be technical and occu-
pation-specific, while "soft skills" are more qualitative in nature—
the *way* you do your job that makes it easier for a team to work
together successfully. For example, Laura is priceless to her legal
team because she knows Internet legislation better than anyone else
in her firm, and is enormously fast—therefore she is able to manage a
very large caseload. Bob, a financial analyst, is heavily relied upon at
his insurance company because he is incredibly accurate in his record
keeping and has a unique knack for communicating "the numbers"
to other departments.

Most people feel less competent in some areas of their core responsibilities than others, then do their best to cover their tracks. Maybe you're good with people, but terrible at numbers; or great at brainstorming, but awful at following through. By being honest with yourself, you can reach out for help or support and improve your contribution to the team.

Take the following value inventory, circling your strengths as they pertain to your current job. Be honest with yourself here.

YOUR CURRENT VALUE ASSESSMENT

SKILLS AND TALENTS

Technical expertise	Communication skills	Organizing skills
Financial skills	Team-building skills	Marketing and selling skills
Presentation skills	Creative skills	Systematizing skills
Leadership skills	Strategic thinking	Analytic skills
People skills	Management skills	
Problem-solving skills	Listening skills	

ATTITUDE/WORK ETHIC

Availability	Flexibility	Reliability
Commitment to completion	Stability	Cooperation
Willingness to go "above and beyond"	Upbeatness/ optimism	Honesty
	Supportiveness	Loyalty
Harmony with company mission	Discretion	Leadership qualities
	Ambition	

EXPERIENCE/CONTACTS

Years in current job	Education	Contacts from personal/ community/schooling
Years in related job at a different company	Years in different position within company	Reputation in industry
Loyal clients/customers	Years as freelancer/ business owner	
Contacts from work	Agents/reps	
Specialized training		

RESULTS/PRODUCTIVITY

Energy	Accuracy	Volume
Follow-up	Independent worker	Ability to take direction
Speed	Good listener	Attention to detail

YES, But . . .   **It's YOU!**
I'm not sure what I'm best at!

Solution: Get feedback! During your next performance review, don't just sit there. Ask your boss questions. Solicit more feedback from your coworkers, even customers. As with directions, if you don't know, ask. Just as entrepreneurs empower themselves by knowing their value (strengths), they are also empowered by knowing their weaknesses. This is just as critical. So if you haven't already, get a fix on them too.

How many of the values circled in your current job are also ones you wrote down in your big-picture value assessment? Were you surprised by how many (or few) qualities you were able to circle under each heading? Do you see which skills you've carried with you from job to job? What about weaknesses? Do any of yours really stand out?

YES, But . . .   **It's THEM!**
Value isn't acknowledged where I work.

Some companies have a "no feedback" culture; everyone just continues with their work, with no time given for recognition or celebration of a job well done. For example, Lisa, a research associate for a major accounting firm, worked tirelessly. In early, out late—but she never received feedback from anyone. By the time it came for her midyear review, she was demoralized and felt like she was doing a terrible job—even though she was three times as productive as the person who preceded her in the position. A boss that isn't clear about what he values most in your work can be difficult for anyone. A boss that's outwardly negative and derogatory can be even worse—you're getting feedback, but only when you do something wrong.

Solution: This demoralizing management style requires a tough skin on your part, and firm confidence in your abilities to get the job done right—no matter how much your boss grumbles. Find one or two people at your job who are upbeat and positive and make you feel good about yourself, and make sure you spend enough time with them to counteract the grumpy people you deal with each day.

Grab-and-Go Strategy #6
Trust Your Truth

People who are comfortable with themselves, who know their value and understand their weaknesses, are more confident. Secure in their identity and role, they are able to more easily navigate the natural challenges in the workplace with more precision, accuracy, and uniqueness. They aren't stymied by the need to look like they know what they're doing even when they don't.

IF YOU HAVE A QUESTION, ASK

When you think like an entrepreneur, you learn to have faith in the skills you possess and are willing to acknowledge what you don't know. Many people are afraid to ask questions. They think that saying they don't understand something will make them look foolish or incompetent. The opposite is actually true. Let me assure you right now, because of the speed and quick-changing nature of industry today, *there are no stupid questions.*

Asking questions is how a business owner customizes his approach to each individual customer and request. Asking questions is a means of making sure you understand what an individual actually means. When somebody asks for a document to be made more "clear," do they mean "outlined" or "more fully developed"? When they say something is "urgent," do they mean the issue needs to be addressed in the next two hours, or by early next week? Only by asking can you be sure.

Most people don't mind answering your queries—it helps them solidify their own thinking.

For example, let's say your supervisor asks you to update the employee manual and gives you a one-month deadline. You've never done an employee manual before, but you're afraid to ask questions because you don't want your boss to think you are incapable of doing the project. A zillion questions run through your mind:

What is the overall goal of the manual? Which areas are most important to cover? How long should it be? Does she want it electronic or paper-based? How often will she want it updated? Should it cover policies applicable to all employees, or zero in on department-specific procedures as well? Are there any examples of manual styles she's seen and liked?

But you ask none of them. Instead, you puff up your cheeks, say, "Sure, no problem," and then go off in a corner, panicking about what to do next. Chances are, you will spend a whole lot of time working on this project—hours will stretch to days, days to weeks— and in the end you will likely produce something your boss won't be happy with, all because you didn't ask. By asking questions, you are tuning in to your boss's view of what she wants—and that means you are already one up on being able to deliver it!

YES, But . . .   **It's THEM!**
My boss doesn't have time to answer questions.

She wants me to figure it out myself and just get it done.

Solution: If your boss is too busy to answer questions, or is relying on you for your expertise, take ownership of researching the project through other people in the company, or with friends on the outside who have done similar projects. Shoot your boss a quick e-mail with your top three questions—keep it short and sweet. And cover yourself with the message, "I talked to a bunch of people, and I think I know what you want. I'll do a draft and send it to you for review—I'll be happy to make the changes." And mean it.

IF YOU SEE ANOTHER WAY, SHARE YOUR IDEAS

Have you ever sat in on a meeting, about to burst with a suggestion, but not uttered one word because you were worried your idea would make you look like a total fool? Then someone sitting two seats away, who has been at the company twelve years longer than you have, comes up the same idea or a similar one, stealing your thunder.

Speak up, share your point of view, and then let the chips fall where they may. Take your ego out of the way. If your boss, coworkers, or customers disagree, or want to do things another way, be gracious, not offended. If your client hears your opinion and chooses to do things her own way, that's fine—do not take it as a personal assault on your intelligence. It doesn't even mean you were wrong. In fact, listening to what you had to say probably helped her clarify her own opinion.

Never fail to bring your unique self to the table. If you do, you risk becoming another cog in the wheel—a yes-man with no real opinions of your own—and that dilutes your unique value.

IF YOU WON'T BE ABLE TO DELIVER, SAY SO!

Trusting your truth means taking full responsibility for delivering on 100 percent of what you are asked to do. If you are having trouble getting something done on time, speak up. Reach out for the help you need, so that you can deliver on time, according to expectations.

If you are not going to get something done on time, let your boss, coworker, or customer know. No one should ever have to chase you for your work. Trying to hide, or hoping they won't notice, puts an unnecessary burden on the person who asked you to deliver for them. You are being passive, and then you end up disappointing your boss.

There is a huge difference between saying no to a project because you don't want to do it, and saying no because you really aren't the best person for the job, and thus it is not in the best interests of the company for you to do it.

If you are asked to do something that you feel you are truly unable to do, that you do not have the skills for, speak up and be willing to learn, or make a suggestion as to a more efficient way to get the job done. If you hide what you don't know, you'll be living a lie, watching over your shoulder, just wasting energy trying to look like you know what you're doing instead of delivering results. And eventually, no matter how much effort you expend, the truth will "out" itself.

IS THE VALUE YOU'RE PROVIDING WHAT IS ACTUALLY NEEDED?

Let's see if what you're offering is what your employer is actually looking for:

1. First, list the top five qualities you think your job requires.
2. Next, list the strengths you circled in the big-picture value assessment.
3. Now, look at how the two lists line up. How many of your strengths match up with the qualities your job requires? Which qualities or strengths mismatch, or are missing? Which areas of your own perceived value are simply not needed? Is there an opportunity, perhaps, to find an outlet for these talents in your job?

When you're confused about your value, or feel as if what you have to offer isn't what your employer is looking for, go back to the

YES, But . . .   **It's THEM!**
What I have to offer isn't what they want!

Feeling like you're making a contribution and are appreciated for it is one of the most honored and treasured qualities in the workplace. People who are confident in their contribution have a higher rate of productivity, are happier, and feel more connected to their jobs. But chances are, only some of your skills and talents are truly valued by your company.

What's important is whether you're comfortable with the skills they *do* value. That said, just because they don't place a premium on everything you have to offer doesn't mean you should hide it under a barrel, or worse, let it dwindle. Are any of your skills unrecognized or underutilized by your company? Has your company expressed a need for this skill from you? Are they tapping into these skills with other staff? Can you ask for a project to demonstrate your ability? Is it possible that your skills and talents are not as good as you'd hoped? What can you do to improve them? What if they really just don't need what you have to offer?

Many professionals in their forties and fifties are catapulted from positions of power to near invisibility by downsizing mergers and business failures. Suddenly age and experience are a liability instead of an asset. When employers don't understand or utilize an employee's sophisticated skills and experience, the effect is stagnating at best, demoralizing at worst. Read any sales skills book, and you will find that the worst kind of salesperson is one who tries to force the customer to buy something he or she doesn't want.

To solidify your relationship to your company and secure your position, tune in to what it *does* want from you, and do the best job you can in providing it.

basics. What can you do to improve the situation? Are you a quick study? Are you open-minded and willing to try new things? Do you have an ability to teach others? That's your value. Be willing to grow in more ways than one. If your value isn't what your boss wants, figure out what she does want, and grow that way. Play the position they need you to play. By concentrating on the areas in which you already do well, you'll regain confidence in your value.

AUDREY

For years, part of Audrey's responsibilities as brand manager included being her company's "public face"—a task she enjoyed more than almost anything else. She loved having the opportunity to communicate the exciting and innovative work her department was producing at various company functions, in media interviews, and at occasional public appearances. And she excelled at it.

Unfortunately, her new boss—the crabby CEO—envisioned herself doing the company PR, and seized Audrey's duties as soon as she started.

This was a major blow and a huge disappointment. So I challenged Audrey to think beyond the roles she'd been playing at this job. For the last five years, she had been tapping into one set of her skills and enjoying them, but I knew she had more inside her. In a sense, it was as though for the last five years she'd been playing the upper register of the piano, but now the audience had changed. She simply had to move to a different part of her keyboard. What else could she bring to the party? Could this difficult transition be an opportunity to discover or showcase other latent skills, talents, and contributions she hadn't yet made? Being the "public face" of her company was something she'd loved doing—but to stay employed and happy, she needed to find other roles she could play just as well.

With the new CEO turning her attention outward, Audrey responded by turning her attention inward, taking on the role of mentoring the staff. Having been at the company for so long, and knowing the mission of the organization like the back of her hand, she found this new position invigorating and rewarding. She was good at it and it enabled her to make a significant contribution. Audrey needed to rediscover *herself*.

Grab-and-Go Strategy #7
Develop Your Vision

Business owners are known for having no problem doing any aspect of what it takes to run their business; they serve the clients, sweep the floors, do the marketing, design the Web site, deliver the packages. They may not love every one of those tasks, but they do each one with attentiveness, commitment, and care. Their ego is rarely bruised by these lower-level to-dos.

Why is that?

Because they have their eye on a higher goal. They are driven by a vision. No matter how miserable a particular task may be, they see something shiny on the horizon that inspires them to move forward. They see the connection between the individual chore (even if it's delivering packages) and their ultimate objective.

It feels good to have a higher purpose. Vision gets you beyond the drudgery of the moment, puts everything in the context of something bigger, and gives significance to every day. Even the most menial tasks are exciting when viewed in the broader framework of your higher goals. Think about it—stuffing envelopes for a fund-raiser aimed at fighting breast cancer or AIDS is meaningful. All the paper cuts are tolerable—they're even a badge of honor.

Developing your vision removes you from fear and uncertainty, focusing you on something bigger than any one moment, or task, or project. A clear vision speeds and elucidates decision making: With your eye on your target, it's easier to tolerate the boundless bumps and dips that come along the way. Those who have a strong vision are determined and stalwart about their goals, but flexible and adaptable on the route to achieving them. They become creative problem solvers, with a talent for seeing multiple outcomes and benefits to every situation.

When you operate from a clear vision, you can see the gift in each experience, how it weaves into the fabric of the journey. That adds a great spirit to your work life. Each encounter and experience offers a gift in the building of your career. You look for what you can get out of it. Eyes wide open, you stay silent, take it in, and learn. Most important, vision infuses your work with energy, enthusiasm, and courage—you aren't afraid to make decisions because you understand their importance in the context of your greater goals. Vision keeps you grounded in the bigger picture.

ARTICULATE YOUR PERSONAL VISION

Your career is a major part of your life. What drives you to be where you are? What, beyond this moment, keeps propelling you forward? What is the vision that inspires you?

Take a minute now to articulate what drives you personally—to say clearly what you are working toward. Developing a vision can be a little overwhelming, but it doesn't need to be complicated.

What does your gut tell you? What do you want? What's making you wake up every day and go to work? Don't feel pressured to articulate your one-year, five-year, and ten-year goals. Vision is often as hard to describe as feeling an impulse, a wish, a desire.

You may be driven to learn as much as you possibly can about your industry, or to develop a reputation as the best in your field. Maybe you want to be a role model for others, or become wise. You may simply be driven to collect experiences so that you can ultimately decide what you want to be "when you grow up." Maybe you are inspired to make customers' lives happier or easier. Often your vision is a dream, a hope, or a belief in yourself and the unique contribution you can make to the world through your work. Perhaps you want to heal the world, or be like someone you admire—a personal mentor, or someone famous in history. Sometimes your inner fire comes from a drive to prove someone who didn't believe in you wrong (your miserable second-grade teacher), or to create the financial freedom to retire early. Whatever compels you, articulate it—it will grow stronger and more inspiring as you acknowledge and embrace it. Don't be shy.

Vision can also be as concrete as specific, targeted goals. For example:

- "Increase my sales revenues by 10 percent every year, until I'm the top earner in the company."   —*Refrigeration salesman*

- "Develop a new body of improvisational exercises that helps actors perform with greater depth and truth."
  —*Theater director*
- "Keep mind and creative juices flowing."
  —*Artist working as gardener*
- "Earn promotion to senior management in two years."
  —*Middle manager*
- "Come up with the next knock-your-socks-off product."
  —*Software developer*
- "Develop my reputation as the most innovative manager in the company, with the strongest team."—*Bonds sales manager*

- "Earn and save enough to launch a nonprofit in ten years."
  —*Nurse*
- "Develop state-of-the-art programs with total enrollment."
  —*Preschool director*
- "Build confidence in every employee."   —*Corporate trainer*

- "Get every student loving to read. Make every child feel good about himself or herself."   —*High school principal*

When you endeavor to define your vision, push yourself to think in terms of your career as a whole; you don't have to limit your vision to your current job (although you can, if you want to). Give yourself permission to dream big.

ADOPT YOUR COMPANY'S VISION

If you're having trouble pinpointing your own vision, another way to find and establish that sense of purpose is to simply adopt, or connect to, your company's. Most companies have a vision that goes beyond just making a profit. Lean Cuisine, for example, is guided by its vision to help people "do something good for themselves." That's their goal for every new product they put on the market. And it makes sense—they are in the business of helping people eat healthier, faster, and easier than ever before. It's a mission that any Lean Cuisine employee could easily adopt as his own.

When you understand your company's vision, you'll be able to keep your role and tasks in perspective with the greater goals of the organization; ensure that you are actually meeting the broad aims of your employer; and understand those tasks in a more meaningful context. Your own vision will become more clear to you once you see how it can feed your employer's goals, and how your employer's goals can feed yours. It's a powerful feeling to have all the resources and brains of your employer promoting your own vision.

SEE THE CONNECTIONS

Every company is an organism whose parts are connected to a whole. Each worker's responsibilities fuel and feed the mission of the organization—whether he's conducting a strategy session or directing the holiday mailing. But when you're bogged down with your own staggering workload, it's easy to lose sight of the whole. How do your tasks fit into that bigger picture?

Each worker must understand and respect the relationship between his tasks and the mission of the company. If you're a salesperson, managing your contact database is not fun. It can be a tedious and frustrating task, but consider the value of that contact information, and the efficiency of having it at your fingertips, to the company. That small task is feeding the greater mission of the company. Once you understand this relationship, you start to see how the people in your company are tied together by a zillion different tiny strings, all pushing, striving, for something bigger.

When I was in college, I took a $6-an-hour campus job because I needed the money. My first day, I was shown what to do. The office manager brought me into a small back room with a copy machine, showed me a huge stack of newspaper clippings, and told me to make twenty photocopies of each article. No explanation of why. I spent the next four hours alone in that back room, no other employees in sight, just opening the lid, placing down an article, and listening to the rushing sound of the carriage moving across the machine. My boss never took the time to explain the context of the job—and I nearly went crazy with the irrelevance of it all. I felt like a tiny cog in a big machine doing a totally meaningless, insignificant task. I didn't even last a full eight hours.

I didn't realize, until many years later, that that office must've been a clipping service—the public relations department for the university. Had my boss explained to me that the articles I was copying illustrated the publicity the university was getting—which enhanced the college's reputation and could lead to more funding—I likely would've been more excited about the job.

Having a strong vision, whether it's your own or an adopted version of your company's, will keep you marching forward. Speeding decisions, elevating you above the drudgery, your vision brings a sense of clarity and purpose to everything you do.

As an exercise, think of the most dreadful task you do. How does it help you fulfill the company mission? How does it help you fulfill your boss's goals? Your own personal vision?

It can be easy to lose sight of your vision when you're stuck doing data entry for hours on end or find yourself in the office working late one Sunday night. But keep working at it, with these tips:

- **Ask your boss:** What do you care about the most? Where do you want me to spend my time? What can I do to help you achieve your goals? Understand what the departmental goals are. It may have to do with building the most cohesive team, or giving people a good work/life balance; the premium may be on face time, or turning work around rapidly. You'll be delivering exactly what your boss wants, and the success and ease that comes with it may help you develop your own vision.
- **Pick up an annual report,** or other marketing materials that your company is distributing to its customers or investors. This is a great way to see concepts and goals your industry is focusing on. Is there anything in those documents that inspires you? That drives you to meet a higher goal?
- **Find a role model.** Is there someone you admire more than anyone else? Do you know them? Have you read their biography,

TIP FOR MANAGER—DEVELOP DUAL VISION THINKING

There are big-picture thinkers and detail people in every organization, and a company needs both to operate. Help your staff connect their daily tasks to the company's vision. Develop your team's dual vision thinking in a staff meeting. Keep them from losing sight of the interrelationship between tasks.

The administrative assistant who thinks everything he does is grunt work will end up resentful, demoralized, and ultimately sloppy in his work. Not understanding the context of his job can lead to the easy omission of a critical task. It's not just people on the bottom rung who need to develop dual vision thinking—the people at the top do too. Senior managers who think purely in big-picture strokes, with no appreciation of the details required to support their initiatives, tend to run their staffs ragged, creating more projects than their staffs can humanly implement. Often their staffs feel disregarded or taken for granted, instead of appreciated. Top-tier performers are the people who can see the importance and relevance of every task, large or small.

Write the company's mission on a whiteboard. Divide the board into two columns, as below. Then have staff call out their everyday tasks—the drudgery, the mundane, the exciting. As they call out the tasks, have the group identify which part of the mission those tasks support, and how.

Vision	*Task*
Personalized client care	Accurate data entry
	Excellent filing and records
	Callbacks on day of inquiry
	Up-to-date product research
New product development	Feedback from customers and POs
	Salesperson's observations on issues
	Vendor research
	Design of logo/packaging
	Marketing and mailing
	Financial record keeping

or seen a documentary about their life? When you're looking for inspiration, a role model is a great place to turn. It's someone you can look up to (not measure yourself against).

- **Picture success.** What has it felt like to succeed before? Write down the triumphs, recognition, and successes you've achieved in your career—no matter how big or small. Have your received any awards? Been promoted? Landed a big raise or bonus? Received a thank-you note from a grateful client or coworker? Completed a new task, or project, you never thought you'd survive with the excellence of a seasoned professional? What drove you to that success? Are any of those reasons transferable to your current work situation? Hold on to those things. Cherish them. Review your list of "wins" whenever you start to doubt yourself.

- **Be fearless.** Maybe you're afraid of not being able to achieve your goals, or not creating a vision that's *right,* or being over-committed in one direction or another before you know what

---

AUDREY

Audrey adopted her company's mission, a statement she'd always believed in, until she could develop a new one for herself. To remain an integral part of the team, she had to adjust, see herself in a new role, and adapt to the new expectations. It wasn't a fast process, and Audrey wasn't always happy, but she made the decision to take ownership and control of her own career. The new CEO was difficult and abrasive and seemingly un-appreciative of her experience and dedication—but Audrey would be damned if that woman would make her run from the career and industry she loved. If Audrey decided to seek new employment, it would be on *her* terms, no one else's.

Audrey came up with an interim vision. The thing that drove her every day was to improve her skills in working with a difficult personality. She focused her energy on developing an inner strength that enabled her to be confident, and trained herself to draw on that confidence no matter what was happening externally. She likened it to being in the army and taking the abuse of boot camp. She tried to see it as an opportunity to develop the offerings and sophistication of Audrey Enterprises.

you really want. Dream big—if you can see it, you can make it happen.

You have the skills to take the reins and guide your career in the direction you desire. Becoming aware of your own choices, value, truth, and vision will inspire you at work every day. It will also prepare you to spend your days choosing what's most important, the next competency in our journey toward making work work.

Chapter Summary
DEVELOP AN ENTREPRENEURIAL MINDSET

Which grab-and-go strategies do you plan to use?

- Embrace your choice.
- Cultivate your value and build on your strengths.
- Trust your truth.
- Develop your vision.

When do you plan to implement them?

What do you think will be your biggest obstacle in applying the strategies?

How will you overcome that obstacle?

What is your motivation for mastering this competency?

Three

CHOOSE THE MOST IMPORTANT TASKS

WHEN YOU HAVE A BUSY DAY, can you confidently zoom in on what's critical, or are you frozen, dead in your tracks, confused where to turn next? Do you complete one task at a time or, in a panicky, scattered state, do a little bit of everything, finishing nothing?

Workers who can consistently decide with clarity and ease which tasks are most important when under pressure are the most prized in every organization. Highly focused in pressure-cooker situations, they rise to meet the challenges of an opportunity-saturated workplace that demands tough calls at every step. Not surprisingly, these employees are also the most calm.

This chapter will help you develop your ability to choose wisely: You'll learn criteria for defining, selecting, and prioritizing your most important tasks, strategies for capturing a complete picture of all you have to choose from, and how to handle conflicting priorities. Once you know how to make crystal-clear decisions, Competency 4, "Create the Time to Get Things Done," will help you manage your day to effectively deliver on those tasks. But first you need to learn how to choose wisely.

Grab-and-Go Strategy #8
Dance Close to the Revenue Line

When it comes to prioritizing, I want you to focus on a very simple concept—everything you spend your time on should be assessed in terms of its proximity to the *revenue line.*

What is the revenue line? It's the point at which your company is actually *making or saving* money. In tough economic times, your ability to make or save your company money is where your greatest value lies—it's where the buck meets the road.

How can you dance closer to the revenue line in your job? Each company is built around either producing a product or delivering a service. Think about how your company measures your results. Is it the quantity of your output, the quality of materials you produce, the size of sale per client, the number of clients you see, the level of donors you woo? Here is an example of five different jobs, and the activities they do that are closest to the revenue line for their companies:

- **Lawyer:** Billable hours and recruiting new clients
- **Journalist:** Writing articles and researching solid sources
- **Nurse-practitioner:** Caring for patients and learning new medical technologies
- **Grass-roots organizer:** Voter contact and volunteer coordination to turn out the vote
- **Publicist:** Booking interviews and coordinating well-attended events

Which of the tasks on your to-do list are closest to your company's revenue line? In most cases, it's the activity that will immediately do the following:

1. Generate revenue (call customer);
2. Create the product or deliver the service (make the doughnuts); or
3. Save the company money (research lower-priced vendor).

The largest portion of your time should be spent on tasks that are, *at most,* only one or two steps from the revenue line. It's not that you shouldn't get to those tasks that are, say, three steps from the revenue line, but the tighter the economy, the more important it becomes to evaluate all of the tasks on your to-do list in terms of their relationship to directly making or saving your company money.

TOP-DOWN PRIORITIZING

Look at the triangle below. Place your tasks closest to the revenue line at the top, and the tasks three steps from the revenue line at the bottom.

The new world of work presents us with a continuous series of knots that need to be untangled. Each time you are faced with too much to do and not enough time, it's easy to feel paralyzed with indecision. Which way do you turn? Where do you start? The point of the triangle is the surest way to work your way through any knot. Loosen the knot by doing something at the point of the triangle first, then use the breathing room that allows to get to second- and third-level tasks.

1 step to revenue		Customer service, product design
2 steps to revenue		Proposals, conferences, meetings
3 steps to revenue		Paperwork, reading, updating files

WHY START WITH THE MOST IMPORTANT TASKS?

You'll always be safe if you start with the task closest to the revenue line, because it clears the decks, providing you with a sense of relief rather than stress. Pleasing your boss or the company enlivens you with a sense of confidence and power—of knowing that you are taking care of what really counts. Working your way from the top down is the surest way to give yourself the breathing room you need to accomplish those two- and three-step tasks.

Most important, when an unexpected crisis arises (and you know it will), you have space to take it on—because you've already gotten the most important stuff taken care of. It's not that these lower-priority tasks are irrelevant; you just shouldn't plan to start your day with them.

Conversely, if you try to structure your time by starting with the lowest-level tasks, you'll *never untangle the knot.* You can't pry open a bundle with a flat edge. You will endure every day feeling miserable, guilty, and weighed down by the two-ton cloud of critical work hanging over your head. That anticipation of the bigger tasks physically slows you down, impacting your productivity.

> **YES, But . . .**   **It's YOU!**
> *Getting the little stuff done first feels satisfying.*
>
> Warming up your day by knocking off a bunch of quick, easy tasks is tempting, but it can provide you with a false sense of accomplishment. The danger in this approach is that the bulk of your energy gets depleted over a bunch of insignificant tasks. First there's e-mail, then a couple of phone calls, then a meeting, then huddles with some direct reports and a quick sign-off on a project budget—then, guess what? It's time for lunch! To warm up after lunch, you start off with another round of e-mail, then a client eats up your midafternoon, and suddenly it's 5 P.M.—and you never got around to, much less finished, the grant proposal—your day's one-step-from-the-revenue-line priority. In fact, you can't even remember what you did get done.
>
> **Solution:** You must retrain yourself to choose the *important* over the *quick,* the *tough* over the *easy,* no matter how intimidating the project may be. Starting too far from the revenue line prevents you from producing the volume of revenue-generating work that your company actually relies on and pays you for. Working from the bottom up puts you in a risky position—when that inevitable crisis appears, you go into heart palpitations. How can you possibly handle this crisis when you haven't even gotten to your most important assignment yet! Completing two or three tasks that directly make or save your company money far outweighs finishing twenty things that are three steps from the revenue line.

If you find yourself continuing to avoid the most important tasks, you must ask yourself what's going on. Are you intimidated by them? Do you dislike the core activities of your job so much that you are actually denying their importance altogether? Jennie was hired as the only customer-service rep in a small service-based company. Her boss directed her to always deal first with clients and prospects. But Jennie felt unsure of herself and found dealing with customers annoying. She preferred to spend her time coordinating logistics and completing administrative tasks. No matter how many times her boss pushed her to attend to clients and prospects, Jennie remained convinced that she was concentrating on the most critical tasks, when that was actually a defense against doing things she wasn't that good at. As a result, sales plummeted and the company lost key clients.

If you are avoiding your most important tasks out of fear or intimidation, take it upon yourself to fix the situation. Brush up on your confidence by taking a class or getting a mentor. Take care of what the company is asking you to focus on, and you will increase your job security dramatically.

DOING THE WORKPLACE DANCE

Of course, your days can't be filled only with items one step from the revenue line. If you ignore all the twos and threes, you'll end up generating your own unnecessary crises—stupid little things left to the last minute that are now roaring back to bite you. By recognizing the revenue-line nature of those detail tasks (e.g., travel arrangements), you'll prevent them from getting out of hand. Making plane reservations isn't difficult, and it doesn't require a lot of time, but the payoff is huge! Without a ticket, you won't make it to the most important meeting of the year—and then where will you be?

Keeping up with the pace and unpredictability of the workplace is

---

YES, But ...   **It's THEM!**
The revenue line keeps changing!

Given today's pace of rapid change, some companies are in constant transition mode as they merge, downsize, move locations, revise their mission, or play catch-up with changes in their industries. All of these factors can be overwhelming—especially in industries like technology, insurance, finance, banking, and telecommunications, where it seems there's some new mission and something new to learn every day. The pace is so fast, and turnover so unforgiving, that it seems impossible to categorize or prioritize anything because you're always up in the air, not knowing where to get the information you need to stay close to the revenue line.

Solution: When prioritizing in times of change, you need to ask, What is the revenue line today? Be flexible. Keep your knees bent, your weight on the balls of your feet, ready to spin on a dime. Don't look to the past during a time of change. Pay attention. Initiate much closer communication with your supervisor and colleagues, letting them know you are on the case, ready to adapt, and willing to work with the changing tides. After all, you all have the same goal: company survival!

a dance—it has a rhythm and a shape. Create a rhythm to your day by doing mostly ones, and then pepper it at certain points with a handful of twos and threes so that you can jump ahead on some deadlines and prime the pump for longer-range payoffs. Figure out which tasks take you the longest and which are the quick hitters.

For some people the ones take the most time, for others it's the twos and threes. For example, my ones—creative work such as writing and speech development—take a lot of concentration; but my twos and threes are approvals, meetings, and phone calls. For a financial broker, the ones are quick, but the twos and threes, like lunches and research, take more concentrated time.

You can texture your days or weeks however it makes sense for the seasons of your business and for your work style. You can spend part of each day on some ones, twos, and threes. Or you can go in cycles—spending several weeks just on one-steppers, and the last week of the month on the two- and three-steppers that have been waiting for you.

But no matter what the cycles of your work, starting each day at the top and working your way out of every stressful moment will leave you feeling accomplished and centered instead of harried and downtrodden. The energy and relief you'll feel from getting these things crossed off your to-do list will fuel you, boosting your productivity for the rest of the day.

Can we eliminate the amount of decisions? No! Can you calm yourself by knowing you are always making the right choice? Yes. Dance close to the revenue line and you'll always be secure.

Grab-and-Go Strategy #9
Capture All Your To-Dos in One Place

The only real chance you have at choosing the most important tasks begins with keeping a complete list of everything you need to do in one place. After all, prioritizing is a matter of relativity—the true question is, What's most important in relation to the other things on your list? Taken one item at a time, everything can mask itself as a critical task.

It's surprising how many people fail to write down everything they need to do in one consistent location. They rely on their memory or haphazardly scribble to-dos in a variety of places: Post-its, envelopes, napkins, planners, notebooks, the computer. For some, their to-dos take the form of chaotic stacks of papers on their desk, intended to be reminders but which blend into visual Muzak after time. This haphazard approach results in lost opportunities and misguided efforts.

You can choose wisely only if you have everything written down in one reliable place. That place can be your planner, a simple notepad, or a computer program such as Outlook. Select only *one* location, and be meticulous about writing down absolutely everything.

During a recent speaking engagement, one audience member asked, rather incredulously, "Come on, do you really write everything down?" My answer was an unconditional yes. If I didn't, anytime I'd look at my list, it'd be incomplete, and then how would I know I was making the right choices? In addition, I'd feel distracted with worry over what I might be forgetting!

People who try to keep everything in their heads often can't fall asleep at night. They have to keep reviewing their list of to-dos in their mind, to make sure nothing falls through the cracks.

Imagine going grocery shopping with this haphazard approach. You jot down a shopping list of stuff you need to buy; then, on your

---

YES, But . . .   It's YOU!
My memory always used to work for me.

It can be hard to train yourself to rely on a single planning tool. One of my clients had benefited from a photographic memory for most of her life. The woman was so fast and brilliant, she'd made it through law school in two years! Her memory was so good, she'd never had to keep a to-do list. Yet by the time she called me, her ability to retain information was slipping. Either her memory was fading or, more likely, the number of to-dos she'd accumulated had exceeded her capacity to remember them. Her follow-ups were falling through the cracks, and clients and peers had started to notice.

Solution: The obvious one was to begin writing things down, but she was extremely resistant to using a planner—it was a blow to her ego, and a complete habit change. She felt a little defeated. To make it more enticing, we indulged in a gorgeous leather planner, which she would enjoy opening several times a day, and trained her to think of this planner as her new best friend, traveling with her everywhere she went. She found that using the planner indeed solved the problem, and put her back in control over her to-dos just like old times. Over the next six months, she still had to keep fighting the gravitational pull toward relying on memory alone. By the seventh month, though, it had become second nature.

YES, But . . .   It's YOU!
I can't decide which planner to use!

With the multitude of choices now available for tracking to-dos, it can be perplexing to figure out which one is right for you. So you end up juggling many systems—and spend more time transferring information between them than actually getting the work done.

Don't let your search for the perfect system keep you in a constant state of flux. Select one system and stick to it. Here are some options to solve some of the classic problems:

- **Find the right size pages.** If paper works best for you, stick with it, getting the smallest size that will accommodate your handwriting and the number of to-dos you juggle each day. A week on two pages accommodates only three to four to-dos per day. For tracking five to ten to-dos, get a one-page-per-day format. For more than ten daily to-dos, or tracking several people's schedules, get two pages per day.
- **Slenderize your binder.** If paper works best for you but you don't like the bulk, switch to a binder with one-inch rings, and keep only two months of daily pages at a time.
- **Get a foldable keyboard.** If you love your Palm but find graffiti writing too slow for to-dos, get a portable keyboard to type in your lists, or enter to-dos on the computer desktop software and hot-synch to the Palm.
- **Marry the best of paper and Palm.** Use the Palm for appointments and numbers, and add a small notepad to your Palm case for recording to-dos. I prefer a dated notepad, with one page per day to keep my planning date-specific.
- **Engage your assistant.** If you have an extremely reliable assistant who's good with time and has impeccable follow-up skills, put him in charge of tracking all of your to-dos. He can enter all of them into Outlook or other software of your choice and print out your lists for you, or you can both access them from the computer. He can also take an active role in prioritizing and reminding you of what's forthcoming because he'll have a fuller picture of everything on your plate, and he's in the best position to protect your schedule when you have big projects. This way, you have an ally in choosing the most important tasks every day.

way to the store, you think of a few more things, but you don't write them down—you figure you'll just remember them. The minute you walk into the supermarket, your mind gets completely overwhelmed by the enticing displays of merchandise and flashy sales signs. You wander the aisles distracted, pondering all the possibilities—Hmm . . . did we need mayonnaise? Ohhh, this looks interesting. Hey, pomegranates on sale, I used to love those. By the time you're done, your shopping trip has taken twice as long as you'd planned, you've bought way more than you needed, and as you unpack, you realize you forgot the aluminum foil. How aggravating.

Write it down, I say!

Having everything captured in one place will free you to make clear decisions, and get a better night's rest.

It may feel like a waste of time to write everything down, but the very act of doing so forces you to think through what you are spending your time on. It gives you a moment to reflect and regroup—so that by the time you do take action, you are doing so with precision and confidence. Running around putting out fires without thinking

---

YES, But . . .   It's THEM!
My company requires me to use their scheduling system.

Okay, so you're a paper person—but you're required to keep your schedule in Outlook so coworkers know where you are. Or, you're very high-tech, but you're forced to enter your weekly schedule onto the company wallboard. This is a difficult situation, because it adds a layer of work and upkeep. Rather than abandon the system that works so well for you, I'd suggest you add the layer of entry. Try to find the most efficient way to do so.

Solution: Build a daily transfer time into your schedule so you can copy info from your system to the company's, utilizing that time to think through and consider the best use of your time and plans. Having a ten-minute daily transfer session can actually boost your precision in choosing the most important tasks. If you are lucky enough to have an assistant or team member who can make the transfers for you, put her 100 percent in charge of updating the company system, giving regular access to your personal system so that she can do so. Don't alternate who does the updates; switching back and forth will cause information to fall through the cracks.

YES, But . . .   It's THEM!
My job really moves too fast to write things down.

In some jobs, the work comes in and goes out at such a rapid pace that you may feel that in the time it takes you to write something down, you could've gotten the task done. This is very common for people who are in "support" positions, such as assistants, brokers, and even executives whose primary job is to manage an entire team and who are always dealing with one crisis after another.

Solution: If every to-do is genuinely instant (i.e., a request comes in, you immediately respond and move on to the next request), there is no need to write it down. But if projects come flying at you and you do them at a later time, you need a recording system. If writing things down takes too long, set up a series of action bins on your desktop, with very specific titles. Rather than label them with vague terms like "Action," "To-Do," or "Pending," diagnose the routine actions you do and label each bin with a single action: "Read and Forward," "Set Appointment," "Submit Expense." This technique will save you an enormous amount of time during the workday that is currently lost to reshuffling your piles to see what's in there.

of their value to the organization is the surest way to burn out and waste an enormous amount of time doing the wrong things.

Grab-and-Go Strategy #10
Remember the 3 Qs and 4 Ds

With all your to-dos captured in one place, you're in a position to choose wisely which ones are the most important. But decision making doesn't always stop so easily right there. What happens when you are facing multiple conflicting priorities? The constantly shifting tides of our industries, customers, and urgencies keep upping the ante, challenging our ability to always know what's right.

What happens when you've planned your whole day around what's important, and a crisis comes up? A key coworker doesn't show up, or a client calls with an urgent, time-consuming need. You hit an unexpected snafu with a project—and it takes much longer

JACK

Jack, a bookstore manager, benefited from the action-bin technique. Much of his time was spent on the store floor with customers, but whenever the store got quiet, he'd go to his desk to catch up on paperwork. Unfortunately the top of his desk was a giant in-box. Everything was marked "Pending" and "To-Do." He'd spend the first fifteen minutes shuffling through the piles just to see what was in there (or avoiding the task because it was so intimidating). By the time he'd picked out something to do, a customer would come back in, and he'd have missed the moment, leaving his desk without having completed a task.

In thirty minutes we sorted Jack's to-dos, discovered ten regular functions ("Special Order," "Sign Check," "Approve Invoice," "Check Stock," and so on), and installed an attractive, roomy stacking bin for each one. Now, when he had a fifteen-minute break, Vernon could go to his office, zero in on one specific action that he was in the mood to do, and quickly process everything inside. For the first time ever, he felt less imprisoned by the piles on his desk, and his productivity skyrocketed.

than you expected. You can't always anticipate the specifics of what you will be up against—but you can be assured that, day by day and moment by moment, you'll be facing the need for rapid decision making. You need to be prepared with specific tools for choosing what's most important with confidence.

Whether it's during a particular crunch time in the business, or on a particular day, our best-laid plans are constantly thrown off course by interruptions, ideas, crises, and opportunities. What happens when you are faced with conflicting priorities? When *everything* seems to be one step from the revenue line? Should you be working on the budget or meeting with a perspective client? Writing an article or laying out a brochure? Attending a professional convention or crafting content for your Web site? Don't freeze. As much as you'd like to hit the imaginary time-travel button on your desk chair and be instantly transported to a beach in Maui, you need to stay and make some tough decisions.

To find your way out of every tangle, once you've determined how many steps from the revenue line a particular task is, start with the 3 Qs (the Three Questions) to determine which task to do first in evaluating conflicting obligations:

1. How long will it take?
2. What is the return on investment (ROI)?
3. When is the deadline?

QUESTION 1. HOW LONG WILL IT TAKE?

All things being equal in terms of distance to the revenue line, you can next prioritize by evaluating how much time a task will take and the relative size of the payoff for the time invested. In other words, if you have conflicting priorities in the top of the triangle, evaluate how much time each task will take, and choose the task that takes the least amount of time but yields the biggest payoff first.

Given the limited time we have to get our work done, it's foolish to look at any to-do list without also evaluating how long each task will take. But people rarely ask this pragmatic question, stopping only to consider *what* they need to do (and perhaps how they feel about each particular item—I like doing this, I hate doing that).

From a purely time-management perspective, knowing how long things take enables you to organize your day realistically. It's pointless to put twenty important things on your to-do list for Thursday if, given the time each item takes, you're really only going to get three done. It is not only better but also necessary to know the limits of your day, so you choose the three most important of the twenty and schedule the others for different days.

Join the ranks of the highest-performing, smartest workers and become an ace at both asking and accurately estimating how long a task should take. Factoring in how long things take makes the intangible factor of time *tangible,* adding objectivity to your workday so that when there's X number of hours to get a few things done, you're more likely to choose the most important tasks. Knowing the limits of your time in advance will ensure you pick the most important tasks.

CALCULATING HOW LONG TASKS TAKE

- Time how long it takes you to do a task three times, to get your average.
- Ask colleagues who have done similar tasks how long it takes them.
- Discuss it as a team. Make asking how long it will take protocol for your department or company.

QUESTION 2. WHAT IS THE ROI?

The length of time any task takes to accomplish figures prominently in determining its priority, especially in relation to return on investment.

Is the payoff big enough, relative to the time invested? Your answer may sometimes lead you to eliminate a certain task that is simply not worth the time invested. But more commonly, asking this question will help you determine the order in which to do your tasks if you are facing the limits of time on a given day.

For example, while on the road doing site visits, Jim, a field manager for an industrial cleaning/waste management company, is notified by a customer he is calling on that something unexpected has come up, and that he will be delayed for their meeting an hour or so. With this sudden window of time thrust upon him, Jim grabs the opportunity to check his voice mail, where there are three messages. He only has time to return one call—which one should it be?

Let's explore Jim's options with the following chart (something you can adapt to your own needs):

Call	Potential Payoff	Estimated time
Call back prospect (warm)	$75,000	45 minutes
Existing customer A (follow-up on proposal)	$24,000	30 minutes
Existing customer B (follow-up on proposal)	$5,000	15 minutes

Jim is tempted to follow up on the warm prospect first because the potential payoff is the biggest. But this task will take longer, and the stakes are higher because it is two steps from the revenue line—a prospect rather than an existing customer. An existing customer is always a surer sale.

Jim really likes customer B—and since it will only take fifteen minutes, he thinks it might be nice to just knock this task off the list. But if he follows up on Customer A first (potentially a payoff five times higher than customer B) and all goes well, he will still have time to give a quick call to customer B in the time he has remaining before his meeting, and bring in another 5K.

QUESTION 3. WHAT IS THE DEADLINE?

If you're looking at conflicting one-steppers with similar time investments and similar payoffs, you can choose which to do first by considering the deadline. This may seem obvious, but at high-pressure

DIANA

Diana, a staff accountant, came in early one morning full of vim and vigor to finally plow through a pile of reports that had been sitting on her desk for weeks. She needed to read and comment on them before handing them in to her boss. On her way to her office, she stuck her head in to see a colleague who happened to be in a mini-crisis—she was having a hard time making a decision and asked Diana for her help. Of course, Diana gave it to her, completely neglecting her own plans. Spending thirty minutes with her colleague paid her in goodwill and stroked her ego; it's nice to be helpful. But the ROI of getting that backlog of reports to her boss was fifty times higher. She should've told her colleague that she was on deadline, and offered to help later in the day. Lack of focus can damage productivity, especially in those short blocks of time between projects.

YES, But . . .   It's YOU!
What if I disagree with what's most important?

If you're making your own judgments about what's most important, regardless of what anyone else says—because you know best—you are in trouble. This kind of behavior is a dangerous breed of arrogance. Watch out. Your confidence is an asset, but not if it turns you into the maverick of your department!

Solution: Your company's values and senior management's concerns should be setting your priorities—not you. Remember, you were hired to provide a service. If there's a conflict over what tasks are most important, there may be a miscommunication between you and your bosses. In this case, continuing to set your own priorities, instead of following those your manager sets for you, could result in serious consequences.

moments like these, you may find yourself tempted to start with the task you are more in the mood to do, or the one you think you can finish more quickly for that sense of satisfaction, rather than the one that is due first. This can be dangerous if it leaves you without

WHAT SHOULD PATRICIA CHOOSE?

Patricia, a senior buyer for a media planning agency, is in a jam! It is Wednesday of her last week before vacation, and everything on her to-do list seems important, all one step to the revenue line, each task requiring a significant amount of her time. She has to arrange to have lunch with one key client before the end of the week to seal a deal; proof and sign off on a proposal; prep for a sales meeting taking place the Thursday before her trip; and rewrite Web content for the firm's Web site, which had been poorly done by a junior associate. She fears that when she goes on vacation, all of her best-laid work plans will fall apart.

Question: How should she handle this, to make sure that this doesn't happen? What do you think Patricia should do first?

- Arrange lunch with key client
- Proof and sign off on proposal
- Prep for sales meeting
- Rewrite Web content

PRIORITY 1

Patricia should call her key client to set up lunch on Friday first (going on vacation for a week without sealing the deal at lunch would really slow down the process on this project). In the event the client is out or on the phone when Patricia calls, there will be plenty of time to call her back and set things up so that Patricia isn't worrying about this all through her vacation.

PRIORITY 2

Next, she should prep for the sales meeting. Why? With her reputation at stake, and management counting on her, getting that out of the way would lighten her load significantly for those unexpected tasks that always have a way of popping up the week before a vacation.

PRIORITY 3

Next, Patricia should proof and sign off on the proposal so her assistant can get it in the mail.

> PRIORITY 4
>
> Last, she should rewrite the poorly written Web content for the firm's Web site; that task is furthest from the revenue line.

enough time to get to the more urgent task that you're neglecting. Always count on the unexpected and be assured that some crisis will almost always come up to prevent you from completing your original plans.

Cover yourself by always starting with the task closer to the deadline, and get that done before moving on.

LETTING GO

The flip side of choosing what's most important is knowing what to relinquish. Letting go is perhaps the most difficult challenge of all, especially for the high achiever in all of us. There's the matter of pride in one's work, fear of getting in trouble, and concern about doing anything other than a perfect job.

There are tasks that you used to be able to do, but given downsizing or changes in your industry, you just can't anymore—for example, following up every single order with an old-fashioned letter, or doing frequent networking lunches. And of course there are the tasks you'd really like to do yourself but simply have to give to a junior person because the stark reality is, you now have many more high-level tasks on your plate. Keeping up with the changes in the world around you requires the ability to constantly reassess what to do, and also what *not* to do—in other words, to "let go."

Groans abound from clients and at seminars when I say the words "let go." It's a concept people consistently ask about and have the most difficulty implementing. What if you're scared that coworkers and bosses will feel like you're avoiding a task or, worse yet, being lazy or irresponsible? What if you just can't stomach the idea of admitting that you can't do it all—lightening your load of even the smallest tasks feels like a denigration of your own self-worth, because you should be able to handle it?

There are some tasks you'll never get to—and holding on to them generates a constant state of guilt and disappointment, feelings that have an adverse effect on your productivity. Facing the real limits of the human capacity to do it all—*your* human capacity to do it all—is a key step in stress management. It's time to concentrate your energy

---

YES, But . . .   **It's YOU!**
I can't let go—I'm a perfectionist.

If you're still expecting yourself to produce huge volumes of work in high-pressure situations that demand you step back and only do what's absolutely critical, you need to rethink your strategy. Focusing more on quantity than quality in this situation entirely misses the point!

    Solution: Lighten up and let go. Producing a smaller volume is desirable because what you are getting done is incredibly important. If you're burned out and have been working fifteen-hour days for months on end, you may have lost perspective, and with it, your ability to see what's most important. See Competency 5, "Control the Nibblers," for more tips on dealing with perfectionism.

---

toward what you can and will do, rather than regretting or deflating over what you won't or can't get to.

    Letting go is easier when you've got some options on what to do with the excess. I offer you the 4 Ds to help you determine what to do with the things that you don't have time for, because you are focused on doing what's most important.

THE 4 Ds (DELETE, DELAY, DELEGATE, DIMINISH)

Use the 4 Ds to lighten your load as often as you can. Honing your ability to use the 4 Ds in conjunction with the 3 Qs is about increasing your efficiency—not about being lazy or avoiding work. It ensures each task is carefully thought through and has a place to go. Your boss/company looks for ways to up efficiency by ridding the workplace of nonessential tasks all the time; you should follow their lead and do the same.

DELETE

Ask yourself, What's the worst thing that would happen if a particular task or project weren't done? Will the company go belly-up? Will you get the firing squad? Give your to-do list a harsh look. You may find an entire category of tasks that should be eliminated to accommodate changes in your industry, your company, or even your own availability. Marianne, for example, coordinated the same community affairs event for seven years. In year eight, management decided to cancel it—the event no longer fit the mission of the company, and wasn't worth its ROI. Deleting the event from the schedule freed Marianne to do other, more important work.

Other times, it's simply a matter of letting go of one or two things on your schedule. Do you really need to attend every "optional" departmental meeting, or write detailed memos to your boss, when you end up just talking about the issue anyway? Let go of the nice but unnecessary.

DELAY

Delay does not mean procrastinate. Procrastination is about indefinite postponement; delaying is about consciously rescheduling something for a smarter time. In some cases it's also about delaying gratification (you'd really like to work on the pro bono design project, but you need to finish your paying gigs first) or saving an important task for a day when you can really do it justice instead of starting it in the middle of a really busy day, when you're better off doing something that requires less concentration.

DELEGATE

It can be difficult to know when to give something to someone else. You may be hesitant to delegate if you feel that everyone else is overloaded, just like you. Or you may worry that someone might not do as good a job as you would. It may not even occur to you to delegate something, because it's always been your job and you are doing it on autopilot.

Follow this rule: If there is something on your list that someone else can do better, faster, or well enough, give it to them. Shifting these tasks from your plate allows a team to accomplish more in less time. It also frees you to make the unique contributions your talents bring to your workplace. (Delegating is an aptitude all its own. For all the how-tos in developing it, see Competency 7, "Master Delegation.")

DIMINISH

Creating shortcuts is a way to streamline tasks. A shortcut can be anything from creating a template for client reports to shaving back on company-wide FYI e-mails.

YES, But . . .   **It's YOU!**
I get swept up in other people's crises.

Are you constantly saying yes to interruptions and other people's agendas and priorities, making it almost impossible to complete your most important tasks? When the person interrupting is your boss, that's one thing. But if you say yes to everyone from your department head to the mailroom clerk, at the expense of your own work, you need to put the kibosh on your runaway people-pleasing nature.

Solution: Learn how to say no graciously, and recognize the critical importance of your own work. Read more about controlling interruptions in Competency 5, "Control the Nibblers."

I once had a client who was a creative director in the advertising industry. He liked reading three newspapers every morning, but with his increasing responsibilities, this was just soaking up too much time. I suggested he invest in a compilation service that provided headlines and lead paragraphs from the major newspapers he liked to keep up with. His reading wasn't as thorough because he didn't get the full article, but if something caught his eye, compelling him to want the full text, he could look it up online.

Use the 4 Ds in conjunction with the 3 Qs as often as you can to hone your ability at prioritizing and to increase your efficiency. It's not a matter of being lazy or avoiding work, but rather of ensuring that each task is carefully thought through and has a place to go.

THE 3 Qs AND 4 Ds IN ACTION

There are three common work situations in which the ability to apply the 3 Qs and 4 Ds comes in most handy: planning your daily to-do list, recovering in the middle of a derailed day, and maneuvering your way through a crunch. Let's see how it works by examining a day in the life of my own business.

One Sunday night I reviewed my upcoming three days, which would be particularly harrowing. Monday, I'd be in the office. Tuesday was a travel day to Maine. On Wednesday I was headlining a Women in Management conference, giving a keynote, two breakouts, and the closing session. I'd be back in the office Thursday and

---

YES, But . . .   **It's THEM!**
My boss has impossible expectations.

Sometimes bosses are so busy and overwhelmed themselves, they don't realize the workload they are piling on you. Or their expectations are so high, they won't let you apply any of the 4 Ds. You must keep producing the same results, but with fewer resources, or your hide is skinned.

Solution: Remember, each of us has the same goal—measurable results for the company. Don't make it a "you versus them" situation. Start by telling your boss that you also want to help meet the objective, that you understand the goal is X by such and such time, and that you don't want to miss that deadline either, but you've kept a log of your tasks and can show that unless a temp is hired, or this task is diminished and another delayed, your shared goal cannot be achieved. It's acceptable if your business is going through a crunch time, but if the business has gone through a permanent change, and management hasn't revamped processes to adjust, it's them.

Ask your boss to help prioritize for you. If you run out of time, which would he or she want you to do first?

Friday, but given the energy expended in two full days of speaking and traveling, I couldn't expect myself to operate at my best.

At this particular time, I was under pressure from quite a few deadlines. I was in the middle of writing this book, my column for *O, The Oprah Magazine* was due, and my daughter Jessi was weeks away from high school graduation.

Here's what I'd hoped to accomplish that Monday:

TASK

Outline book chapter 3
Polish October column
Rehearse presentation for Wednesday
Do media interview
Call in payroll
Sign computer contract
Review seminar drafted by staffer
Check in with two clients
RSVP Volunteer Business Council
Jessi—reserve restaurant for graduation luncheon

This was a lot to accomplish in one day. Perhaps some things would have to go. There was no way to evaluate what was possible in this format until I further analyzed my list with the 3 Qs.

TASK	STEPS TO REV	TIME	ROI	DEADLINE
Outline book chapter 3	1	3 hrs	High	Friday
Polish October column	1	1 hr	High	Today
Rehearse presentation	1	2 hr	High	Today
Do media interview	1	¼ hr	High	Today
Call in payroll	1	¼ hr	High	Today
Sign computer contract	1	¼ hr	High	Today
Review seminar drafted by staffer	2	1 hr	Med	None
Check in with two clients	1	¾ hr	High	None
RSVP Volunteer Business Council	3	¼ hr	Med	Next week
Jessi—reserve restaurant for graduation	3	¼ hr	High	Friday

When added up, this totaled about nine hours' worth of tasks. Although I usually work about nine hours a day, that schedule was too tight; it left little room for unexpected questions and issues that might come up that would need immediate attention. So I applied the 4 Ds to lighten my load and leave room for surprises.

Review your own task or to-do list for tomorrow or next week, filling in "Steps to Rev Line," "Time," "ROI," and "Deadline." How does that change your view of your plans for the day? Are your plans realistic? Are they feasible? Can you lighten your load by applying one of the 4 Ds?

Even my best-laid plans are occasionally derailed for one reason or another. In fact, most days call for a few bars of pure improvisation—when you either throw your hands up and deal with the emergency, or do a little reordering to make room for the *new* most critical item. Maybe a project takes longer than you expected, a coworker, boss, or client calls in with a crisis, an opportunity must be pursued immediately, or your kid calls with a problem at school. Derailment can occur for any number of reasons.

When the world decides to move beneath you, especially without asking first, take a pause, step back, reevaluate, and reshuffle, always making sure you're coming back to land on what's most important. Mix and match the 4 Ds on these days, keeping them in your back pocket, to trade tasks in and out when you need to.

What happened to me that Monday?

I'd planned to work on this chapter for just one hour, from 10 to 11 A.M., then move on to my other projects. Well, at one-thirty, I

4 Ds	Task	Steps to Rev	Time	ROI	Deadline
Diminish	Outline book chapter 3	1	3 hrs	High	Friday
	Polish October column	1	1 hr	High	Today
	Rehearse presentation	1	2 hr	High	Today
	Do media interview	1	¼ hr	High	Today
	Call in payroll	1	¼ hr	High	Today
Delay	Sign computer contract	2	¼ hr	High	Today
Delegate	Review seminar drafted by staffer	2	1 hr	Med	None
Delay	Check in with two clients	1	¾ hr	High	None
Delegate	RSVP Volunteer Business Council	3	¼ hr	Med	Next week
Delegate	Jessi—reserve restaurant for graduation	3	¼ hr	High	Friday

found myself still working on the chapter. I had hit the "zone"—true inspiration in writing that made the time fly—and it seemed crazy not to follow through on it. However, as I looked up from my work, there was a decision to be made—should I keep riding my momentum, or downshift and return to my plans for the day?

The most important thing I did was stop for a moment to check my to-do list.

Three things leapt to my attention from my daily plan: ·

> Polish October column (1 step)
> Review presentation for Wednesday (1 step)
> Call in payroll (1 step)

I felt compelled to attend to each of these "one-steppers." Though I probably could have sweet-talked my editor at the magazine into giving me more time, I knew that postponing delivery would hold up everyone in the production department from doing their work.

Theoretically, since I wasn't speaking until Wednesday, I could have delayed reviewing my presentation until Tuesday on the flight to Maine. But the truth is, I feel much calmer and more confident reviewing my material two days before a speech, when I actually have time to make a change, than the day before. This was a big gig (one step to the revenue line), and of course my reputation is on the line when I'm on stage. I want the client who is paying me to feel good about their investment, and a good performance often leads to additional gigs. All right on top of the revenue line, with a big ROI!

Conjuring up the hanging-off-the-ledge image from Competency 1, I decided it was wisest to let go of the chapter and move on

> **HOT TIP!**
>
> Never stray too far from your to-do list! As tempting as it was to just keep going, checking your list at key pulse points during the day will prevent you from getting sideswiped by surprises and unnecessary urgencies.

to my other critical tasks. I had nearly finished drafting the chapter on paper and was excited to be transferring my notes to the computer. I spent about twenty minutes wrapping up and established a good place to start fresh on Tuesday. And because I'd just lost nearly two hours of my day to the chapter, I used the 4 Ds to reorganize the remaining tasks on my to-do list, including some new tasks, calls and e-mails that had come in that needed my attention.

YES, But . . .   **It's THEM!**
Everything on my list is a one-step.

Either because your job has grown, or because the staff of your company has shrunk, everything on your plate is critically important to the revenue line of the business.

Andy was an environmental engineer at an architectural firm. He'd been with the firm for five years, and had worked hard to learn the business and earn the respect of his peers and partners. A few years ago, his firm endured several rounds of layoffs. Andy held on to his position because people thought he was smart, hardworking, and productive. But as the firm continued to hemorrhage staff, he became a victim of his own success—partners piled on project after project, with barely any breathing room. After two years of bare-bones efficiency, Andy simply wasn't able to manage all that was critical.

Solution: Keep impeccable records of your daily results—log what you accomplish every day and what you wanted to get to, but couldn't. Then make a case to your boss about the benefits of a new hire—potentially a sizeable increase in revenue, and a staff morale boost. If approaching your boss about a new hire is out of bounds, reset your priorities with your boss. Is there something you currently do that could be handled by anyone else, or not done at all?

A 2002 study by Office Team suggests that today's workforce has too much to do and too little time in which to do it. In fact, 84 percent of managers surveyed feel that average employees are "somewhat to significantly overburdened." According to the Families and Work Institute and others, over the last twenty years, jobs have become less secure and more time-consuming—especially in troubled economic times, when employees are asked to do more with fewer resources. Such is the new work reality. No one values the frills anymore—managers and companies see the bottom line with a bald eye. What they want, and frankly expect, is for your most critical work to be done. Choosing what's most important, then letting go of the rest, will boost your productivity, reduce stress, and keep moving you higher into that top tier of workers.

In the next chapter, let's look at how we can find the time to actually achieve all the important tasks.

Chapter Summary
CHOOSE THE MOST IMPORTANT TASKS

Which grab-and-go strategies do you plan to use?

- Always dance one or two steps from the revenue line.
- Capture all of your to-dos in one place.
- Prioritize from the top down.
- Remember the 3 Qs and 4 Ds.

When do you plan to implement them?

What do you think will be your biggest obstacle in applying the strategies?

How will you overcome that obstacle?

What is your motivation for mastering this competency?

Four

CREATE THE TIME TO
GET THINGS DONE

FRANCINE

Francine is a publicist for a large public relations firm. When we started working together, she was on probation for failing to deliver her most important creative tasks—strategic planning, developing media contacts, and attracting new clients. If she didn't start producing results, fast, her livelihood was in jeopardy.

Francine had developed a reputation around the office as a deadline misser who created chaos in her colleagues' workdays. The production people had grown accustomed to shoving Francine's material in at the last minute, and the art department often had to work into the night because Francine was so late in getting them her stuff.

There's no doubt that Francine was working extremely hard, but her bosses asserted that she wasn't working efficiently. There was little to show for her efforts. Instead of the big, strategic work, she was choosing to do basic meat-and-potatoes stuff, like editing press releases and dealing with caterers' questions about seating arrangements. Francine was somehow mistaking being busy for being effective and creative.

I asked why she wasn't getting to her creative work. "Daily urgencies keep crowding out the important stuff" was her immediate reply. After all, *someone* had to revise copy and deal with contracts for publicity events. A nonstop stream of tiny details left her with no time in her day to concentrate.

"I can't find time to concentrate during the day!" is the universal cry of the new world of work.

We work and live in a staccato environment. E-mails, faxes, meetings, crises, and constant pressure create a naturally frenetic cadence to the workday. Tasks that require short bursts of attentiveness (ten-minute calls, e-mails, spontaneous conversations with clients and coworkers) are easy to get done, but responsibilities that require more time and deliberation, like writing and analysis, are harder to tend to. Often, as was true for Francine, those bigger, more thoughtful tasks are where you have the opportunity to shine and make your most valuable contribution. Therefore, it's really dangerous to your job security if those items are back-burnered or overlooked.

The most valued employees at any company manage to get things done—the little tasks *and* the creative work—despite the distractions.

How much do you accomplish each day? Do you turn work around quickly, or does it get backed up on your desk? How are you with deadlines? Do you often leave others waiting for indefinite periods? Is your office the company's black hole? Nothing feels better than getting stuff done. Regardless of your best intentions and the overall quality of your work, if stuff isn't done in a timely way, your value to your organization is compromised. Period.

But we all know work isn't about the number of hours you put in, it's about what you actually get done. You must periodically ogle top performers in your company who routinely leave while it's still light out, and still manage to produce enormous amounts of work. Are they just whiz kids—blessed with a speedier brain? Or are they managing their day better, using their time at the office more efficiently?

The fact is, just because the world moves at this crazy, presto pace doesn't mean your work necessarily fits that description. Knowing how and when to pull away from that staccato energy to focus on longer, broader strokes is critical to turning your day around.

Think of texturing your day in terms of Morse code: a series of *dashes*—tasks that require blocks of concentration, an hour or more of quiet time, like writing, design, or analytic work—and *dots*—quick phone calls, e-mails, signing checks, approving invoices, and so on.

It takes a conscious effort to create the time for dash work in a dot-defined world. You need to pull away, close your door, and protect the space. Here are four techniques to help you create the space to do the dashes so that you can boost your productivity—and increase your value.

Grab-and-Go Strategy #11
Avoid E-mail for the First Hour of the Day

Audiences gasp when they hear me say this, but let's cut to the chase: E-mail is the biggest time-suck of the modern workday. We interrupt ourselves every five minutes to check our in-boxes, hoping for something more interesting, more fun, or more urgent than whatever we're working on in that moment. Checking e-mail interrupts continuity in our thought process, and not surprisingly, our productivity plummets as a result. E-mail is undoubtedly the world's most convenient procrastination device. How many times before making a difficult call, or starting a challenging project, have you said, "Well, let me just check my e-mail first"?

E-mail plays a leading role in the development of our supremely impatient culture, where everything has to be "now, now, now!" People expect immediate responses, because an immediate response seems possible. Or you may feel driven to return your boss's or colleagues' e-mails first thing in the morning so that they know you are in the office. But just because messages arrive instantaneously in your in box doesn't mean that you have to respond immediately. Not everything is urgent, and not everything is e-mail—some projects, requests, decisions, and correspondences take time and thought. You need to fight this unhealthy speed-freak impulse and press your internal pause button. Don't let technology take away your time to think and apply your higher-level self to tasks.

Change the rhythm of the workday by starting out with your own drumbeat. The most dramatic, effective way to boost your productivity is to completely avoid e-mail for the first hour of the day. Instead, devote that first hour every day to your most critical task. When you devote your first hour to concentrated work—a dash—the day starts with *you* in charge of *it* rather than the other way around. It's a bold statement to the world (and yourself) that you can take control, pull away from the frenetic pace, and create the time for quiet work when you need it. In reality, if you don't consciously create the space for the dashes, they won't get done.

When I say NO E-MAIL, I mean it—don't even peek at what's in there until your hour is up.

Why not?

Think about it: E-mail is really nothing but a bunch of interruptions and distractions that appear in your in box without an invitation. Even checking your e-mail for a minute is a surefire way to open up all the different drawers of your brain and immediately distract

---

YES, But . . .   **It's THEM!**
What if my livelihood depends on checking
e-mail/messages first thing?

There are some jobs that absolutely require you to check e-mail first thing in the morning. If you work in a 24-hour production cycle, instructions may come in overnight that you need to fulfill upon arrival. Or if your boss leaves requests overnight that she expects to be done first thing in the morning, then it is imperative to check e-mail first thing.

  Solution: You simply need to adjust the NO E-MAIL ZONE to a different time of day—I recommend grabbing the first available hour after the immediate requests are handled. So maybe for you, it's no e-mail for the second hour of the day. But I warn you, once you're open for business, it's hard to pull away.

---

your mind with a zillion other issues. Once that happens, prolonged concentration on anything, critical or not, is nearly impossible.

FOCUS ON YOUR MOST CRITICAL TASK

To make your first-hour policy work, decide the night before exactly what you are going to tackle during that hour. Ask yourself, If tomorrow flies out of control, what *one* task (not two or three) would I be thrilled to get done—what can I do to earn my salary by 10 A.M.? Deciding the evening before will give you a chance to mull it over in your sleep and on your commute to the office that morning. Once you arrive, you can hit the ground running, instead of wasting half of your precious hour figuring out what you should do. Try it. Turn off your e-mail alarm, turn on your voice mail, and walk into your office with a single focus—completing that critical task. Don't drop in on a friend. Put on your blinders and tear into your task. The energy you'll feel from accomplishing it will fuel you all day long.

  Think about it—if you postpone your most important task, it hangs over your head all day, weighing you down with dread and guilt. If you knock it off first thing in the morning, the relief buoys you up all day long, literally energizing and boosting your productivity as you tackle the rest of the items on your to-do list.

FRANCINE

Using this technique, Francine got herself off probation. Though initially shocked at the concept of no e-mail first thing, I wooed her into making it a lovely ritual—she came in at 9 A.M. with a latte, had all her reading material assembled on a special table, and outfitted it with an incandescent lamp. Francine devoted this first enveloped hour to reading trade journals and brainstorming new market strategies.

Her biggest fear was that her boss, who often sent e-mails overnight, might need something from her first thing in the morning. At my suggestion, she spoke to her boss and explained the plan, letting him know what she would be doing for the first hour . . . and that if he needed anything done before 10 A.M. he could, by all means, knock. Since her boss was the person who put her on probation, he was completely supportive.

The morning hour became Francine's favorite time of day: Getting something critical done so early restored her confidence and bolstered it for the rest of the day. It also gave her the physical experience of full concentration—an experience she could repeat throughout the day, as needed. Victory over that first hour gave her a model to understand how it *is* possible, and beneficial, to create quiet time. This helped her assert control over the rest of the day as well.

MANAGING E-MAIL THE REST OF THE DAY

E-mail is not evil. It is just a little dangerous.

It has had two profoundly positive effects on our efficiency—first, by providing round-the-clock availability, so you don't have to coordinate schedules to communicate, and second, by automatically keeping a record of correspondence. Bottom line? E-mail can save or steal time, depending on how you manage it.

In a survey of 2,447 adults, the Pew Internet and American Life Project found that there are two types of e-mailers: average and power.

Average e-mailers receive about twenty e-mails per day and send five; this involves about half an hour per day. Power e-mailers receive at least fifty e-mails a day and send out a minimum of twenty. Which one describes you?

The most interesting thing about this study is that whether you are an average or power user, the total time e-mail probably entails each day is between thirty and ninety minutes. That's really not so bad. The question is, Why does it feel like much more than that? How come it seems as though you spend over half your day on e-mail? It's because you are probably checking it all day long, several times per hour, interrupting your concentration to just see what's in there. Opening and closing e-mails only to save them as new is poor e-mail discipline.

Even if you avoid e-mail for the first hour of the day, it still has a way of eating your time alive. Let's look at other ways to loosen the grip of e-mail.

- **Keep your e-mail alarm off.** Check e-mail at designated times of day—e.g., 10 A.M., 2 P.M., 5 P.M. If an issue is that critical or urgent, someone will call you. Ninety percent of the time, things can wait.
- **Process e-mails fully during your e-mail sessions.** Respond immediately to e-mails that can be answered in two minutes or less. For e-mails that require more thought or research before responding, schedule a specific time later in your day to take care of the matter, and respond then.
- **Say what you need in the subject line.** In many cases, you can write everything you need to in the subject line, keeping the body of the e-mail wonderfully blank—"Please schedule staff meeting for Friday 11 A.M.," "Lunch meeting set for 1:30." Similarly, if you need an immediate response, say so in the subject line—"URGENT"—and ask others to do the same.
- **Start longer e-mails by telling the reader what you need from her/him.** A little note like "Please review and advise," or "Can you double-check the numbers below?" will save the recipients time, focusing their thoughts as they read.

TIP FOR MANAGER

Create an e-mail protocol for your office, to get staff on the same page and save everyone time. Use any of the tips in the section above, along with any of your own, to speed up productivity by making e-mail communication more effective.

YES, But . . .   **It's THEM!**
I get 100-plus e-mails a day.

Some jobs bring enormous amounts of e-mail.

Solution: Try one or more of the following suggestions to manage them efficiently: (1) Set filters on your e-mail to pre-sort by sender, so you can process e-mails in priority order. You can deal with different categories of e-mail at different times of day. (2) Have an associate or assistant read and summarize all of the e-mails you receive as CC, FWD, or FYI, bulleting the highlights and letting you know which ones really do require your attention. (3) Time how long it really takes to process e-mail, and structure your day accordingly. (4) Take your e-mails through the 4 Ds in Competency 3—delete, delay, delegate, diminish.

- **Stick to one or two points per e-mail.** Long-winded e-mails that require scrolling down the screen don't match people's attention span on the monitor. It's much more efficient to write a separate e-mail for each issue than one twelve-page letter to catch someone up on ten complicated matters.
- **Create stock responses to routine requests.** This will help spare you the trouble of rewriting the same message over and over— "Thank you for your inquiry about employment. We aren't currently hiring, but will keep your résumé on file. Someone will follow up with you if a position becomes available."
- **Limit FYIs.** They clog e-mail boxes, confuse recipients, and waste their time. Never send an FYI without telling the reader at the beginning of the message why you think it would be of interest to him, and what you want him to do with it. FYA (For Your Awareness) can be used for political purposes—for example, to keep a colleague or boss aware of an issue that is brewing so that he will know to hold on to it . . . in case.

Substituting e-mail for all human contact is a mistake. Some people hate when a coworker or direct report who sits eight feet away from them writes an e-mail instead of speaking in person. Use the warmth and personal touch of a phone call when the nuance of how you are saying something matters, and meet in person to form stronger bonds or when you need to spread out project work or brainstorm with a group. As a general rule, use e-mail to convey dot-like information; discussions about creative, lengthy work—the dashes—should be done in person.

Grab-and-Go Strategy #12
Beware Multitasking

Once thought to increase productivity, multitasking has since been discovered to do the exact opposite.

NeuroImage, a science journal, has determined that managing two mental tasks at the same time significantly reduces the brainpower available to concentrate on either one, ultimately damaging the quality of your final product.

The *Journal of Experimental Psychology* found that it takes your brain four times longer to recognize and process each thing you're working on when you switch back and forth among tasks. This means that if your day is a random free-for-all, in which you hop from task to task in no particular order, your work will literally take much longer because of the real time you lose switching gears.

Think about it. If it takes you fifteen minutes to get oriented to the new task every time you switch gears, and you switch gears ten times a day, there's two hours and twenty minutes of wasted time. But that's not the worst of it. Severe multitaskers experience a variety of symptoms, including short-term memory loss, gaps in their attentiveness, and a general inability to concentrate. In other words, a growing body of scientific research asserts that multitasking can actually make you less efficient and, well, less smart.

If you instead concentrate on one task at a time, and group similar

FRANCINE

Every time Francine was asked about the status of her bigger projects, her response was that she was "working on them." And she was, but nothing was ever completed. Her coworkers and boss were stupefied as to how she could work such long hours and never finish anything. They figured she was being inefficient—probably chitchatting, languishing over decisions, overcomplicating tasks, or procrastinating.

When I pressed the issue with Francine, her explanation was far from what anyone would've guessed. Her intentions were noble—she was genuinely trying to manage her overwhelming workload. But her particular method was ineffective. That's why she had nothing to show for her efforts.

Francine explained that whenever she was faced with too much to do (which was every day), the way she calmed herself down was to work a little bit on each task. This way, she figured, she at least got everything started, giving her some sense of being in control. She approached her day like a plate spinner in a circus, constantly switching from project to project and giving it a little spin. Unfortunately, the very method Francine used to calm herself down made her boss and coworkers frantic. No one could do anything with something that was "almost done."

Francine's constant multitasking approach was preventing her from being a productive, useful member of her team. Intellectually, Francine was easily convinced that it would be far preferable to have 50 percent of her projects 100 percent done than 100 percent of her projects 50 percent done. But breaking her multitasking habit would be difficult; working on one thing at a time was counterintuitive. She needed to be retrained away from her natural impulse to do a little of everything—and trained to focus on one task at a time and see it through to completion.

tasks, you could be one of those people who leave the office in time to coach your kid's soccer team! And get just as much work done! Not only does multitasking have a quantitative impact on your day, it can also damage the *quality* of your work.

Do any of those symptoms sound familiar? Do you think your work suffers from too much multitasking? Think of the quantitative gain—

don't you want your work to be the highest quality possible, so that you'll save time not having to redo it? Study after study has found that doing only one task at a time helps you get more quality work done in less time.

DETERMINE YOUR CONCENTRATION THRESHOLD

Once you've invested the effort to create the time for the dashes, make sure your concentration abilities are up to the job. How long can you ignore all distractions and give 100 percent of your attention to one task? Ten minutes at a time? Thirty minutes? Two hours? Four hours?

We each have a different concentration threshold. Find out what yours is. How long can you give one task your undivided attention before you begin to feel saturated, distracted, or antsy to take care of something else? Study yourself—you may be surprised what you learn.

At the height of your threshold, there's an enveloping feeling that *anything* would be better than what you're currently doing. It's like your skin no longer fits your body; you're jumpy. Or you feel the pull of checking in with the "outside world." You need to move around, check e-mail, check voice mail, go to the water fountain.

For some, focusing even for ten minutes on just one task can be pure torture. Others delude themselves, believing they can concentrate for two hours, but upon closer inspection they realize that they actually interrupt themselves every thirty minutes by checking voice mail and e-mail and filing their nails. In many cases, the office around you may be buzzing so furiously that a twenty-minute break in the action is the most time you'll ever get.

YES, BUT ...   It's YOU!
What if I miss something important?

Sometimes we get caught up in believing that we might be missing something—so we keep checking e-mail, wandering around the office, and chatting on the phone instead of shutting the door and focusing on our own work. The fear of being isolated from what might be happening around you keeps you from getting through your to-do list.

Solution: Try working in fifty-minute bursts of quiet time, giving yourself the final ten minutes of every hour to check e-mail, pick up messages, and touch base with the group.

Once you know your threshold, begin to build up your tolerance. If you start at ten minutes, add five minutes, then five more, and five more, increasing to twenty, then thirty minutes. Your goal is being able to focus for a full hour. There's no easy way to do this—it's simply a matter of forcing yourself to hang in there, postponing curiosity and satisfaction for just five more minutes. You'll be amazed how much you can actually get done in a full twenty minutes of complete focus.

FOCUS ON THE JOY OF COMPLETION

Gallup surveys have shown a direct correlation between job satisfaction and achievement. People who accomplish a lot are driven by a certain joy of completion—the thrill of crossing things off their to-do list. It's often what keeps them focused when the going gets rough on a particular task—they have their eye on that victorious feeling of crossing it off, or handing it to their boss or colleague: Here, it's done!

An adrenaline high gets triggered when things are finished. That sense of accomplishment is highly energizing, and keeps you tackling one task after another all day long. Francine, for example, found this to be a new way of thinking. She had always been focusing on "What can I start?" rather than "What can I finish?" She had to turn that around.

Here's the key: Once you know your concentration threshold, break your tasks down into the increments in which you can concentrate. This way, you can enjoy the sense of finishing things in the time allotted. You can get something *done*—actually completed—during your period of focus.

Let's say you're responsible for planning a sales meeting. There are many aspects to this project and ideally you'd love to clear out an entire week where you could shirk all your other responsibilities and just get this done. But that's not realistic. In fact, the longest block of time you can ever get to concentrate on the dashes is thirty minutes. Each time you get a dashlike block, instead of just planning to "work on it," ask yourself, What specific tasks can I complete in thirty minutes?

- Come up with a theme for the meeting.
- Review last year's attendee list, and cross off the names of terminated employees.
- Add new names A–M.
- Add new names N–Z.
- Call three possible speakers for agenda.
- Draft e-mail to staff soliciting speaker ideas.
- Send e-mail to staff soliciting speaker ideas.

The idea is to focus on completion—what can you get done?

This way, you can report to the powers that be what you have accomplished—not just say, as Francine so often did, that you're "working on it." They get a sense of where you are, that you are making progress and producing results. This helps them plan their next steps and schedules. You become emboldened, encouraged, energized by the sheer joy of completion!

Grab-and-Go Strategy #13
Stretch Time by Planning

One of the primary causes of multitasking is worry. Without a plan for when you are going to do things, you fall into the trap Francine did, scattering your efforts. An enormous amount of hidden time is lost to indecision—wondering what to do next, failing to give a task your full focus, because you second-guess yourself. This? Or that? Without a plan, you don't know; and that fear and anxiety makes you resort to a scattered approach, because if you don't do it now, you don't know when you'll get to it.

The best way to get your work done, no matter what your job title, role, or position, is to have a plan for your day or week that determines *when* you do *what*. A to-do not connected to a *when* doesn't get done.

People who plan their day find that time stretches—they are suddenly able to get so much more done, yet the day seems calmer. You can concentrate confidently in the moment, assured that there is a time and place for your other responsibilities. Having a plan frees you from confusion and distraction over what you should do next, or worry about what you might be missing.

GROUP SIMILAR TASKS

A powerful way to minimize the time lost to switching gears all day long is to group similar kinds of tasks. This pattern can be as simple as paperwork in the morning and calls in the afternoon. Or you could organize your pattern into sections of the day to concentrate on each of your core responsibilities—generating reports, then e-mail, then meetings, then research and filing.

If you set aside an hour to do all your sales calls, even if each one is only ten minutes, you'll stay in the sales mind-set and get through them faster, and perhaps even more skillfully. Something you say in your first call may inspire you to take a new tack with your second call, and so on. Batching calls is faster than one at a time.

Of course, as with finding your quiet hour, you should try to plan your day around your energy cycles . . . or your industry's natural flow, or your boss/coworkers' schedules.

SAMPLE DAILY PATTERNS

People at every level of an organization can create a routine for themselves that allows them to stay focused in the moment. Even people whose jobs are based solely around supporting others, like a customer service rep, an administrative assistant, or a full-time manager, can assert some control over the beginning and end of their days for critical paperwork, filing, creative work, and strategic planning. Here are some examples at varying levels of an organization:

- **A middle manager.** Francine's schedule is a series of dashes and dots. Following her first quiet hour, she checks e-mail. The morning is her peak energy time, so she'll then dive into a series of concentrated tasks until lunchtime. She uses lunchtime for developing media contacts and new clients, and by 2 P.M. she is back at her desk, checking e-mail again. This time, she gives priority to e-mails from external people—caterers, media people, and so on. The afternoons are reserved for all the day's crises—four full hours of dots.

9:00–10:00	Reading, strategic planning (dashes)
10:00–10:30	E-mail—internal (dots)
10:30–12:30	Writing/concentration tasks (dashes)
12:30–2:00	Media and client lunches (dashes)
2:00–2:30	E-mail—external (dots)
2:30–5:00	Open for any crisis (dots)
5:00–5:30	E-mail—all (dots)
5:30–6:00	Wrap up loose ends (dots)

- **Administrative assistant.** Anna is an office information manager. It's her job to keep the office humming. She is responsible for data entry, computer backup, bank deposits, mail processing, and any urgencies that arise. Every day brings something new, but even with that unpredictability, Anna has managed to create a routine that enables her to handle the chaos calmly. By getting her routine tasks (and, in this case, the "dots") out of the way in the morning, Anna is more comfortable working on project-driven ("dash") tasks in the afternoon. Does her boss periodically need something NOW? Absolutely. But since Anna has a pattern to her day, she can relax, concentrate on the moment, and have a baseline to keep coming back to.

8:00–12:00	Routine tasks (dots)
12:00–1:00	Lunch
1:00–5:00	Project work (dashes)

- **Executive, crisis manager.** Connor's primary job as the director of inpatient care at a mental hospital is to be available at all times to the psychologists he is supervising to help them troubleshoot problems. If Connor gets a call, he needs to react immediately. He does his case reports for the first hour of the day and spends the rest of his time putting out fires. His door is always open to his staff, and patients are encouraged to call with issues and questions. At each and every lull, he returns calls and e-mails. What works about this structure is its simplicity—by predetermining what's done with downtime to the second, he never squanders a moment wondering what to do next. Tasks that require more concentration than phone calls and e-mail are written directly into his schedule as appointments with himself. Because he's incredibly disciplined about sticking to his schedule, the most important, thoughtful tasks get done—and he's able to keep his pledge to return *every* call and e-mail the day he receives it.

8:00–10:00	Reading, reports (dashes)
10:00–5:00	Crisis management, meetings (dots)
All "down time"	Returning calls (dots)

WORK WITH YOUR ENERGY CYCLES

For maximum productivity, try to coordinate your pattern with your natural energy cycles. The morning is best for many people, but if your brain doesn't kick into gear until later in the day, you may need a different time. Attempting to concentrate at a time of day when you're sluggish is highly inefficient—a project that would normally

---

YES, But . . .   **It's THEM!**
My job hours are irregular.

Erratic schedules don't lend themselves well to a time structure. If you work different shifts every week or are a part-timer, producer, or freelancer, your schedule changes all the time. So how do you create pattern?

Solution: Either plan each day one day in advance, or take a broader view by creating a pattern that spans weeks or months.

YES, But . . .   **It's YOU!**
There will be days when I can't stick to my plan.

Sure, there will be circumstances under which you will have to cast your day to the wind! Which is why your pattern is a *general* structure—one that is designed to work *most of the time.*

Solution: For the occasional emergency that simply can't wait, drop your plan and go full steam ahead. On every other day, having the discipline to stick to a routine will keep you grounded as you move swiftly through your day with confidence and clarity.

---

take you one hour at peak energy time can end up taking two or three. And remember, everyone, no matter what their job title or step on the totem pole, needs at least one hour a day for quiet, concentrated work.

The nice thing about using the first hour for your critical, dashlike tasks is that it's often easier to resist the gravitational pull of outside demands before you get involved. It also seems reasonable to "delay" people for an hour, at the most, since you will have the whole rest of the day to address their matters once you "open shop." Grabbing quiet time once the chaos has begun is extremely challenging, because you feel the tug of calls waiting to be returned, coworkers lined up outside your door, meetings demanding your presence, crises needing attention. It's hard to concentrate when you feel like you *should* be doing something else.

If you can't, or don't, take the first hour of the day, use the following suggestions to make it easier to pull away:

- Build in a transition ritual. Get up for a stretch thirty minutes before your quiet hour and walk around to see if anyone needs something before you go "into the hole."
- Be consistent. Train your boss, and all the people you work with, to know when your quiet hour is. Let them get used to it. They may even copy you.
- One of these three times could work for a quiet hour: between 12 and 2 P.M. (when much of the world is out to lunch and would reasonably expect you to be); from 3 to 4 P.M. (much

ALICIA

Alicia was the fashion director for a beauty magazine. Two weeks a month she was in the field doing photo shoots. With her days running twelve to fourteen hours, messages would build up because it was impossible to call people back. The other half of the month Alicia spent back in her office, designing and planning the next shoots, and finally having a chance to meet with staff and return calls and e-mails.

When I met Alicia, she complained that her two weeks in the office were less productive than she'd like. While she was in the field, a million ideas for projects, calls, and tasks would occur to her. But by the time she got back to the office, she'd usually waste the first week just trying to get reoriented and remember what she'd wanted to do. By the second week she'd finally get in gear, but never with enough time to get everything done. All she needed was a plan, and a way to make sure she was prepared for her time in the office.

We added a section to the back of her planner called "Back at the Office," so that while she was in the field, whenever an idea occurred to her she could write it down. Then, the day before her return to the office, Alicia would review her lists, plan the next two weeks, and hit the ground running on her first day back.

Week 1	Field shoots
Week 2	Field shoots
Week 3	Staff management, correspondence, planning next shoot
Week 4	Staff management, correspondence, planning next shoot

YES, But . . .　　　　　　　　　**It's THEM!**
I'm constantly bombarded by interruptions.

Do drop-in visits, e-mails, phone calls, meetings, a disruptive coworker, or the location of your desk/office make it impossible for you to get things done in a timely manner? Kerri was renowned for being one of her company's most productive employees. When people needed something, she was the go-to person; she'd know the answer to the question, and if she didn't have it, she'd find it. Her workstation was located in a very busy area of the office, which she liked, because it made her so accessible. But it also made her an open target for interruptions, preventing her from getting things accomplished.

Solution: If this describes your situation, you might need to do some of your most concentrated work from home. Also read Competency 5, "Control the Nibblers."

---

later than that is too hectic, with people trying to wrap up projects for the day); or the very end of the day, between six and seven or seven and eight, after everyone else has gone home (this is purely a lifestyle choice).

- Close your door (if you have one), put on voice mail, turn off your e-mail alarm.

Remember, this is a self-imposed meeting with your critical tasks; it's just like being in a meeting with any other customer or client. So no matter what is going on out there, it's perfectly reasonable to ask people to wait—up to fifty-nine minutes—for you to be available again. Remind people that the outcome of that hour—a measurable result—will make everyone you work with happy.

The techniques presented in this chapter are meant to boost your productivity—but not at the expense of expunging any spontaneity from your workday. To some degree, asides with friends at the vending machine and a little time spent daydreaming now and then are just as important as making time for your "dash" tasks. There's no denying that many of our most creative bursts have resulted from an unexpected phone call or an impromptu brainstorm that might never have found its way onto our schedule. In fact, the camaraderie and teamwork between coworkers gives any office its unique energy. If we were all solitary automatons, simply checking off one to-do after another, the workplace would be lonely; most of us would never last

TIP FOR MANAGER

Institute a department-wide "quiet hour" policy. It's a way to make sure your people designate the time they need for critical work, without feeling guilty or remiss in shutting people out. Designate one or two times every day when the whole department or company puts their phones on voice mail, turns off e-mail, and refrains from interrupting one another. This could be the first hour of the day, the end of the day, or between 12 and 2 P.M., depending on what's reasonable for your industry.

With an institutional quiet hour in place, people will naturally start to synch their schedules with their boss's and coworkers', so they are available to meet one another at the same time.

One client institutionalized the quiet hour at her firm by using a gong—the striking of the gong signaled the beginning and end of each quiet hour. Managers should ask every employee to list one or two types of tasks that both demand a longer period of concentration and are difficult to set aside time for—client work, reading, proposals, reports, research. Make it official. No meetings. No voice mail. No e-mail responses. Quiet hour for all.

YES, But . . .   It's YOU!
The only quiet time I can get is when I am exhausted.

Obviously, we can't always get quiet time when we are at our peak energy level. The broker whose best time of the day is the afternoon may have to be at his best in the morning, when the deals are made.

Solution: Fortify your energy by preplanning. Identify ways to boost your energy, aiming for the healthiest means to do so. Take a brisk walk, exercise, get up for a stretch, eat a power bar or other healthy snack. Awareness is everything. Consciously managing your energy throughout the day by proper planning, rather than mindlessly grabbing a candy bar or fifth cup of coffee, will help you produce more in less time and stay healthy.

the eight, ten, or twelve hours of work each day. (To learn more about working well with others, skip ahead to Competency 8.)

Now that you have the proactive skills to get more done every day, it's time to address the nibblers, little things that steal time from our workday when we aren't looking—interruptions, meetings, perfectionism, procrastination. Let's tackle them head-on.

Chapter Summary
CREATE THE TIME TO GET THINGS DONE

Which grab-and-go strategies do you plan to use?

- Never check e-mail the first hour of the day.
- Pay attention to your natural energy cycles.
- Beware of multitasking.
- Stretch time by planning.

When do you plan to implement them?

What do you think will be your biggest obstacle in applying the strategies?

How will you overcome that obstacle?

What is your motivation for mastering this competency?

Five

CONTROL THE NIBBLERS

FRANCINE

We met Francine in Competency 4, "Create the Time to Get Things Done." A publicist whose job was in jeopardy because of her failure to deliver on her most important tasks, Francine got herself off probation and regained her job security by implementing the skills I'd taught her. She marveled at the boost in productivity concentrating on one task at a time afforded her, and the e-mail-free morning quiet hour had become her favorite time of day. "Planning works" became her byword.

About a month after our work concluded, I checked in to see how Francine was doing.

Most days—when she stuck to her plan—she was happy and successful. But every few weeks she felt her old bad habits of taking a casual approach creeping back up on her. On those days, she would forget to plan, yield to bouts of perfectionism, or allow herself to get sucked into hours of office chitchat. Every time she was deterred from planning her days, her productivity took a dive; she now needed the tools to fight the gravitational pull of her old habits.

Francine was falling victim to "the nibblers." How could she stop herself from slipping?

The nibblers are distractions that gnaw at our ability to concentrate, threaten our productivity, sabotage our plans, and steal hours every day. These insidious saboteurs, defined here as perfectionism, procrastination, interruptions, and meetings, have likely ingrained themselves into your everyday routine—stealing five minutes here and ten minutes there, threatening to hijack one workday after the next. Competency 4 armed you with the tools to build a framework for your day, and that's a great place to start; but maintaining your productivity and success in the workplace means juggling a stream of disruptions imposed by both internal and external factors.

Do you remember when you first learned to drive? If you were anything like me, you learned in two stages. The first step was driver's ed, which definitely covered the basics for taking control of the vehicle—steering, accelerating and braking, three-point turns, road signs, horn etiquette. It was an education in offensive driving— proactive techniques for maneuvering the car in a perfect world, where everyone followed the rules.

Then my father gave me a series of lessons in defensive driving. He showed me how to handle a car in relationship to the real world. A brilliant driving teacher, he taught me to think ahead and be prepared for real contingencies—like reckless drivers, skidding on ice, and hydroplaning in light rain. He also made me aware of my own inclination to go too fast, ride the brake, and drift to the right. Being prepared for these scenarios was the real key to being safe and successful on the road.

Competency 4 was the driver's ed version of getting things done. Those strategies work, every time—they're the basics. But it would be unfair of me to stop there, because that's not the full story. It's time for the advanced course—the defensive driving lessons: preparing yourself to tackle the real contingencies you will encounter as you travel toward completing your to-do list.

KNOW YOUR BLIND SPOTS

In driving, of course, it's critical to know where your blind spot is. Similarly, you need to anticipate your blind spots at work.

No matter how disciplined or focused you are, everyone deals with the nibblers to one degree or another. It's unrealistic to think you could avoid them altogether. Whether it's a conference call that goes on too long, a coworker who hounds you with a zillion questions, or your own tendency to procrastinate on your toughest tasks, things happen that can throw even your best intentions off track.

What counts is how you deal with them in the moment, and how you maneuver your way back to being in control. Which nibblers are you most vulnerable to?

NIBBLER 1. PERFECTIONISM

Perfectionism is a sticky wicket. On one hand, upholding strict standards of excellence helps many people and companies compete. On the other, that same striving for perfection can spin into a paralyzing trap that halts projects and generates undue stress.

Perfectionism, when left unchecked, can lead to dangerous work standstills. It's a burden that can zap the joy out of work and create physical health problems, from increased anxiety to high blood pressure.

NIBBLER 2. PROCRASTINATION

To procrastinate is to indefinitely postpone or to avoid performing a task out of anxiety, rather than time constraints or logic. Procrastination involves unfocused wandering. Instead of spending time on something productive, procrastinators waste their energy taking multiple trips to the coffee machine, checking their e-mail, rearranging their pencil drawer—anything to avoid the dreaded task.

NIBBLER 3. INTERRUPTIONS

"Got a minute?" "Can we have a quick meeting?" "Is this good enough?" "Can you help me with this?" "Can I run something by you?"

Interruptions are sudden requests and demands that you hadn't planned on dealing with at that moment. Dealing with interruptions, perhaps the most menacing nibbler, is a delicate balance. When you work with other people, you want to be supportive and keep the work flowing; yet if you take every single interruption, you'll pay a high price in your own productivity.

NIBBLER 4. MEETINGS

Meeting overload is one of the most common complaints among my clients—many lament spending half their week in meetings that are mostly a waste of time. Whether you're the leader or a participant, there's little more aggravating than meetings that start late, go on forever, and fail to resolve a darn thing.

Well-run, useful meetings provide enormous value—they can solve problems, generate ideas, save you time, clarify direction, tighten work bonds, build teamwork, and reignite passion for your individual projects. Because this is an arena in which you are so much at the mercy of other people's work habits (or lack thereof), knowing how to get the most out of meetings—without them getting the most out of you—is a fine skill.

The nibblers have a funny way of working together that can make it difficult to tell when it's you and when it's them. Have you ever welcomed a phone call or other interruption so that you could put off a meeting with a difficult direct report? Or let a meeting run on too long because of a drive to resolve something perfectly?

Regardless of how the nibblers manifest themselves, or whose responsibility they are, my main objective here is to prevent them from stealing more than their fair share of time, and teach you techniques to put yourself back on track, whenever you get derailed.

Expect the unexpected. Instead of throwing your hands up helplessly, be prepared with recovery tricks. If you go into denial or succumb to wishful thinking, you will get caught in the same traps over and over again. Use the following tips, techniques, and strategies to battle back all four with a plan.

Grab-and-Go Strategy #14
Crunch Your Container

Just like the trunk of a car, your day is a container in which you need to fit a certain number of tasks. When you carefully arrange things inside, you can fit so much more in (as you learned in Competencies 3 and 4). But also like the trunk of a car, the bigger the space, the more stuff you have to haul around.

Once you start thinking of your day as a physical entity that can only hold so much, you realize you can exert control over its size and shape. You have the power to choose: How many hours do you want your container to hold? How long is your workday? How long do you want it to be?

Too often, we get into a rut with our work hours, falling into a pattern where we automatically put in, for example, ten hours a day. Subconsciously, we believe our worth is measured by the number of hours we stay at work. It's as if we say, "Hey, my work may not be done, but I'm working hard, so no one can call me to task. After all, I've been here for ten hours!"

Working long hours is the easy way to fulfill our obligations. But good work is not about the hours we put in; it's about what we actually get done.

If you consistently work longer than an eight-hour day, I challenge you to break the rut you've fallen into by crunching your container and stealing time back from yourself. Think of it as a reward for all you've accomplished so far—you deserve it! ZAP—your workday just got thirty minutes shorter. If you are used to leaving the office at seven-thirty, make seven your new exit hour. Accustomed to leaving at six o'clock? Get yourself out the door by five-thirty.

This may seem ludicrous—the workday is too hectic as it is, why apply even more pressure? Because it puts the fear of God in you, that's why. Think of yourself on a really tight deadline. Do you dawdle? Do you chitchat? Absolutely not!

Chatting with colleagues, getting a snack, redoing work that's already done, and surfing the Net are all habits that, left unchecked, waste time every day. How do you dillydally? Do you gravitate toward long business lunches when you could accomplish similar results over the phone, do too much research on simple issues, or let personal stuff, like paying bills and talking to friends, intrude at work?

List your top three time-wasters here:

1. _____
2. _____
3. _____

Now, how do you to keep these time drains in check? First, simply become aware of them. When you see yourself slipping into a less productive mode, stop dead in your tracks and ask yourself these three questions:

- Why am I doing this?
- What is the gain?
- What is the risk?

The more you recognize your saboteurs, the less likely it is that you will let yourself get away with it.

Look over your list of top three time-wasters. Every time you catch yourself doing one of these things, put a checkmark next to it and write down how much time you lost. Most studies show that one hour per day is lost to inefficiencies. Crunching your container eliminates thirty minutes of that wasted time.

So shake yourself—look alive! If you put a fire under your tail every day, you'll jump to it to get the work done.

Crunching the container is the best and most efficient way to eliminate the majority of the dillydallying you do everyday. But beyond

MICHELLE

Michelle approached me after a seminar in which I had been presenting this strategy. She told me how she had used it herself, and how it had changed her life. A workhorse who'd prided herself on putting in twelve-to-fourteen-hour workdays, she'd never taken breaks for lunch, or even dinner. She was always there on the job, stoic and true. But at the age of thirty-three, she weighed 275 pounds and was beginning to experience panic attacks, insomnia, and heart palpitations. After an emergency hospital trip, with a heart attack scare, she swore she would "clean up" her work life. She promised she'd leave work promptly at 6 P.M. every night and go to the gym.

At first she was scared of becoming dispensable at her job (losing her old reliable identity), but to her surprise, her productivity at the office soared. It was completely counterintuitive, but by crunching the container of her workday, she got much more done.

Go figure. She hadn't realized the number of ways in which her workhorse self had been wasting time every day. Her increased productivity led to promotion after promotion. She's now the special projects director for her old company, and has since started her own nonprofit, dedicated to helping women in business. She still firmly sticks to her eight-hour workday, and manages to get more done in a week than most people get done in a month. She's also lost 130 pounds, has kept it off for eight years, and has never felt more healthy, productive, or valued by her clients, coworkers, and family.

that, you may encounter bigger obstacles—internal habits that are harder to break, and the external expectations of other people. These are real, significant obstacles to effectiveness that deserve to be focused on one at a time.

Grab-and-Go Strategy #15
Apply Selective Perfectionism

More than anything else, perfectionists are looking for security. Problem solvers at heart, perfectionists often feel invigorated by a rush of adrenaline every time they go deep and start refining the nu-

FRANCINE

Francine's worst nibbler was the paralyzing grip of perfectionism. Her boss had told her many times that it was more important to get things done, than to get them done perfectly. Like so many organizations, they had pared back on staff and let go of certain tasks, projects, and events altogether to cut costs. Francine's eye for excellence and perfection had always been an asset to her company. How could she be expected to lower her standards now, just when she was recovering from probation?

On an intellectual level, she knew that she occasionally lost her perspective, crossing the line from truly enhancing a project to simply becoming counterproductive. Sometimes she'd find herself working hard to perfect something that she knew didn't really matter—like writing a simple in-house memo or an e-mail to a colleague.

ances. "Airtight" results make them feel safe—they are fulfilling their own expectations, while immunizing themselves against criticism or complaints about their work.

Perfectionists tend to evaluate everything they do in one of two grades, either perfect or a complete disaster—there is no in-between. This approach is demoralizing, degrading, depressing, and unimaginative.

A lack of perspective leaves perfectionists feeling crushed by the weight of their own expectations. They are constantly mad at themselves for not getting to that reading pile, or failing to return every single phone call and say yes to every single request.

Perfectionism has its place—you can and should hang on to your eye for excellence—but apply it only where it really counts. In the unique stresses of today's workplace, every perfectionist (including Francine) needs to undergo an *evolutionary* adjustment, and develop what I call *selective perfectionism*—the art of deciding which tasks need to be perfect, and which ones can just be good enough.

Apply a version of Paredo's 80/20 law, the economic theory that 20 percent of the population earns 80 percent of the income. Only 20 percent of your tasks need to be completed with absolute perfection—plans for clients, products that are sold, information distributed to the public, materials sent to the top 20 percent of your clients . . . Save your perfectionist eye for tasks and projects that are essential to the revenue line of the business.

The more adaptive and facile your perfectionist muscle is, the better the contribution you can make to your company, while keeping your own health in order.

Take the perfectionist in you to task, with these tips:

- **Ask yourself who the critic is.** Who does that voice in your ear *really* belong to? Usually, it's not the people you work with, it's someone in your past—a harsh parent, teacher, coach, or sibling, or yourself. Recognize that the critics you're railing against may not exist in the present and may no longer be relevant. So ignore them! Pay attention to the people who understand the work you're doing and have a hand in its evaluation.

- **Practice doing one thing less than perfectly.** Start with a lower-stake task—something that your rational mind knows doesn't need to be perfect—and allow yourself to do a so-so job. Who knows, your version of "good, but not perfect" may be someone else's version of great.

- **Back away.** When you work on something for too long without any breaks, you reach the point of *diminishing returns:* the state in which you spend hours and hours getting almost nothing done, or worse, fixing things that weren't broken by second-guessing your first, best impulses. Recognize when you are reaching that point and force yourself to back away. It will save you hours of futile effort and time spent redoing work done in a fog of poor judgment. Better yet, get a second opinion. Hearing what one or two people say, whose opinions you respect, is a way to give yourself some distance and perspective.

- **A deadline is a beautiful thing.** And if one isn't handed to you, impose it on yourself. Focus on completion—remind yourself that something done imperfectly *on time* is often better than something done perfectly that's late.

- **Delegate the small tasks you obsess over.** There are tasks that simply take you twenty times longer to do than they would take someone else—and that amount of time is compounded if you insist on doing them flawlessly. Know your limits. If you are struggling with a task that someone else can do faster, better, or good enough, let it go. (See Competency 7 for more guidance on successful delegation.)

- **Limit the number of revisions you grant yourself.** Perfectionists often revise things to death, because they can always see ways to make an improvement. Computers make it far too easy to keep changing your work. Track yourself for a week to see how many times you tend to revise documents. If it's normally seven times, pare yourself back to six, then eventually five, or four. Once you hit your targeted number of revisions, stop! Recall the days before computers, when editing wasn't so easy, and fight back a little.

- **Recognize degrees of excellence.** When I first started speaking professionally, I knew when I'd hit a bull's-eye performance—it felt like I was "hanging ten," riding the waves of the audience's emotions with perfect timing. Each person hung on my every word; the room was so quiet that a cell phone ringing would make everyone jump out of their skin. When I didn't hit that mark, I was crushed, disappointed, and mad at myself. I felt like I had failed the audience.

  But feedback forms would tell me just the opposite. To my great surprise, the audience expressed having loved the presentation and gotten enormous value from it. I'd be mystified—were they just being nice?

  I discussed this perplexing phenomenon with a more seasoned speaker at a National Speakers Association convention one summer. He gave me words of wisdom I'll never forget. Jamie knew what a perfect performance, felt like, but had come to the realization that it was impossible to hit a 10 every time. Because he was a trained speaker with well-developed material, he'd learned to trust his skill set. His audience would enjoy and garner something from his speech, even if it was less than perfect. So each time he spoke, he figured as long as he hit at least a 7 (which was also excellent—the audience could never tell the difference between a 7 and a 10), he could live with himself and feel good about his performance.

No matter how much anyone assures you that good enough is good enough, it can still be hard to release your own need to do everything at an equal level of perfection. Your harsh evaluation does not necessarily align with other people's perceptions of your work.

One of the most important real-rules driving lessons my father impressed upon me was that I was driving much more than the steering wheel. Before he even let me stick the key in the ignition, he had me walk around the car and see how far this big metal machine extended in front of and behind me.

Perfectionism requires the development of similar points of reference; when your need to polish things to death runs amok, it comes from a skewed perception of your work in relation to other people.

Just as a car is bigger than you think, your credibility and reputation for excellence extend beyond any single thing you do. You've got

FRANCINE

Francine learned to fight her perfectionism every day, and began by practicing doing one small task less than perfectly. She skimmed a proposal and forwarded it to her boss with a quick handwritten note, rather than investing an hour in carefully typing a memo covering every thought. She enjoyed the lighter feeling of selective perfectionism, yet for several months she felt like she was getting away with something. But the other shoe never fell; no lightning struck. She survived. And her boss was absolutely satisfied with her comments.

The real test came when her boss sent back one project with corrections. Her first reaction was panic—Francine felt like she had utterly failed. Her boss assured her that the corrections were nothing more than that, a request to change a few lines here and there. He reiterated that he valued getting things out on time more than anything else—so some things would be perfect and others would require revision, but at least the work would be flowing. In time, Francine learned to tolerate the corrections and not take things personally. She trusted the contribution she was making, so she could keep getting things done.

a body of work in front of you, and a body of work behind you. Perfectionists are unforgivingly harsh on themselves, feeling the need to "prove it" on every single task, forgetting the ways in which they've already proven themselves in the past, and will in the future.

Besides, so what if your work needs correcting? Perfection, after all, is very hard for others to measure up to. Imperfections are endearing—it makes you more accessible, easier to relate to, and lets other people have a job to do. You really aren't in this alone.

Grab-and-Go Strategy #16
Replace Black-and-White Thinking with Shades of Gray

Procrastination means doing nothing. And doing nothing has an impact. Your action, or *in*action, dramatically affects the people around you. Your procrastination on tasks makes it difficult for other people to get their jobs done, their work may be stalled, and the quality of your work—done at the last minute—may suffer. If you wait until the last minute to start a project, and then at 5 P.M. go to a colleague to ask for help, they may not be there for you.

If you frequently fall victim to procrastination, study yourself for a couple of weeks by keeping a log. Do you procrastinate about everything or only some things? Some people procrastinate primarily on big projects; others tend to avoid the little, boring, or annoying tasks.

Procrastination is a self-saboteur (in other words, it's definitely *you*) that is closely related to perfectionism. It involves stalling on starting or finishing something out of anxiety rather than logic.

One of the best ways to combat procrastination is to identify the cause of your hesitation the moment it occurs. Getting to the heart of the matter will help you find the solution.

- **The task is too big.** Often we are intimidated by the size and scale of a task. You don't know where to start, or have the feeling that if you do start, you'll barely make a dent—so why bother?
- **Performance anxiety—the fear of making a decision.** Demanding, risky, and requiring courage, some of the tasks on your list are intimidating for one reason or another. You may be worried about making a mistake, or not feel confident in your ability to get the job done.
- **Fear of what comes next.** Sometimes we put things off because what's next is something that makes us really anxious. Hiring a new employee means change and risk. Completing a difficult new staff-policy memo means facing the disgruntlement of the masses.
- **We work better under pressure.** Some people thrive on the adrenaline rush that comes from leaving things to the last minute. It's a thrill, it's a little dangerous, and they love the victory of rescuing themselves from near disaster. Other people work better under pressure because it takes the edge of performance anxiety off. This is where procrastination meets perfectionism. Perfectionists often leave things to the last minute because it takes them off the hook—subconsciously they feel that if the work isn't perfect, they have a built-in excuse. It's not a reflection on their abilities, they just didn't have enough time.

Taking an all-or-nothing approach to any project is unwise; being sophisticated in the workplace involves the ability to think in nuances. Learning to think in shades of gray takes the pressure off—it stops you from procrastinating and frees you to move forward.

- **Break it down into smaller tasks.** It's not about doing it all or doing nothing. Keep yourself from always delaying tough projects until another day by breaking an overwhelming task down into smaller, manageable thirty- to sixty-minute bites. Outline a critical memo one day, flesh out the introduction the next day, the body the day after that, and give it a final polish on the fourth day. Mark Twain once said, "The secret of getting ahead, is getting started."

- **Slip in sideways.** Sometimes it's hard to start a project at the beginning, but if you start on the second or third step, something less threatening, you can get into the water. When you're writing a letter, for example, the opening paragraph may be the most difficult. If you're stuck, try jumping to the body of the letter and outlining the four bullets you want to cover first. Get that out of the way, and the intro may come easier.

- **Do a fast and sloppy version.** Anne Lamont's best-seller *Bird by Bird* has a chapter titled "Shitty First Drafts." That's one of the best pieces of advice for procrastinators around. If you can't get past the first paragraph, relax your standard and write whatever comes to mind to get a whole draft on the page. Assume it will be awful. Allow it to be dreck. Rush to get it done early (which is the opposite of your tendency to push deadlines to the last minute). One you've got anything on paper, you'll be relieved to at least have something done, and you can make corrections with the extra time.

- **Focus on the payoff.** What one thing are you hoping to gain from completion? When filling out expense forms, think about what you will buy with the reimbursement. While slugging through that annual report, imagine the special bonus that may be coming your way. If you take your eye off the particular task, and focus on the happiness and success you'll gain from completion, you can often keep yourself moving forward.

- **Remember past victories.** Just because you're experiencing a setback doesn't mean you're doomed to fail! You have made your way through similar challenges in the past; have a little faith in your record and charge forward with confidence. If you're having trouble, reach out to a friend, colleague, or boss for a pep talk.

- **Set time limits on difficult tasks.** Setting aside either too much time or not enough time can make you procrastinate. Setting aside an hour to do expense reports? Minimize the torture by shrinking it down to thirty minutes and get as far as you can. Trying to write a customer letter in thirty minutes and can't get

---

TIPS FROM THE MASTERS

Anita Riggio, an author and illustrator of children's books, uses a simple kitchen timer (or stopwatch) to help her push through procrastination. When she's having trouble getting started on a project, she grabs the timer, sets it for twenty minutes, and stations the device next to her computer or near her drawing table. For the next twenty minutes she forces herself to sit tight and stay focused on the work. By the time the bell rings, she's usually engaged enough to keep going. If she's still having trouble after twenty minutes, she gives herself another chance, repeating the process up to two more times (to make a full hour). Could this strategy work for you?

---

started? Try giving yourself an hour and see if that does the trick. Similarly, work with your need for pressure by moving your deadlines up. If something is due in two weeks, drive yourself crazy to get it done by this Friday. If it's due in three days, get it done today.

- **Choose the best time of day.** Plan to do things you tend to procrastinate on at your peak energy. Dedicate at least thirty minutes to getting those things off your plate, so the rest of the day can feel like a reward. For help in building your concentration abilities, see Competency 4.

Finally, if you're procrastinating to the point of paralysis, try fantasizing about worst-case scenarios. Take a five-minute break to focus on what you're scared of. Allow your mind to run wild with the most horrible outcome, and find the humor in it. What's the worst thing that could possibly happen? Are your worst fears well founded?

If you still can't get moving, you might as well give in. Give yourself permission *not* to do something; completely take yourself off the hook for the day. And then, just for the heck of it, and because it doesn't matter anyway, go ahead and spend fifteen minutes on it. Our best, most creative work often emerges when it just doesn't matter. Release the pressure, throw your hands in the air, and do one for the Gipper! And if nothing gets done, so be it. Reschedule the task for another, fresher day.

Grab-and-Go Strategy #17
Anticipate Surprises

The key to defensive driving is anticipation—it's all about predicting what the other guy will do next. My father taught me to expect everyone on the road to break all the rules. Speed limit 55 mph? Expect people to push 80. Signal before turning? Don't count on it. Pass only on the left? Fat chance.

The same is true of interruptions—you can outsmart them with keen anticipation. Not all interruptions are the same; likewise, not all interrupters are the same. You could be disrupted by a phone call from your biggest client . . . or your spouse. Both break up your flow—but they are of a decidedly different breed.

It's one thing to handle interruptions on a case-by-case basis; it's a taller order to break a deeply ingrained habit that you, and the peo-

---

CATHRYN

When Cathryn came to me, she was sinking under the weight of a superhuman workload. Bright, ambitious, and talented, she'd started her new job as a program associate at a community health center two years earlier, and had quickly won praise due to her willingness to help on any project.

She had become the designated "go-to" person at her center. The good news was that her willingness to pitch in had yielded the reward of new and more important responsibilities. The bad news was, these new assignments took a different level of commitment, and with the constant stream of interruptions, she had no time to get to her work. She was in a rut—stuck believing that her value was tied up in being available for "anything at anytime," and worried that abandoning her do-it-all approach would disappoint everyone. So she never said no and kept piling it on. In fact, she kept inviting the requests, saying yes with a smile on her face and dread in her heart.

Cathryn was trapped in her childhood belief that value and validation come from being able to do for others. She needed to change her definition of hard work.

Value, I explained, doesn't come from being able to manage 1,001 projects and please everyone. It arises from a personal, concentrated connection to what you do best.

ple you work with, have grown accustomed to. If you are someone given to extreme people-pleasing, change involves shifting old patterns and altering behavior.

The people most vulnerable to being overrun by interruptions are those who feel responsible for everyone and to everyone. My goal is to get you off autopilot, teaching you to weigh and measure each situation. You can exert more control than you think.

EXPERIENCE THE REALITY

Even if you feel like you're fairly experienced at handling interruptions, it's good to pay attention. Study the real time lost to interruptions every day, and the importance of each one. Track yourself for a week or two. Know who is likely to interrupt you, and why, and understand your own proclivity to be railroaded by someone who bursts into your office begging for help, or that tendency to reach for the phone every time it rings.

Each time you are interrupted, whether it's by someone else or yourself, note the time, and how the interruption came—via e-mail, telephone, or drop-by visitor. Then grade the importance and urgency of the interruption: A = critical and urgent; B = important but not urgent; C = unnecessary and not worth the time. Your log may look something like the one below.

SAMPLE INTERRUPTION TALLY

Time	Who	Via	Issue	Length	Grade
9:15 A.M.	Office manager	e-mail	Approval for ordering monitors	:10	B
11:20 A.M.	Boss	Call	Evaluation for new hire	:25	A
11:45 A.M.	Customer	Call	Confirm delivery dates	:05	B
1:40 P.M.	Coworker	Drop-by	Discuss boyfriend problems	:35	C
2:30 P.M.	Boss	Drop-by	Plan board presentation	:15	B
3:50 P.M.	Son	Call	Have I seen his soccer shoes?	:05	A
4:25 P.M.	Coworker	e-mail	Opinion on her proposal	:20	A

The best way to prevent unnecessary interruptions is to think and plan ahead. Use the following strategies to outsmart the interrupters—and your own compulsion to say yes to every Tom, Dick, and Mary.

- **Calculate your daily interruption ratio.** Each type of job allows for a different ratio of planning—how much of your day can be proactive (i.e., planned tasks) and how much is reactive (i.e., unplanned tasks). Study your log to determine the average time lost to interruptions each day, giving special focus to A- and B-level interruptions. If together they add up to two hours of interruptions a day, and you work an eight-hour day, your ratio of proactive to reactive time is 75:25. In other words, on any given day, you can only plan six hours of work, and must leave two hours per day open to allow time for the inevitable interruptions.
- **Choose two or three people who can interrupt you, any time.** Make a short list of key people (definitely no more than five) whose interruptions you will always take, no matter what you're doing. These are people where the buck meets the road—probably your boss, the company president, one or two key clients, and your spouse or child (in case of an emergency). Then fight your own impulse to please the pushy people who will try to wriggle their way onto your short list.

HOT TIP! X MARKS THE SPOT

If you need to stop in the middle of a project, make it easier to pick up where you left off by writing yourself a little "Next Action" note. On a brightly colored Post-it, placed directly onto the document, indicate where you left off and write down the very step you need to take next. For example: "Read last three pages, write summary, highlight changes, check the address, draft closing paragraph." Investing a minute to mark your spot before you stop will save you time currently lost to getting reoriented.

According to study by the Institute for Advanced Management Systems, it takes at least twenty minutes to get back to the level of concentration that had been attained before the disruption. Leaving a Next Action Post-it can eliminate that reorientation time completely.

YES, But . . .   **It's THEM!**
People always take more time than they say they will.

Some people have no sense of time; others are notorious for saying they only need five minutes when they really mean thirty.
They minimize how much time they need just to get their foot in
the door.

Solution: Know who you are dealing with. If it's your boss,
you need to shrug your shoulders and just give her the time she
needs. If it's a chatty coworker or client, try outsmarting him.
Offer him double the time he's asking for, then stop the interruption in its tracks. For example: "You only need five minutes?
I can actually spare ten, and then I've got a [conference call,
meeting, appointment, fill in the blank]." When the time is up,
stop, whether or not the discussion is over. A few experiences
like that, and your time-hogging colleague will plan his time
with you attentively.

- **Defer everyone else to a better time.** Postponing dealing with an
  interruption enables you to prepare yourself to discuss the matter in a more focused way. Remember, just because a coworker
  brings you something the moment it happens doesn't necessarily
  mean it's a crisis! Some issues are urgent, but most can wait. Build
  several "open" times throughout the day to funnel interruptions,
  so that everyone is handled—but on your schedule, not theirs. On
  most occasions people are fine waiting, especially if you get back
  to them when you say you will. (See Competency 4, "Create the
  Time to Get Things Done," for tips on how to create a pattern to
  your day that allows time for interruptions.)
- **Rehearse a few, comfortable catchphrases** to help you handle
  interruptions, so you are not caught off guard. You don't have
  to say no to everyone, just those people who have no sense of
  boundaries, who always take longer than necessary, who talk
  on and on and take advantage of your time. Be prepared for
  them with an automatic response—"I'm in the middle of finishing a project, can we talk this afternoon?" "I'm on a really tight
  deadline, can we catch up before the staff meeting?" "Gosh, I'd
  love to help you out . . . but this week is impossible." That'll
  make it easier and more natural to defer interruptions in the
  moment.
- **Create a buffer.** Have someone (like an assistant) screen your

phone calls and e-mails, or put your voice mail on and turn your e-mail alarm off. Encourage people to leave a specific message (with your screener or on your voice mail), indicating what they need and the best times to call them back. If your office or desk is akin to Grand Central Station, look for creative ways to set up your space so you're less likely to give in to distractions. Moving your chair or setting a plant on your desk can have a cocooning effect, fending off potential interruptions and helping you stay focused on the task at hand.

- **Ask how long it will take.** Every time you're interrupted, ask how long the person needs (fifteen minutes? forty-five?). Tell them you want to know so that you can clear your schedule to

CATHRYN

For two weeks, Cathryn tracked and analyzed her interruptions. Though some had high value, the majority were clearly the result of people being spoiled by her enthusiastic offers to help. Cathryn could see that at least 80 percent of the interruptions were unneccessary matters that people could really handle on their own. Her goal was to eliminate the least important interruptions and create a 50:50 ratio to her day—50 percent for program development work and 50 percent for spur-of-the-moment drop-bys, phone calls, and meetings.

She reviewed the log with her boss and got his sign-off on what she could drop and what she should always help with. He was completely supportive of a shift in the way she spent her time—he was looking forward to the results of her attention on higher-level projects.

Then, for the first time, during a staff meeting when she was asked to take on an extra project, she mustered up the courage to simply say *no*. Cathryn told her coworkers how her job had evolved since she started and explained that she would no longer be available to help on certain things. To Cathryn's shock, her coworkers were fine with the limits she had set—no one screamed, no one was mad at her, everyone welcomed her decision and adapted to the change. Cathryn had always hoped they'd all intuit that she was overwhelmed, but now she understood that this was an impossible expectation. Everyone else was too busy handling their own workload to keep track of hers too.

> ### YES, But . . . It's YOU!
> #### *I hate saying no!*
>
> Of course you want to be reasonably accessible to the people
> you work with. But an over-the-top need to be liked, to be the
> hero, to be valued, can be a trap—if you spend you entire day in
> helper mode at the expense of completing more critical, rev-
> enue-driven tasks. If you thrive on the martyr/rescue role, you'll
> do anything for anybody at any time, because the approval at
> that moment feels good. Remember that people-pleasing in-
> cludes more than the person standing in front of you at that mo-
> ment. For each interruption you say yes to, ask yourself who
> you will be disappointing. Who else did you promise to delieemr
> something to? The next time you're working on a project for
> your boss or a key client, and someone comes to you begging
> for help, decide whose disappointed face you can tolerate
> least—the person in front of you or your boss.

give them the focus and attention they really need. If you can't
swing twenty minutes now, reschedule for later when you have
more time. Holding people accountable to the time they ask for
helps them be more efficient, too.

- **Begin the conversation with "What can I do for you?"** not
  "How are you?" "How are you?" is an open invitation to chat
  and warm up. "What can I do for you?" immediately focuses
  your interrupter on getting straight to the point. It's professional and gets you both down to business. This enables you to
  handle the interruption in the least amount of time possible.

Grab-and-Go Strategy #18
Make Meetings Worth Their While

Meetings keep people from working on other revenue-generating
tasks—like responding to customers, designing new products, court-
ing new business, and so forth—but few people realize the huge tab
poorly run meetings can run up. Calculate the cost of who is coming
to your meetings, by using the chart on page 134.

Considering the cost, if a meeting is called, there should be a payoff. In this era of impersonal, rushed communication, it's easy to get
isolated from one another, and meetings can have value—if:

CONSIDER THE COST OF MEETINGS

Figures reflect a forty-hour workweek, excluding benefits.

Salary level	½ HR	1 HR	2 HR	3 HR
$30,000	$7	$14	$28	$42
$50,000	$11.50	$23	$46	$69
$70,000	$16.25	$32.50	$65	$97.50
$90,000	$21	$42	$84	$126
$100,000	$23	$46	$92	$138
$125,000	$28.50	$57	$114	$171
$150,000	$34.50	$69	$138	$207
$200,000	$46	$92	$184	$276

Chart adapted from *Managing Effective Meetings* by Harold Taylor, 1977.

1. They have a clear purpose.
2. Only the essential people are included.
3. They are as concise as possible.
4. They will benefit from the in-person aspect—i.e., not achievable by memo, phone, or e-mail
5. They end with a clear plan of action.

DIAGNOSE THE PROBLEM

What causes meetings to go awry? Why do they fall off course? Whether you are the meeting leader or just a participant, consider if any of the following factors make your meetings a drag. A quick fix may put you right back on track.

- **Inconvenient time.** If a meeting is scheduled at a bad time of the day or month—when everyone has other pressures on their minds (like finishing the annual report, or getting out the door for the weekend)—it will be hard to get people's full attention. Participants are less likely to come prepared, because they are scrambling to meet some other deadline. Morning meetings may catch the height of most people's energy, but that time is probably better used for more concentrated, solitary work. Also beware of late-afternoon meetings, when people are tired and spent from the day. If late in the day is your best option, keep participants lively with refreshments and invigorating discussion.

- **Too long or too short.** Given the staccato nature of our work-day, discussed in Competency 4, it's just too nerve-racking for anyone to be away from their work for too long. It's better to break an overly ambitious agenda down into a few different parts and stay within the time alotted than push to cover too much at once. On the other hand, if you don't allow enough time for everything to be discussed, participants will be frustrated that their time was wasted talking about something that saw no resolution, and will probably require another meeting to follow up. An ideal meeting length matches the attention span of participants with the breadth of the topic discussed.

- **Unclear agenda.** When a meeting is vague in its intention (What is to be resolved?), it will be impossible for participants to stay on topic. Similarly, if participants don't know the agenda in advance, they can be caught off guard and innocently take the meeting in the wrong direction. Even meetings with stated agenda topics will inevitably give rise to unanticipated obstacles, ideas, and side paths—determining which issues are relevant, and which are beside the point, is a challenge. Also, beware of those who come with their own hidden agendas and are determined to talk through issues, no matter what.

- **Wrong mix of people.** In a great, effective meeting, you can feel the room buzzing—everyone is engaged, connected, and interested, all striving toward a common purpose. But when people are not connected to the topic, the energy plummets, as people slouch in their chairs, engage in side conversations, appear bored, check wireless e-mail, or do other work. Bored participants don't make for a great meeting, but that situation is not nearly as explosive as a meeting where a particular set of colleagues are known to butt heads on every issue. You may value each of their views privately, but in a meeting, their difference of opinion turns into a long, drawn-out argument that no one has time for. Do your best to keep those people from coming to the same meetings; meet with them separately, if you have to. If the battling duo must attend, seat them on the same side of the table, with several people between them. Their eye contact will be limited, minimizing the chance for all-out conflict.

MEANINGFUL MEETINGS

Whether you are the meeting leader or a participant, there are ways you can prevent useless, time-wasting meetings. Prevent the most common pitfalls, discussed above, with these tips:

LEADERS

Question the value of each meeting. Can the purpose of the meeting be achieved as effectively through a memo to the staff? Is there anything on the agenda that could be better accomplished in a series of one-on-ones, or via phone or e-mail?

Question the value and consider the cost of each participant. Make certain that every person at your meeting is an essential player—remember the "cost chart." Each person you invite sacrifices a big investment of their time, and the company's money. For example, if one participant is presenting an idea and is only required for that part of the meeting, give him the timetable and have him come just for that portion.

If you are respectful of people's time, they are more likely to contribute and feel good about the meeting, instead of being resentful, detached, and difficult.

PARTICIPANTS

Ask if you must attend. Does it feel like there are other things you could be doing with your time that would better serve the company's mission? Sometimes your boss might invite you to a meeting so you don't feel left out—or she may need you to help support her by being a good role model.

If you are required to attend meetings that you think are a waste of your time, talk to your boss. Ask what the value of your attendance is (you may be missing their intention, and once that's clarified, you can go as a more active participant). If after that conversation, you still think there is a better investment of your time, bring it up to your boss again, but this time explain that you could spend an extra hour working on project X, or attend the meeting. See what she says; after all, she has an investment in your productivity as well.

Can someone go in your place, as your representative? Ask yourself if someone else (like a trusted assistant) can go in your place. Similarly, alternate attending weekly meetings with a team member— keep each other updated on the most important information, and any follow-ups that are required.

The executive director of a nonprofit used to attend every meeting the development department had. As the public face of his organization, he wanted to understand the background of every campaign the development team was initiating. But the development team met all the time—with full department meetings at least four times each week, which often went on for at least an hour.

Development-team members actually relished each meeting—they brainstormed, shared daily updates, talked about hot topics in the development world—but these were details the ED didn't necessarily need to know. Eventually he decided to only sit in on one development meeting each week. The development director could keep him apprised of important issues that didn't come up in the larger meeting, and he would still feel connected to the team.

Question the length of the meeting. Time spent in meetings keeps people from working on other revenue-generating tasks. If someone has agreed to meet with you, consider it an honor and respect their time. Limit the meeting length to thirty minutes. You'd be surprised how much can be done in that brief amount of time.

Ask if the meeting can be shorter. In smaller meetings, suggest that the topics covered be limited to accommodate a shorter time frame. For larger meetings, ask if you can attend only the portion that directly relates to you. Make your case by explaining the other work you will tend to in the time not spent at the meeting.

Control lateness. Use odd start times, such as 27 or 41 minutes after the hour, to control lateness. People are far less likely to be late for a meeting that starts at 11:27 than one at 11:30. Designate an official timekeeper to watch the clock for every meeting, and rotate that role among attendees. It's their responsibility to regulate the meeting so it doesn't go overtime, and they'll have an invested interest in doing a good job—they could be on the other side of the clock the next time around.

Show up on time. And let people know that you are there. Volunteer to be the timekeeper. Your meeting leader may feel uncomfortable cutting people off, either for political reasons or because it's just not their managerial style; but if you are the clock watcher, it takes the onus off of them.

Create a clear agenda for each meeting, limited to *three* topics. Any more than that is too ambitious, too overwhelming, and almost assures that the meeting will run longer than you originally planned. Announce the goal of the meeting—are you there to explore an issue or resolve

Ask for the agenda of each meeting beforehand (even if it's just you and one other person). Having a stated agenda will focus you and the person who has requested the meeting.

(continued on next page)

it? Be specific about what exactly is to be resolved. Knowing the purpose will keep people on target, and prevent everyone from going too far down a road that there aren't answers for yet.

Have meetings standing up. It's surprising how much gets done.	**Offer to have the meeting in someone else's office.** It'll be easier to excuse yourself when the meeting is over than it is to kick people out of your office.

No matter how hard you try, meetings will fall off course. That's the nature of human beings. Instead of helplessly yielding to the derailment, be prepared with some recovery tricks to get the meeting back on track.

MEETING OFFENSES	LEADERS	PARTICIPANTS
Rambling off topic	**Have someone record side issues in a notebook called the "Parking Lot"** and schedule follow-up meetings to address these issues in a timely way. A Parking Lot will capture important questions/issues that may be off the agenda, but deserve to be considered in their own time and place.	**Rehearse recovery lines.** When someone goes off track and the leader doesn't catch it, ask, "Is this something we all need to be here for?" "That's an important topic, why don't we schedule a separate meeting on that?" "This seems off topic—can someone write that down in the Parking Lot?" "Seems like this level of detail should be hammered out one-on-one."
Dealing with latecomers and rudeness	**Start on time—regardless of who's there.** And don't stop to catch the stragglers up on what they just missed. People who are late will be embarrassed into showing up on time next time.	**Be prepared.** If certain meetings always start late, bring work to do while you wait, or plan ahead to confer with a coworker about another project when you arrive. Capitalize on that time, instead of letting it be wasted.

	Ban wireless e-mail devices and cell phones during meetings. It steals time and focus from the task at hand.	
Lack of decision making by end of meeting	Leave a fifteen-minute wrap-up time for every meeting. State what was resolved, even if it wasn't everything you'd hoped to achieve. If a second meeting is required, select the date then and there. Publicly agree on next actions—who will do what and by when? Assign deadlines, and be sure you, or the meeting secretary, records these actions. Don't let anyone wiggle out with a vague "I'll let you know." If they can't give you a delivery date at the meeting, set a deadline for when they will get back to you. Don't yield to the temptation to figure things out later— once the group disperses, all hope of clarity goes with it.	Follow up, follow up, follow up. If the meeting leader fails to end his session with specific next actions, take the initiative to ask what happens next. Follow up with the meeting yourself. Writing a short e-mail after the meeting, or making a quick phone call, can ensure that you get done what you need to (even if it wasn't clear in the meeting itself) and aren't blindsided by a task, or project, that wasn't apparent.

Conquering the nibblers is mostly a matter of awareness, combined with a few well-rehearsed techniques. But remember, no matter how diligent you are, you will never eliminate the nibblers totally. It's up to you to control them by recognizing and fighting your inner demons.

Be easy on yourself; know that you are bound to make mistakes and will get caught by the nibblers along the way. Review this chapter periodically to give yourself a refresher course, or to master new techniques whenever you need them.

Chapter Summary
CONTROL THE NIBBLERS

Which grab-and-go strategies do you plan to use?

- Crunch your container.
- Apply *selective* perfectionism.
- Replace black-and-white thinking with shades of gray to prevent procrastination.
- Anticipate surprises by calculating your daily interruption ratio.
- Make meetings worth their while.

When do you plan to implement them?

What do you think will be your biggest obstacle in applying the strategies?

How will you overcome that obstacle?

What is your motivation for mastering this competency?

ORGANIZE AT THE SPEED OF CHANGE

MARK

Having been the top salesman at a medical supply company, Mark was promoted to sales manager because of his impressive track record. Mark's chronic disorganization had not been a stumbling block to his salesmanship, but in his new role as manager, where he now had to deal with volumes of corporate memos, reports from his field reps, and mountains of other paperwork, his mess was catching up with him.

Mark's desk was a sea of paper. He rarely even knew what was there. He was often afraid to take calls from his field reps because he wouldn't be able to find what they wanted to ask him about.

Before meetings, Mark would find himself scrambling to locate his materials for the agenda. His disorganization was now slowing him down and holding him back professionally; he felt ineffective and looked bad to his bosses and coworkers. If he wanted to move up the next rung on the company ladder (and he did), he needed to improve his organization skills first.

He kept trying to find the time to get organized, but that time never came. The phones never stopped ringing, the meetings never ceased, and the intense scramble to close deals was always there.

Every hour of every day at work, we are bombarded with information that comes to us in myriad forms—memos, regular mail, e-mail, reading material, computer attachments, handwritten notes, phone messages, business cards. In order to seize opportunities and beat the competition, we must be able to separate information we need from what we don't at lightning speed, without missing a beat.

It's the great irony of the modern workplace that the volume of information we have to process—and the speed at which we have to process it—requires us to be exceptionally organized, yet that very same pace leaves us virtually no time to *get* organized.

The costs of messy desks, briefcases, and computers are huge: When we let stuff pile up, we end up paying for it in hours lost looking for misplaced information, overlooked ideas, wasted space, and in some cases, a bad reputation.

I'm sure you don't need to be convinced of the benefits of being organized—you probably crave order every day. What you don't realize is that knowing how to get and stay organized is a critical competency. Top-tier workers can find what they need, when they need it, swiftly, calmly, and clearly.

But, as with my office organizing clients, your desperation to get organized is choked by the very limited amount of time you can devote to this project. These days I'm lucky if I'm able to get my clients' attention for three to four hours; then *whoosh,* they are swept back up in the pressure to produce. So I've had to invent ways for them to make quick, dramatic improvements in the least amount of time.

I will share those techniques with you in this chapter, so that you can find what you need when you need it, feel light on your feet, make a glowing impression on your colleagues and clients, and feel comfortable in your space.

Each technique is designed to take fewer than four hours—a speedy turnaround compared to the twenty-four hours it usually takes to completely overhaul the average office. Spend as much or as little time as you need to meet your goals.

Grab-and-Go Strategy #19
Build on What Works

No one is disorganized everywhere: There are always sections of your office—even if it's just one desk drawer and the bookshelf—in good order. Mark had his reference materials in impeccable order: He kept binders with ad rates at his fingertips, and he tacked up-to-the-minute ad schedules to the bulletin board next to his phone. The accessibility of this info enabled him to assemble proposals and quotes and close deals quickly.

The problem area was his management-related stuff—expense reports, corporate forms, and procedure memos, most of which came in the form of paper, were spread out all over his desk. Handling these were a new responsibility for him, so it's not surprising that it was in disarray.

Instead of waiting for enough time to open up for you to overhaul your whole office, let's target the areas that do and don't need fixing and understand why. By breaking up the project in this way, you can zoom in to any one area and fix it relatively quickly, then get back to the projects on your plate.

First, let's be clear on what being organized means. In the most straightforward terms, being organized is not about whether your space is messy or not—it's about the effect of the clutter on your productivity.

Pinpoint the problem. You could be facing one (or all) of three critical problem issues:

- **You can't find things.** This is the biggest problem of all. If documents, information, and materials get lost in your system (or lack thereof), your efficiency and the quality of your work plummet. Period. You squander an enormous amount of time (sometimes as much as two hours a day) searching for misplaced items. You procrastinate on key projects because you're worried you won't be able to find what you need.
- **Other people can't find things.** Perhaps *you* know where things are, but no one else understands your system. As a member of a team with whom you share information, you may be creating problems if others can't find things in your space when you are out. Have there been complaints? An assistant who doesn't understand your system can't be as helpful as an assistant who knows the system and is a part of it. There's also nothing worse than being on the road—desperately needing a document—and not being able to tell someone where to find it. This wastes time and sometimes reduces the trust your peers and boss have in you, which can stunt your career.
- **You're out of storage space.** The accumulation of material, unchecked and unweeded, in your office results in a space that is cramped with visual clutter. Just looking at it saps your energy; you automatically use brain power to think, When will I ever get to it? The decisions about what to keep and what to

toss aren't easy, and in the heat of the busy workday, many people just don't bother.

Each specific problem requires a different solution.

PROBLEM	SOLUTION
You can't find things.	Redesign or tweak your systems.
Others can't find things.	Label your existing system.
Overstuffed space.	Weed out or add storage.

Your workspace consists of eight primary areas. Which ones are *really* causing you a problem—and specifically what *is* that problem? Inventory these potential trouble spots to find out what's working and what isn't by creating an inventory chart, as shown below. For each area, indicate whether the problem is that you can't find things, others can't, or you're out of storage. Naturally, you can have more than one column checked for each area—for example, if you can't find things it's likely that your coworkers would be hard-pressed to locate things in your office as well.

Next, prioritize: Which area is having the biggest effect on your productivity? What area is worst for you? Fixing which area would

OVERSTUFFED AREA	I CAN'T FIND THINGS.	OTHERS CAN'T FIND THINGS.	OUT OF SPACE.
1. Desktop			
2. Paper filing system			
3. Computer filing system			
4. E-mail			
5. Rolodex/contacts/database			
6. Briefcase			
7. Reference/reading materials			
8. Supplies			

instantly make you more effective on the revenue line? A streamlined filing system, so you could follow up on prospects currently lost in your system? Or your desktop, so you have a clear space to work and meet with coworkers? If there are several areas in which you can't find things, always tackle the area that you spend the most time in, because it will provide you with the biggest sense of relief and power.

Grab-and-Go Strategy #20
Create a Road Map for Your Colleagues

If you can find things but others can't, you are probably what I call "messy, but organized." You work from a visual memory, and can remember exactly where things are in each stack. There is a method to your madness—the system *works for you*—so don't change a thing. Give your coworkers, boss, and direct reports access to your files by equipping them with a road map to your system.

There are several ways to do this.

- **Label clearly.** Using a label maker and a series of same-colored Post-its or squares of paper, give a title to every stack, drawer, shelf, and folder in your office. If you are a "master piler," place a colored sheet of 8½ by 11 paper atop each pile, or tape a label to the edge of the shelf under each stack. Indicate on the outside of each file drawer and bookshelf what the contents are—either by broad category (Clients, Marketing) or a specific inventory of the contents (Appleton, Brittany, Catering, Dance Companies, and so on).
- **Create a file index.** Even if your filing system isn't perfect, it's easy to create a one-page guide to where you've stored everything. Begin simply. Open each file drawer (or box) where you keep your records, and list the contents. Example: "Top drawer of black filing cabinet: corporate paperwork—health insurance, expense reports; middle drawer: Appleton, Brittany, Catering, Dance Companies, Equestrian Societies; bottom drawer: marketing budget, promotional materials, Web site updates, marketing campaigns, and Web site info.; stacks on top of the credenza: annual reports, P & L's by month." Give a copy of your file index to your assistant or coworker, and carry a copy with you while you travel. This way, anyone can find anything in your office regardless of whether you are there or not.
- **Use photos.** Take a picture or draw a floor plan of your office, indicating the contents of each pile of "stuff."

YES, But . . .   **It's YOU!**
I don't want *people to be able to find stuff!*

Sometimes desktop chaos serves a conscious purpose—to keep people out of your office and out of your way. Several of my clients admit to using the piles of stuff and chaos in their offices as a wall to hide behind—to be less transparent, more protected, to always look busy, and thus less interruptible. The need for such a barrier does not necessarily mean that you are avoiding accountability or responsibility. More often, it's just a work style for the more solitary and creative among us who like to go deep into their work and lose themselves for hours and prefer not to have people barging in on that concentration all the time. Also, there may be materials we legitimately don't want others having access to—private sources of information, or confidential records.

Solution: If this is your situation, separate what's confidential from what's open access, and lock up the confidential materials. Clear out a concentrated workspace, and then divide the materials in your office into logical and consistent groupings—even if you keep hiding behind those towering stacks. In other words, it can be organized, but messy—enabling you to find what you need, and still look confusing to other people.

Creating a road map for most offices usually takes no more than an hour if you know where everything is, and it's well worth the effort. No one likes to feel out of control, and providing a direct translation of your system will help coworkers feel more confident, and less aggravated, when they have to grab something from your office or return an item.

Providing a road map to your coworkers is similar to what you and your spouse or partner might do at home with household accounts and tax/legal papers. Even though one person is probably responsible for paying the bills, every household member should know where to find vital documents in an emergency, just in case the bill payer isn't available. The same general rule applies to coworkers. It's in your best interest, if you are out sick and an angry client calls in demanding a status report, that instead of dragging your flu-ridden self into the office and contaminating everybody, you can place a quick call and direct someone else in your office to *easily* find what's needed.

TWEAK YOUR EXISTING SYSTEMS

Organizing at the speed of change sometimes means having faith in your old basic systems and integrating things into them, so you spend less time redesigning or learning new technology.

The best place to look for solutions is wherever you are already organized and most comfortable. Study your systems and identify what really works. (Is it your computer filing system? Paper files? Rolodex?) Instead of trying to invent creative new systems for the disorganized area, just mirror the systems on the other platforms that already work for you. Similarly, you can go back to what *used* to work. I frequently encounter clients who once had a system that worked, but abandoned it and can't remember why. As we grow in our jobs and our responsibilities change all around us, we often make the mistake of thinking our systems need to change as well. How

---

ELOISE

Eloise was a successful commercial real estate broker. With no fewer than four power lunches every week, she had always been meticulous about her schedule and had developed a reputation for remarkable punctuality and nary a confused date, through her reliance on an elaborate paper-based system, which combined her desk calendar with a color-coded Post-it note system. She would never have altered her method, but a close coworker (who had employed a similar technique) went digital with great success. Eloise loved the idea that her assistant could keep the lunch schedule without her help, and having a digital system would keep her desk looking cleaner and more professional.

Eloise switched over to a networked schedule, and within the first month and a half she missed two lunch dates—more than she'd dropped in the previous five years combined. By the time we started working together, she'd been a nervous wreck for four months, but remained steadfast in her determination to make that networked schedule work. The first thing I asked was, What was wrong with your old system? "Nothing," she said. Why did you switch? "Because I thought I should. My other system seemed really old-fashioned." Is the new system an improvement? "No." Do you want to switch back? "Yes!" Eloise and readers, you have my permission.

many times have you placed a bet that technology will offer a better solution, only to return to your old faithful manual system in time?

KNOW WHERE TO KEEP THINGS

Most people get thrown off when it comes to deciding what items should live where. If you're confused, here's a few general guidelines:

ANCHOR YOUR SYSTEM IN PAPER OR COMPUTER

The real key to finding information is having only one place to look. Yet establishing any consistency to your information management system is a challenge because there are so many mediums to work with—paper files, computer documents, e-mail, voice mail, handwritten notes, business cards. When any one document can be found in multiple locations, you are bound to have trouble putting your hands on information when you need it.

To avoid confusion, anchor your organizing system either in paper files or on the computer, depending on what makes more sense for your work and what is most comfortable for you. While some jobs are 90 percent computer, 10 percent hard copy, others are just the opposite. Do what's most natural to you. You can even choose the best medium for each type of information—see the example below of eight types of information, each anchored in its own medium.

Information System	Anchored In
• Client/project records	Paper—e-mails printed and placed in client folder
• Reports	Computer—best for reusable templates
• Contact information	Rolodex
• Procedures (meeting agendas, forms, templates)	Computer—printed in binders for staff access
• Ideas for improvement	Paper—because all handwritten notes
• Financial records	Computer
• Directions, dates/schedules	Paper files
• Research material for current projects	Bookshelf—including books, periodicals, Web

ESTABLISH A POLICY OF ONE-WAY ENTRY

If you keep your calendar on the computer but find yourself making appointments when you are at a meeting and scribbling them on

---

YES, But . . .   **It's YOU!**
I hate putting things away.

Often we have a great system, but it falls apart because we are moving so fast. Lack of upkeep is never so apparent as when we remove a document from a file/folder and fail to put it back before going on to the next project. Unfortunately, the next time we go to the original file, there are major materials missing, and we have no idea where they are.

Solution: The best way to prevent this unfortunate situation is to avoid ever removing things from original files. Keep master files intact and print out a working version of a single document for a meeting or travel—this may cost you more in toner, but it will save time and money later by ensuring that nothing is ever lost. You can also just carry the whole file with you to a meeting or on the road, reducing the burden of having to reassemble files upon your return.

---

paper, enter them on your computer the minute you get back to the office rather than rely on the written record. If your database of business contacts is on the computer and you collect a business card at a conference, enter that information in your computer's Contact Manager, and toss the card away.

Alternatively, if you prefer to keep all phone numbers in an old-fashioned Rolodex, and someone e-mails you their cell phone or other contact information, automatically transfer it to your Rolodex. Remember: *There should be just one place to look!*

If it's hard to motivate yourself to take the time to put things away, change your outlook. You're not putting things away; you're positioning them for their next use. Remind yourself how great it will feel to look for the phone number of an important business contact, and voilà! It's right there in your database, the first time you check.

LEAVE YOURSELF A BREAD-CRUMB TRAIL

If you must remove individual documents from folders, make it extremely easy and mindless to return items to their original homes by leaving yourself a bread-crumb trail. When you remove a paper from a file, put a Post-it flag in the spot from which you removed the document (the bread-crumb trail), and place a matching Post-it on the actual document. This way you don't have to "remember" where a

---

YES, But . . .   **It's THEM!**
Other people don't put things away.

You may be extremely diligent about always putting things back in their place, but your project partners are horrendous. They consistently take documents out of the shared files (client files, marketing materials, and so on), and fail to put them back.

Solution: An outguide, a flat manila sheet the size of a file folder, with a printed log on the front, will help you create a bread-crumb trail in shared files. When someone removes a folder, they place an outguide in the spot, indicating the name of the file removed, with the person's name and the date. This way, if you go looking for a folder and it's not there, you'll see noted on the outguide: "Luke took the such & such file on 6/9/03." You know where to go to find the reference material you need.

---

document was pulled from. When you get back to the office, all you need to do is match up the Post-its to put the papers away. Three minutes is all it'll take to return everything to its original home, as you match up Post-it flags.

STREAMLINE YOUR BRIEFCASE

Overstuffed, disorganized, chaotic briefcases are a source of backaches when you schlep them around, and embarrassment when you end up rummaging through them messily in a meeting and can't find what you need. When your briefcase is streamlined, organized, and filled with just what you need to feel in charge of your time, proud and together when meeting with a client. It's also a sort of microcosm for your office; by organizing your briefcase first, you will inspire yourself to tackle other areas of your files and desk.

Divide the contents of your briefcase into two types—"permanent items" (calculator, business cards, pens, glasses) and "transient items" (files, reading material, and materials you are transporting from one place to another). Establish sections of your bag for each category of items. For example, the front divider for communication tools and your planner, the middle section for transient files, the inner pocket for personal items and money.

Limit what you carry.

Be realistic.

Never cart a project home, or on a business trip, unless you have planned a specific time to work on it. See Competency 4 for scheduling time to get things done. Establish weight limits for yourself—no hardcover books and no files thicker than one inch should go with you on the road.

Clean out your briefcase daily, emptying out old files, itineraries, extra pens, pencils, and business cards you collected in your travels. Having your briefcase together will make you feel lighter, grounded, and give you ideas on how to set up your office as well.

Grab-and-Go Strategy #21
Rearrange Your Desktop

If the quick fixes above did not make it easier for you to find things, let's go a level deeper. A cluttered desktop is one of the most visible and annoying problems in the workplace. There's no room to work, it can be hard to concentrate, and it makes a very bad impression on coworkers, clients, and bosses. If your team has taken to leaving things on your chair so you won't miss them, you know you're in trouble. Organizing your desktop is the fastest way to regain control of your office and will often buy you the time you need to go deeper—refining some of the inner systems that need attention, or throwing things out.

An archaeological expedition of most desktops reveals a combination of unsorted mail, projects in progress, things to discuss with others, items to file, spare supplies, and abandoned coffee cups. If those things are mixed together, the sea of confusion makes it hard to know where you are with any of your projects. Half the battle may be in knowing what's new and what's not. Typically the ratio of material is: things to do, 1:3; things waiting to be filed or routed elsewhere when you have time, 2:3.

Banish the anxiety-provoking vagueness by dividing each space in your office or shared cubicle into three visually distinct zones that reflect the flow of papers across your desktop: "In," "Working," "Out."

These three zones create a tangible, visual depiction of the path projects and to-dos take across your desk. Make sure you place the In Zone close to the door, or on the corner of your desk, for easiest access to all concerned. The Working Zone should be in the middle of your workspace, occupying the largest portion of your desk and storage space inside. The Out Zone should be stationed on the opposite side of your office from the In Zone, or on a credenza or lateral file behind your desk. See figure 6.1.

FIGURE 6.1

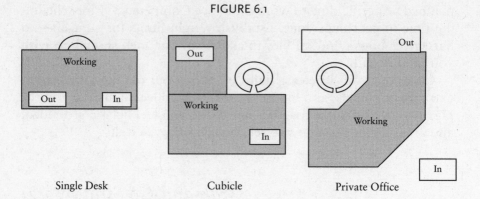

Single Desk   Cubicle   Private Office

Here's what to put in each zone, and how to keep them pure:

IN ZONE

New material only, including mail, memos, projects, and requests that you haven't read or dealt with yet.

- Consider having one deep in-box, or a series of boxes, subdividing the material you process into broad categories. (For example, an assistant to two executives might have two in-boxes, one labeled "From Peter," the other, "From Adie.") Subdividing the In Zone reduces time shuffling through the new stacks if there are certain items you always go to first, or a category of items you like to process simultaneously. Generally speaking, the higher the volume of new information you get on a daily basis, the more helpful it is to subdivide your In Zone by categories.

WORKING ZONE

This area stores everything that is in process, along with all the items you need to get your work done. This includes your project files, reference materials, calendar, phone, contact lists, pens, pencils, and paper clips. Everything you need to do your work should be stored at your fingertips. If you have to get out of your desk chair to assemble materials, you'll waste a lot of time throughout the day.

- Differentiate between *transient* papers and *permanent* files. Transient materials are things that come in, require action, and then leave your office almost immediately, to be further han-

HOT TIP!

Don't let items stay in your In Zone indefinitely.

One client always referred to her in-box as the "Hell Hole." She never took the time to really go through every item, so it was a constant mishmash of new and old, a sea of paper confusion. When she finally dug in to clear some space, it could occupy an entire afternoon.

Clean your In Zone out at regular intervals—it can be several times a day, or weekly, depending on your job and the quantity of material that comes in. Processing the In Zone takes time. Figure out how long it takes you to process the contents and work it into your schedule on a regular basis. Most important, when you do process the new material, be decisive and move things forward. *Avoid glancing at items in your In Zone and then placing them back down, putting off dealing with them.* Once you look at a new item, assign it a next action and move it into your Working Zone for processing.

dled by someone else (checks to sign, invoices to approve, memos to comment on and forward). Therefore, transient items are best kept on your desktop. Permanent files are the routine topic-, project-, or client-based folders that you are working with all the time, as part of your core responsibilities. These are best stored inside your desk drawers or file cabinets within arm's reach of your desk chair to minimize desktop clutter (although a piling system within the work zone is more effective for some people).

- Create space by storing archival materials outside of your Working Zone. Archival records are from projects you have completed and will probably never refer to again, but are required to keep for tax or legal purposes. There's no need to clutter your limited office space with those items. Move them out of your office, and into common file areas or deep storage. Keep an inventory of the archival materials you send to storage in your permanent files so you can remember what's there and retrieve them if you ever need to.

OUT ZONE

This is where you place work you have completed and need to send elsewhere—items to file or mail, assignments you are delegating, or responses to requests from coworkers, colleagues, your boss, or your assistant. Once you place it in the Out Zone, you are done with it.

MARK

When we rearranged Mark's desktop, we discovered that 10 percent of the papers were new, 10 percent were things waiting to be filed, and 80 percent were what he called "pending items"—ideas and notes for upcoming meetings, and reports sent to him by his field reps to discuss or which he had printed out to forward to or review with them.

We rearranged his desktop as follows: We placed one in-box on the corner of his desk closest to the door, so his assistant could drop all new materials there.

Instead of keeping pending material on his desktop, I suggested we create a transient system in the lateral-file drawer that was right behind his desk chair (which was sitting mostly empty, I might add!).

In the top drawer, we created one folder for each of his field reps—eighteen folders in all. Each time a field rep sent him something to discuss, Mark would drop it directly into that person's "pending" folder. Every time Mark made a note or collected something he wanted to share with one of his reps, he'd place it directly into the specific field rep's folder. When he had a rep on the phone, he could instantly go to her folder, pull out the relevant materials, and be prepared. And his desktop was clear!

Mark's Out Zone was comprised of two out-boxes on the far end of that same lateral file, one labeled "To Do," the other labeled "To File." His assistant could clean out those boxes several times a day, as needed.

In simply rearranging Mark's desktop, we created a tangible, visible flow to his work that was reassuring to him. He could think clearly, and he could always get his hands on the information he needed in an instant. Most important, he had a system that supported him in his new role as manager—he always felt prepared when his sales reps called.

- As with the In Zone, you can have one large out-box or a series of boxes, subdividing the out materials for quicker processing, by person or function.
- If you routinely meet with several different people, you might want to designate a separate out-box for each one, so you can just grab the stuff and go to a meeting with them, ready to discuss or forward all your completed materials or assignments. The purpose of subdividing the out-boxes is to minimize the time you or your staff have to spend re-sorting the contents to move them to their ultimate destination.
- Clarify who is going to clean (collect the materials from) the out-boxes—will it be you or your staff? If others, they will need to have access to your Out Zone. If you will be doing the "cleaning" and forwarding things to their destinations, make sure you schedule the time into your day, week, or month—or the Out will stay In forever.

Grab-and-Go Strategy #22
Weed as You Go

As I noted at the beginning of this chapter, accumulating unnecessary information weighs us down physically, emotionally, and psychologically, preventing us from making decisions nimbly to match the pace of the workplace.

We all know we *should* weed, but answering the questions "Do I need this? Do I want this?" can be taxing in the heat of the moment. Who has time to slow down to make those decisions when you are working so hard? There's too much ambiguity to deal with—and we tend to save our decision-making capacities for client projects, products or services, and performance-related issues, anyway.

Yet while we put off decisions about what to toss and what to keep, the stuff keeps piling up.

KATY

Katy was a brilliant, successful entertainment agent with an enormous executive office—large enough to hold a massive oak desk, several floor-to-ceiling bookshelves, and a large meeting table for six, plus two credenzas and four lateral-file drawers. Her office was also wheezing under the weight of tens of thousands of documents stacked on every visible surface and all over the floor. She was so notorious for her clutter, I was told that she'd be my biggest challenge in the history of my business.

When I went to meet with her, I quickly realized that the disorganization was an optical illusion. As she toured me through the piles, she was able to identify what was in each one. This was not a situation of her not being able to find what she needed. Katy was a "piler." She was so focused on her work that she never took the time to throw anything out and instead formed piles, each with an identity. Only the top six inches of each pile was current; the rest was old and could stand to be thrown out, but Katy could never bear to take the time. Her habit was to clean out whenever she moved to another job, and she hadn't moved in seven years!

Katy was not too concerned about what others thought of her office. She didn't even care that there was nowhere for anyone to sit. There was always the conference room for that. She liked to work in solitude, so she could fully concentrate on her calls, deals, and strategic planning, coming up for air and meeting with others on her own timetable.

But the clutter had started bogging her down, clogging her creativity with its visual oppressiveness of "things closing in." The mass of stuff was so overwhelming that even the air in her vast corner office was stagnant. Together, working side by side, we spent two solid weeks weeding out old, outdated, unnecessary materials.

The secret to avoiding a situation like Katy's is to weed constantly. And to make that process easier, you need to remove the burden of day-to-day decision making over what to keep and what to purge. Use the following eight questions to make decisions easier:

- Does it tie in with the core activities of your work?
- Will it help you complete a current project?
- Does it relate to a viable opportunity?
- Will it help you make money?
- Do you refer to it on a regular basis?
- Do you have time to do anything with this information?
- Would your work be affected if you threw this away?
- Are there any tax or legal reasons to keep it?

Now create "weed-as-you-go" lists for each area of your office. Use these examples as jumping-off points to customize your lists according to your own business and needs. Post them on your bulletin board, or on the wall next to your desk, so that weeding each day is fast and automatic.

WEED AS YOU GO—PAPER

- Old manuals and reports that have since been updated.
- Anything that someone else has the original of, and which you can replace if necessary.
- Hard copies of documents and reports, if the original is kept on the computer.
- Duplicates: Keep original document in a plastic sleeve for protection, keep one copy on hand, and toss the rest.
- Early drafts of letters, proposals, and reports: Keep the best (the final) and toss the rest.
- Unsorted mail over three months old.
- Product solicitations (don't worry, they'll send you new ones whether or not you want them).
- Files inherited from a coworker or immediate predecessor: Send to deep storage if you've never referred to any of them.
- Literature and promotional materials from companies you aren't interested in. And even those you are. If they have a Web site, and you have their number, why keep the hard copy?
- Invitations/conference brochures: Decide if you want to attend the event. If so, mark the date in your planner and toss the invite.
- Dated, unread reading material (newspapers over one week old, journals over three months, books you've had for years but never read).
- Literature from past conferences containing information you already know.
- Internet printouts: Toss the paper, but keep the Web site address on file.

WEED AS YOU GO—COMPUTER FILES

- Delete or burn on disk anything older than two years that has not been used.
- Identical documents with different names.
- Early drafts and versions of documents that are now finalized. Keep only the final.

YES, But . . .   **It's YOU!**
I want to know everything!

Research and learning are crucial in the new world of work. But we're deluged with information from a million sides at once and can often be caught up in the paranoid fantasy that (a) we should know it all, and (b) everyone else in the world is probably more on top of things than we are.

Solution: To get over your fear of throwing out reading material for fear of missing something important, remember that while there may be something new and interesting in those pages, you are a smart person who can pull great ideas from all around you. Sometimes it's an act of faith in the universe. The information you do catch will be the information you can use—and it will find its way to you. Most important, keep in mind that there really isn't that much more information available—it's just the same information recycled and available from many, many more sources. Choose your most reliable source or two, and let the rest go.

- Games or programs that you never use. *Don't* delete any operating or program files unless you're an absolute computer whiz.
- Graphics/pictures you've downloaded that are now clogging up your hard drive; burn on CD if you want to hang on to them.

We acquire and collect information, but have no organized system of retrieval. Material ends up piled on every available surface, brimming from briefcases, and toppling from bookshelves. To work wisely, you need to filter information carefully, then condense it into a form that's easy to retrieve and use. No one I have ever met gets to the bottom of her to-read pile. So don't feel like a failure if you don't either. Instead, congratulate yourself on having an active, curious mind.

Then follow these three steps to keep from getting swamped:

- **Be selective.** Select key areas of interest and/or specialization as a focus for your learning and research. Within these areas, select your most effective forms of learning. Do you prefer to read books, magazines, and newspapers, take workshops and courses, search for information on the Internet?
- **Pare it down.** Don't save anything that you already know, or anything you're unlikely to need. Condense, clip, and purge whatever you can before filing.

TIP FOR MANAGER

Develop retention guidelines. Encourage employees to weed by developing and distributing guidelines about what to keep and what to toss. You can develop retention guidelines by checking with your legal department, as well as HR and Accounting. The American Association of Records Management has retention guideline instructions on their Web site. You'll make it easier for employees to save valuable storage space. You can use the weed-as-you-go lists as inspiration for what you want them to toss as well. Once guidelines are developed, circulate them, and celebrate with an annual file-clean-out day, when you give your people time to get organized and weed. Order pizza, have everyone dress down, and clean out. If you think it's not worthwhile, consider the cost of storage per square foot, or the cost of a critical client bid gone AWOL. The smartest organizations pause every six months or so, allowing their people to weed, winnow, and streamline their files so the company can stay lean, light, and efficient.

- **Store it where you can retrieve it.** File it where you can access it easily. Logical retrieval is the first consideration when you're filing your research materials.

WEED AS YOU GO—E-MAIL

- All junk mail.
- Anything received as a CC or FWD—let the originator be responsible.
- Simple niceties and chatty e-mails.
- E-mails related to scheduling meetings and lunches.
- General announcements (meetings, events) that you've already accounted for.
- Early strings (save the final string only, which includes all correspondence).

WEED AS YOU GO—ROLODEX/CONTACTS

- People who moved years ago who you have no interest in reconnecting with.

TIPS FROM THE MASTERS

"My whole goal is to empty my e-mail in-box as thoroughly and ruthlessly as I can. I don't save anything. A request comes in; I answer it, then hit delete. The only things I file are critical e-mails from my boss and his boss. But once I've read and dealt with one of their e-mails, I move it into their folder. You'll never find more than a dozen new e-mails in my in box. I refuse to let accumulate more than will fit on one screen. If I have to scroll to read my new e-mail, I've broken my rule. And if there are floating unread e-mails or e-mails I haven't dealt with in three months, I just hit delete—that means they just weren't that important."

—Realtor

TIP FOR MANAGER

Create e-mail retention guidelines to help your employees weed their e-mail systems. Many companies have started instituting guidelines to employees for what e-mail to save and what to purge. For example, *The Wall Street Journal* reports that the Steak Escape, a franchise chain, has issued a directive banning BCCs throughout the company, and has instructed that only senders and receivers archive their e-mails and that employees copied on e-mails are to delete them regularly. This policy is designed to save space on the company's network and reduce the amount of confusion in each person's e-mail box. Use the weed-as-you-go lists here to start your own policies for what employees should keep and toss.

- Any old business cards sitting in the bottom desk drawer for over three years.
- Any name you can't remember.
- Unsolicited business cards handed to you at a networking function, when you have no idea whose they are.
- All paper business cards, once entered in computer/address book/database. (Why save them?)
- Phone numbers without a name.

YES, But . . .   **It's YOU!**
I'm scared to let go of anything. What if I need it?

The fear of letting go of information can be paralyzing. But if you hang on to everything, it renders all of it useless because the volume is so overwhelming. Huge piles and overstuffed files are simply too intimidating to sort through to look for what you want. So, most people end up saving but never looking back.

Speedily clean out your computer and e-mail files by taking advantage of the sort features. On Windows Explorer, go to the menu bar, choose View, then choose Arrange Icons By, then select the sorting method: name, date, size, or type of document, and so on. On your e-mail program, you can usually click on the menu bar above any column (date, subject, sender) and the mailboxes will automatically arrange e-mails according to the column you clicked.

Instead of thinking about what to get rid of, think of what you really want access to. There's a human limit to how much we can process and retain. Keep the piles manageable, so that they are approachable. Don't save anything unless you have a surefire way of retrieving it. If you have something, and you can't find it when you need to, or you forget that you had it in the first place, you might as well throw it out. Don't save anything that you can't trust is up-to-date.

WEED AS YOU GO—SUPPLIES

- Outdated stationery, business cards, and envelopes with the old company address or your name misspelled.
- Leftover, dated literature, event invitations, and announcements.
- Freebies and promotional items you don't like or want.
- Old, broken, uncomfortable pens, pencils, and bulky permanent markers (where do they come from, anyway?).
- Outdated supplies (like old printer cartridges and the broken hole punch).

"AUTO-SAVE" LISTS FOR PROJECTS AND CONFERENCES

Weed-as-you-go lists are excellent for managing the daily deluge. But I'd be remiss if I ignored two of the most common wellsprings of massive quantities of paper—big projects and conferences, for which the accumulation of material builds up at a rapid pace. You plan to distill all those project file folders and binders or tote bags full of seminar handouts into what's valuable and what isn't as soon as the pace slackens. But you rarely do, or you rarely spend the time it takes; before you know it, you're on to the next project or off to the next seminar, and when they're over, there are more bulging file folders, stuffed binders, and packed tote bags to add to all the others in your office.

You can nip this problem in the bud by creating auto-save lists, which will speed up the distilling process as you go so that you will never have to—Yuck!—go back.

FOR PROJECTS

Create an auto-save list and tape it to the inside cover of each project folder or binder at the beginning of each project. At the conclusion of the project, schedule a twenty-minute weeding session and just follow your auto-save list of what to keep and what to toss. *Do not* consider the project complete until you've completed the distillation. These twenty minutes are a time-and-resource-saving investment in your future. Brainstorm common projects for which you can create auto-save lists. Here are some examples:

AUTO SAVE—CLIENT PROJECTS

- Original bid
- Signed contract
- Final project designs
- Correspondence (notes, e-mails, letters)
- Meeting summaries
- Contact info

AUTO SAVE—PUBLICITY EVENTS

- Final version of press releases
- Press list
- Invitation list
- Seating chart
- Final budget
- List of attendees

> ### HOT TIP!
>
> If you delegate the distillation process to a junior staffer, avoid insecurity over any potential "maybes" that might get saved or tossed by mistake by clarifying your auto-save list with a companion weed-as-you-go guide (for example, "Weed as you go—all drafts, except final version"). If you manage a staff, make sure your direct reports follow the same policy.

AUTO SAVE—SPEAKING ENGAGEMENTS

- Final version of remarks
- Master copy of handout
- Signed contract
- Conference promo materials
- Meeting planner contact info

FOR CONFERENCES

If you attend a lot of workshops, seminars, or courses, you probably come home with an armload of material. Check your track record— if you actually take the time to look through the canvas bag stuffed with materials when you get home, well done. But if you end up shoving that information, still intact in the bag, into the far recesses of your desk, along with the forty-two other abandoned binders and totes, you've got to distill!!

Instead of feeling compelled to save it all, sit down with the pile of material and weed every night in your hotel room by reviewing the material you brought back over the trashcan.

AUTO SAVE—CONFERENCES

- Business cards of people with whom you will absolutely follow up (no need to save unsolicited cards)
- Handouts from seminars where you learned something NEW (no need to save information that confirms what you already know)
- Brochures from products you intend to buy
- Handouts, seminar notes on things you will use, or information you will act upon

HOT TIP! THE GOLDEN NUGGET BINDER

As you go through every handout and seminar, note all the tips, facts, and information that is new to you and that you will use on a sheet of paper, then transfer the sheet to a loose-leaf binder (or appropriate topic file) marked "Golden Nuggets." In addition to saving on storage from having tossed all the non-nuggets, writing all the Golden Nuggets down has another benefit: It will help you retain the information, making you more likely to apply it.

MARK

Once we set up a paper flow and filing system for Mark, he felt so much better. His productivity increased exponentially. Even more important, his confidence and effectiveness as a manager blossomed. No longer fearful of phone calls from salespeople in the field, he responded quickly, and with precisely what they needed. Since he felt like he really knew what was going on, he could direct and support them. Organizing his office enabled him to spin on a dime, and kept him in touch with his sales reps. He was able to use the information at his fingertips to plan inspiring and informative sales meetings and maintain his systems as his department grew. His sales force grew, and he was able to grow with it.

If the clutter in your office is affecting your productivity because it prevents you from finding things, distracts you, or negatively influences people's perception of you, it's time to address the issue.

Just fix one thing at a time, go back to work, and a month or two later, come back to this chapter and apply the next technique. This way, you can get organized in the least amount of time possible, and feel free to swoop back into the projects on your plate, feeling buoyed instead of stymied by the state of your space and information.

Chapter Summary
ORGANIZE AT THE SPEED OF CHANGE

Which grab-and-go strategies do you plan to use?

- Create a road map for colleagues.
- Leave a bread-crumb trail.
- Rearrange your desktop into In, Out, and Working Zones.
- When it comes to reading material, keep the source—toss the paper.
- Weed regularly with weed-as-you-go and auto-save lists.

When do you plan to implement them?

What do you think will be your biggest obstacle in applying the strategies?

How will you overcome that obstacle?

What is your motivation for mastering this competency?

MASTER DELEGATION

CLAIRE

A news writer for a national trade magazine, Claire was a five-foot-one dynamo transforming her industry. Working alone, she was a one-woman wonder, churning out cutting-edge stories from an office as wild as her mane of curly black hair. Claire's eyes sparkled with a sense of adventure, and her face was always on the verge of a huge, warm smile.

Claire's success was breeding success. The magazine was so pleased with her innovativeness, they kept giving her more and bigger assignments. Claire delighted in the recognition, but her workload had become impossible. She was missing deadlines, missing details, and missing documents. Help!!! She raised the white flag to her boss. It had gotten to be too much for her.

Rather than shrinking her workload, Claire's boss rewarded her with additional personnel—a full-time assistant and a full-time associate editor—so that she could produce more and exponentially increase her contribution to the publication. Wow! What an opportunity! She was being promoted to head her very own department—but uh-oh, what to do with these people? Claire was not an experienced delegator; she'd never had to manage a staff of her own before. How should she divvy up the work? What could she expect from her new staff? Where would she find the time to explain assignments or supervise their work? And if she was having difficulty keeping track of her own responsibilities, how in the world was she to stay on top of theirs?

Learning to delegate effectively is a critical stepping stone in the development of one's career. As Claire found, the opportunity for a promotion and the need to learn how to delegate go hand in hand.

Delegating is a powerful yet complex skill with a slightly double-edged allure: Done skillfully, this competency boosts productivity and builds cohesive teams. But done improperly, it consumes more hours than a fire-breathing dragon consumes trees.

Few people are trained in how to delegate effectively, and even fewer come by it naturally. Whether you are promoted to a management spot, like Claire, assigned a summer intern, given your first assistant, or asked to supervise a computer consultant, you are usually left on your own to figure out what and how to delegate. With little formal guidance, many people doubt their abilities. Then there is the perfectionism issue—no one will do it as well as I will. And the glory issue—what if someone else gets the credit?

Ninety percent of my office-organizing clients request delegation coaching, because they are aware of the potential benefits but truly perplexed on whether they are doing it right. The high-speed, high-pressure environment we all work in makes effective delegation at once important and nearly impossible. Time. Tasks. Trust. Delegating is a competency that presents the Three-Question Quandary:

- **A question of time.** There's not enough time to do it all yourself; there's not enough time to explain what needs to be done; and there's not enough time to let people make mistakes. Like Claire, most people who delegate are multitasking, having to divide their time between supervising others and getting their independent work done. What's a person to do? How do you strike a healthy balance?
- **A question of tasks.** What can, and should, you delegate? How do you determine the best distribution of labor? Which tasks are appropriate for others to do, and which should you always reserve for yourself? Whom do you choose, and how do you know if a person is up to the job?
- **A question of trust.** To delegate is to depend on someone else to perform a task or set of tasks for you. It's a relationship built on trust—and it takes courage, and diligence, to build that trust. If you are not accustomed to relying on others, if it's not in your nature to trust people, or if you think that you do everything best, you will be reluctant to delegate. Building trust can be especially challenging given the frequently changing cast of characters at work. What if your coworkers are all much less experienced than you?

DID YOU KNOW?

A 2002 survey of 1,400 chief financial officers, from a random sample of U.S. companies, asked people to identify their most "effective time management tool":

- 38 percent said delegating.
- 37 percent said taking greater advantage of technology tools.
- 15 percent said spending less time in meetings.

Robert Half Management Resources, 2002.

What's the danger in never learning to delegate properly? The danger is that you'll always feel crushed under the weight of your own workload, hold yourself back from promotions, and eventually burn yourself out, exhausted and overburdened. The danger to your company is a slowdown of growth as work gets backed up in your office.

This chapter will help you overcome the three-question quandary. Rather than being an insurmountable time-suck, you will discover that sharing the workload is one of the *best* uses of your time, yielding great results for the energy you invest.

The examples that follow will focus mostly on delegating to assistants and direct reports (people specifically assigned to support you), although the principles work as well in multidirectional delegation situations (when delegating to a coworker, boss, consultant, or customer).

Grab-and-Go Strategy #23
Break the Habit of Total Self-Reliance

The biggest obstacle to learning to delegate successfully is the (conscious or unconscious) insistence on doing everything yourself—a stance that is sometimes a matter of psychology, sometimes a matter of habit. When you are used to working independently, it may not even *occur* to you to delegate. You just plow forward as if on autopilot, and do whatever needs to be done.

Extremely self-sufficient people don't think hierarchically about work. They have no problem doing any aspect of a job—no job is beneath them. This is a highly admirable quality—until it locks you into a time bind you're not even aware of. How many things do you

CLAIRE

Claire and I began masterminding the new roles for her department by brainstorming a list of responsibilities that her assistant, Lisa, could take over. My first suggestion was for Lisa to
begin answering Claire's phone, which would help to eliminate
the constant stream of interruptions Claire experienced every
time it rang.

Claire was hesitant; she liked the nonpresumptuous air and
accessible image answering her own phone projected. She didn't
want to look like she was hiding behind her assistant. But upon
my assurance that we'd train Lisa to distinguish VIP calls that
should immediately be put through but take messages from
everyone else, she was willing to give it a try.

Claire then expressed concern over whether her phone line
could actually be technically wired to forward directly to Lisa's
desk. Without missing a beat, she declared she'd call tech support to find out and began making a note in her planner. I
stopped her in her tracks. "Why don't we have Lisa look into
that?" Claire smiled that charming smile. She hadn't even
thought of asking Lisa! *Time saved: 45 minutes of research;
1 hour of phone time per day.*

---

do on a regular, knee-jerk basis that someone else could probably do
just as well?

One doctor I worked with always made all of his own travel
arrangements, even though he had a top-notch secretary and several
receptionists who were happy to plan trips for him. When I asked
him why, he explained that there were so many choices to be made—
which airline, which flight, seat, hotel—and he had particular tastes
when it came to traveling. He felt it was faster to just do it himself rather than take the time to explain all his preferences. Yet in a
fifteen-minute conversation, I was able to uncover the thinking behind his decisions, which we made into written guidelines:

- Flight time preferences: If it's a morning flight—not before 10
  A.M., to avoid rush hour. Evening flights—never book last flight
  of the day, in case of delays or cancellations. Choose second or
  third to last flight of the day.

- Prefers an aisle seat, as close to the front of the plane as possible. Always request bulkhead or exit row.
- Doesn't like to fly in small prop aircraft on a "puddle-jumper flight." Willing to fly earlier or later if a jet is available.
- For frequent-flier mileage, books airlines in this order—first, second, third choice.
- Hotel preferences: nonsmoking, king-size bed, lower floor, as close to the elevator as possible to avoid time-consuming walks down long halls.

With these guidelines written up, his secretary (or if she were busy, any of his receptionists) could book his travel, and at the very least narrow his options down to minimize the time he spent researching flights. *Time saved: 4 hours per month.*

It can be difficult or uncomfortable to explain your reasoning behind various choices because you are a private person. It may even feel embarrassing to you to share some of your thinking because it's too personal—like the doctor, who may not love the idea of others knowing he prefers jets to prop planes. But where would you rather see that doctor spend his time—four hours a month making travel arrangements, or taking care of patients? Everyone has their idiosyncracies, and breaking past the self-consciousness is well worth the time saved.

YES, But . . .   It could be EITHER.
If I don't do it myself, it won't be done well.

Ah, the common cry of the super self-reliant. It's tricky belief to let go of, because sometimes it's true. Here's a quick way to determine if it's you, or if it's them:

If you are dealing with an inherited staff (one you didn't hire or train yourself) or are the only senior person in a company that hires ambitious, smart, but inexperienced newcomers to save money, it may well be true that you are the only one who does things well. (It's them!)

However, if you have never been able to find anyone who meets your standards of excellence (even among the people you have personally hired and trained), the issue is more likely your own inner power struggles, misperceptions, and perfectionism run amok. (It's you!)

HERMAN

Herman is a finance director who'd pulled himself up by his bootstraps from junior associate to senior analyst, a tremendous success story. Herman's main setback was that he could never find a competent assistant. The scene in the cubicle outside his office was like an episode of the sitcom *Murphy Brown*—a new person occupied the position every three to six months. "I don't really know how to delegate," he confessed, adding that he'd been suffering from anxiety attacks. Unable to find anyone dependable, Herman did all his own filing, scheduling, calls, and searching for documents—while simultaneously managing million-dollar accounts!

We helped Herman define the job description for a high-level assistant. He needed someone organized, fast, and sharp as a whip, who could keep up with him and the complexity of his work. We prescreened the candidates and recommended three extraordinary applicants. Herman rejected every one of our top candidates, and went instead for someone much less experienced, passive, and, quite frankly, not very bright.

Why would someone do this?

In a word: insecurity.

Herman always felt like he was holding on to his success by the skin of his teeth. Though he always came through for clients, he was convinced they'd shudder if they knew how chaotically he worked behind the scenes. He was ashamed and embarrassed of his disorderly ways. The idea of bringing someone competent and organized in to work with him was threatening. He would rather just do everything himself than risk being found less than competent.

Two months later, I got a call from Herman. This new hire was so incompetent, she was doing nothing to alleviate the pressure. In fact, things had gotten worse. He was spending an enormous amount of time worried about what she was doing wrong and correcting her mistakes. No surprise!

Luckily we were able to reconnect with one of the candidates, who was still interested in the position. As scared as Herman was of being "found out" and criticized, he took the risk (with great reassurance from us!). The new assistant was fabulous, and was able to hit the ground running within a day. Within two weeks we got an elated call from Herman: "Why didn't I do this before? She's a dream come true. Smart, fast, and respectful! We're getting so much done—and get this, she thinks I'm really smart! Not one word or snide remark about the piles and mess. She just gets in there, finds what we need, and fixes the problem. She's been developing systems for us left and right."

Save your time for what you do best, and delegate the rest.

It takes a tremendous amount of courage to delegate effectively. If you are afraid to delegate out of fear of someone seeing your messy side, take heart. *Nobody is perfect.* Your daily attempts to "hide" your imperfections don't work as well as you think they do. People know—and they *still* respect your hard work and intelligence. Imagine the sense of relief (and heightened energy) you'll feel once some of the tasks you don't excel at are off your plate.

It may not be in your nature to depend on anyone but you. Break the habit and the irrational belief that you are the only person who can do things right. It's time to discover that other people can offer fresh and wonderful ideas. Focus on the fact that, like you, most people are responsible and like to make a contribution.

YES, But . . .   **It's YOU!**
I'm afraid I'll no longer be needed.

A resistance to delegating can also be a reflection of your own insecurities about being replaceable. If you can train others to do what you do, you'll no longer be needed. Of course, there are certain responsibilities you should never delegate. The real purpose of delegation is to free you to focus your time on your highest-value tasks, and the first step is to identify which tasks you should *never* delegate. Delegating is not about getting rid of the stuff you hate and only doing what you enjoy. It's about making sure that the best person to do a job is doing it. Review your job title, job description, performance appraisals, and conversations with your boss. What is your company counting on you and you alone to do? What is *your* unique contribution? Do *not* delegate the following:

- Tasks that reflect precisely why your company hired you in the first place.
- Tasks where you're the only one with the expertise to make tough judgment calls.
- Tasks directly on the revenue line, where your unique talents shine.
- Tasks that bring you joy and define the meaning of your job.

Now that we've isolated what you should always retain ownership of, to assure the highest quality deliverable, go back over your to-do list. Pretty much everything that didn't make the cut above is delegatable. Identify tasks that are *not* the best use of your time. What takes too long? What tasks aren't you good at? You should consider delegating any task that someone else can do better, faster, or good enough. Delegate all of the following items:

- Tasks that deplete you of energy or time you need for more critical activities.
- Tasks you honestly aren't that good at doing.
- Tasks that belong on someone else's job description.
- Tasks you are doing out of habit, or comfort . . . but are not the best use of your time.

And as to being replaced: If you delegate tasks effectively, you will still be viewed as responsible for the increased productivity of your department. When the people under you thrive, it makes you look good, not weak. If you really thought about it, you would probably agree that other people's need for you is not tied up in your ability to perform just one task, or your ability to handle several tasks at once. You were hired on the basis of a complete picture, one that encompasses all the unique skills, ideas, and experience you bring to the party that are viewed as valuable. You need to believe in your own strength, knowledge, authority, and ability. So let go of tasks that other people can do, and free yourself up for new projects.

YES, But ...   It's YOU!
I enjoy doing some of those tasks!

This reservation is extremely common among people who've been promoted up the ranks and are now supervising others but haven't quite gotten comfortable giving up the tasks they loved. Consider the star salesperson promoted to division manager who still likes to get on the phone and close deals. We all gravitate toward what we are comfortable doing and can succeed in.

Solution: Periodically treat yourself to doing old, familiar tasks; it can be invigorating (like having a cool glass of water on a hot day). Just don't make a habit of it, or you'll stagnate your growth (as well as that of the people you should be delegating to).

Grab-and-Go Strategy #24
Pick the Right Person for the Job

Once you are convinced that sharing the workload will help you, the next secret to successful delegation is picking the right person for the job. Pick the wrong person, and you'll end up spending more time explaining, chasing down the work, and correcting mistakes than you actually saved.

There are three levels of delegatees to consider assigning a task to. Each will require a different investment of time on your part.

- **Expert.** Giving the task to someone who can do it better or faster than you is the ideal scenario because it requires the least tutelage on your part and therefore saves you time instantly. If there is no one on the expert level available in-house, see if you can hire an outside person—a consultant or an experienced temp.
- **Equal.** Giving the job to someone who is just as qualified as you are reduces the amount of time you must spend explaining and passing the task off to a minimum, and offers a high likelihood that the work will be done just fine. It may be handled differently than you would do it yourself—but the objectives will be met, and you will have freed up significant time to deal with the more important tasks on your plate.
- **Beginner.** Giving the job to someone who's not as skilled as you are is a leap of faith. It requires the biggest investment of your

time by far, but there can be great rewards. Pick someone who's just starting out, and you may develop a loyal helper who feels privileged and grateful for the opportunity to learn. His fresh approach may solve more problems than you anticipated, and teach you a thing or two as well.

The goal is to match each task to the person assigned to it according to the *best fit*, so that the work is done well, on time, and with the least amount of activity on your part. There are also two categories of tasks that can be delegated:

- Noncreative, repetitive tasks done regularly (generating regular reports, crunching numbers, answering phones, routine correspondence, preparing packets, confirming meeting attendance)
- Special projects, onetime or infrequent tasks (creating a brochure, launching a new initiative, planning an event, designing a product, researching and acquiring a new computer)

This distinction will help you when you are determining whether the task is worth the effort of delegating.

For routine tasks, it is almost always worth investing time to record the steps on paper and train someone else. An initial investment of time will free you up for years to come.

For special projects, consider the scope of the undertaking. If it would take you longer to explain the project to someone than it would to do the project yourself, and the project won't have to be repeated in the future, it is more efficient to do it yourself. But beware of your laziness in deciding whether or not to delegate a task—it can be tempting to keep it for yourself just because you don't feel you have the energy to communicate what you need to someone else.

What routine tasks or time-consuming projects are on your schedule that you've been hesitant to explain to someone? Look for those that have been sitting for a while because you haven't been able to find the time to do them. Is it worth offloading a particular responsibility to an assistant, direct report, or fellow coworker, who could take it over for you?

When looking at each task to delegate, ask yourself two questions:

1. Does this person have the skill or capacity to do the job?
2. Does this person have the motivation to succeed?

Remember that you have options to choose from: There are coworkers and direct reports, assistants, consultants, clients, even bosses, to hand things off to, each with their own set of interests, strengths, and weaknesses. Delegating gives you an opportunity to build and strengthen relationships.

QUESTION 1. DOES THIS PERSON HAVE THE SKILL OR CAPACITY TO DO THE JOB?

How do you determine someone's capacity to do a job? Keep in mind that different people take to different types of tasks. Here are some qualities you can use to evaluate whether a person is up to the job. Some people thrive on repetitive tasks (where routine and attention to detail is paramount), and others live for variety (people who enjoy the challenge of projects, and possess excellent follow-up skills and judgment).

Pick the best match between the task and the person you are delegating it to. Base your decision on what you've seen her do successfully in the past—have you noticed her to have any of the following attributes? Is she:

Good with people	vs. Good with processes
Thrives on routine tasks	vs. Thrives on variety
Able to multitask	vs. Prefers one task at a time
Likes precise directions	vs. Likes to be creative
Sticks to a rigid schedule	vs. Works flexible hours until the job is done
Slow and methodical	vs. Fast, works in general broad strokes
Self-directed, keeps own deadlines	vs. Requires frequent reminders
Unable to make decisions	vs. Has excellent judgment
Thrives on starting new things	vs. Thrives on completion
Communicates clearly	vs. Frequent misunderstandings

By matching the task to the person's strengths and style, you are likely to get a willing helper, who will gobble up the assignment and succeed.

MAKING THE MOST OF YOUR ASSISTANT

Below are the common areas an assistant can help with, divided into two columns. The first column depicts basic functions requiring the ability to follow specific instructions that any beginner, or even someone who is experienced but less confident, should be able to perform. The second column describes higher-level functions requiring greater

TIPS FROM THE MASTERS

"I've learned a lot through the years about who to delegate to and even hire. The people that work out the best may not start out knowing the most or fit into that box exactly the way you would have liked. But the people with the best attitudes, the ones that come in and say, 'I want to work for you, for your company. I want to learn this,' are the people that are successful, because they're not just doing the job; they are hungry to work and to learn, they can kind of come in and hit the ground running. These are people that want to learn and really love what you're all about. And are just enthusiastic, really want to start."

—Bureau Chief

judgment that a more experienced, seasoned, or competent assistant can master. These will require you to sit down and train that person in how you think, but are well worth looking into.

Use these lists to speed your efforts to get the most out of your assistant. Cherry-pick functions that would be helpful to you, and begin assigning the tasks. My suggestion is to start with the basics, and then increase responsibilities to the more advanced functions.

ASSISTANT	BEGINNER—REQUIRES ABILITY TO FOLLOW DIRECTIONS	EXPERT—REQUIRES JUDGMENT AND EXPERIENCE
Phones	Take complete messages and forward to appropriate dept.	Filter calls and troubleshoot problems
		Dispense information
Mail and e-mail	Presort into categories	Read, summarize mail
	Toss/delete junk	Stock answers—certain inquiries
	Assemble packages	Forward to relevant others
	Type stock letters	Draft letters, edit boss's drafts
	Address packages	Custom assemble materials
	Sends faxes	Draft faxes
Filing	Maintain existing system	Design/streamline system
	Put things in right places	Weed folders postproject

Schedule	Type appointments	Prioritize and schedule appointments
	Types to-dos	Remind boss of upcoming dates
	Confirm appointments day before	Pull relevant files and brief boss
	Arrange transportation	Keep boss on time
	Get directions	Meeting planning
	Make reservations	Block out time to do projects
	Type itinerary	Assist on to-dos
Manage contacts	Enter new contacts	Weed database/recategorize
	Vigilantly update changes	Mail merge for mass mailing
Client/staff care	Send birthday cards	Clip and send articles of interest
	Order flowers/gifts	Write thank-you notes
		Fulfill special requests
Reports/memos	Type as dictated	Generate reports—requires writing, editing, financial software skills
		Summarize memos
Supplies/equipment	Keep supplies in stock	Troubleshoot computers
	Call and supervise repairs	Research vendors/reduce costs
Marketing	Send out packets	Oversee brochure production
	Assemble huge mailing	Design mailing materials
Meetings	Book space	Pull relevant files
	Confirm attendees	Take notes
	Order refreshments	Attend in place of boss
	Order A/V	
	Assemble materials	
Projects	Independent schedule	Marketing budget
	Errands	Research

QUESTION 2. DOES THIS PERSON HAVE THE MOTIVATION TO SUCCEED?

When deciding who to delegate a task to—whether it will be an on-going responsibility or a onetime job—consider what motivates each person. Some people are motivated by the opportunity to learn, while others appreciate the chance to show what they are capable of. Some will thrive on the opportunity to boost their value to you and to the company, and others are simply motivated by their paycheck.

If you give people tasks that will help them further their own goals,

TIP FOR MANAGER—IS HE *REALLY* TOO BUSY?

In lean times, and with lean staffs, everyone might seem over-worked. But all too often I see managers doing the work of their direct reports, or even things they'd normally ask their assistant to do (such as making a lunch appointment), simply out of not wanting to impose too heavily on the other person. When someone you have authority over says he is too busy to take over or perform a task for you, it behooves you to take a closer look at how he is spending his time. If you're busy with your own work, it can be easy to lose track of what you've as-signed, or forget how long it should take. Is he really too busy—or is he being inefficient with the use of his time?

Solution: Ask the following questions when someone seems overwhelmed and unable to take on a high-priority task you want to delegate:

- What are you currently working on?
- What can I do clear off your plate so that you have time to do this project?
- Is there a process you are doing that is taking too long? How can we streamline it for you?

Then review his to-do list, helping him reprioritize to make time for the new task. Or when you review his to-do list with him, you may change your mind about the importance of the new task—and perhaps decide to divert it to someone else on staff. For suspiciously inefficient employees, ask them to keep a log for a week or two recording what they do every day to ascertain where their time goes, and so on.

they will want to be on your team and perform with excellence—be-cause they will feel you are looking out for their best interests.

Grab-and-Go Strategy #25
Create a Clear Division of Labor

The goal of delegation is a clear division of labor—each person should have a clear set of responsibilities that he is fully accountable for. Vagueness creates overlap between people and prevents them

CLAIRE

In order to divide the labor effectively between Claire, her associate editor, Monique, and her assistant, Lisa, I asked Claire for a list of everything her department would be responsible for producing. In no time, she rattled off her list: three large investigative articles and the material for three monthly columns, plus developing a pool of talented outside writers and continuing to deliver innovative, fresh ideas.

When I asked Claire what excited her the most, those elfin eyes lit up as she talked about the big investigative news pieces. She was excellent at coming up with ideas and playing spin doctor to the angles of all her stories—that made sense. It was her innovativeness that had prompted her promotion to begin with. Her staff could pitch in, but ultimately it would be Claire's responsibility to lead the team in idea generation.

At first she wondered if she should delegate the research on those pieces, but then she explained that it's during the research phase that the angle for her story crystallizes.

We came up with a plan (see figure 7.1) whereby each person could fully concentrate on her role and master the skills involved in delivering that work. The consistency of the clear division of labor removed the burden of rethinking everybody's jobs each month, and would help to avoid any confusion about who was responsible for what.

When you delegate tasks that you are used to doing yourself, you'll find that you not only save the actual time it takes to do the assignment, you also clear your head space.

Claire was in the business of ideas, and buried in her daily heap of mail was often the germ of a great news story. But sorting through it all was so time-consuming that it would sit unopened and untapped for months. By delegating this task to Lisa, who would pluck what looked relevant and attach a brief summary to the outside of her recommendations to Claire, the department was able to do more in less time, and move aggressively forward to fulfilling its mission to keep providing a wealth of cutting edge material to readers. *Time saved: 2–3 hours per day.*

from taking ownership, like a volleyball game where someone across the net spikes the ball, and no one on your team digs because they think someone else has it covered.

FIGURE 7.1

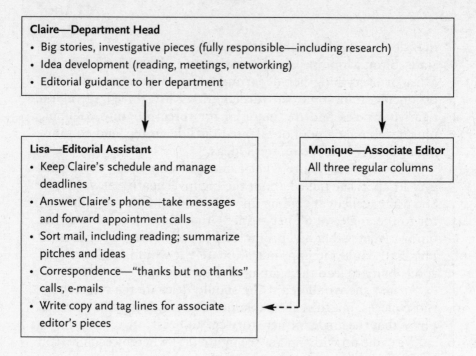

Grab-and-Go Strategy #26
Delegate One Skill Set at a Time

Since delegation and supervision take time, one way to reduce the risk of losing hours explaining, evaluating, and correcting work is by delegating one skill set at a time. Especially if you don't know someone's abilities very well, make it easier on yourself to evaluate them by focusing on one skill at a time. For example, with a new assistant, you may want to first see how closely she follows instructions. Teach her how to answer the phones, and see how she does. Next, you might want to check her organizing skills. Have her rearrange the supply closet and evaluate the result. This gradual approach keeps both delegatee and delegator from being overwhelmed. Starting small is also a good way to give yourself a little practice, while leaving you enough room to experiment with your delegation style as you go.

SLOW DOWN TO THE SPEED OF PEOPLE

Delegating effectively requires giving clear instructions, being available for guidance along the way, and evaluating the job when it's

CLAIRE

Claire's associate editor, Monique, needed to be an ace on three fronts: editing, writing, and idea generation. Diving right in, Claire haphazardly threw Monique a little bit of everything in the first three days—she brought her to an ideas meeting, gave her a writing assignment, and a small piece to edit. She wanted to test her abilities and make her feel like part of the team. Well, understandably, Claire was then totally overwhelmed by trying to evaluate the woman's work—it was too much to think about all at once.

I suggested that Claire start smaller, beginning with Monique's known area of strength—editing—so Claire could give 100 percent of her attention to evaluating that skill first. Starting with your delegatee's strength gives her a chance to succeed early on, and you a chance to gain confidence in her abilities. If Monique's editing (her primary responsibility) wasn't up to snuff, nothing else really mattered. Claire would discover early on that she wasn't right for the job, saving time she would have invested in assessing her other skills.

done. How do you communicate everything that's important, leave nothing out through false assumptions, and not sound patronizing? How do you give someone a sense of ownership, but still communicate what you want? And when you still have a ton of your own responsibilities to tend to, where the heck do you find time to explain, supervise, and evaluate your delegatee's work?

No matter how rushed you are, it's essential that you slow down to the speed of people. This isn't easy because managing others requires a wholly different rhythm than doing your own work. When you are working on your own projects, you may be revved up, hyper-focused, deadline-driven, and intense. Then along comes someone needing an assignment or direction, asking questions, wanting input. It's hard to shift gears.

Yet the worst mistake to make is to resort to the *dump-and-run* approach, whereby you give out the assignment and never bother to review the person's work. It's demoralizing and insulting, and can easily be interpreted that you "just don't care," sapping your delegatee's enthusiasm for the next assignment.

Your delegatees will feel appreciated when you discuss a project, review their work, or even help them brainstorm solutions to a prob-

---

TIPS FROM THE MASTERS

"Effective managing is about building relationships and getting people to talk to you. Even if you're sitting in front of a computer all day, your job as a manager is to build relationships with other people. That's what greases the wheels."

—Store Manager

---

lem. Putting in that time gains you their respect—and that's where you get the real power and influence. And save huge amounts of time.

There are many ways to keep the actual process of training, explaining, assessing, and, if needed, correcting, as efficient as possible. Here are some key elements:

1. **Be clear on the outcome, creative on the path.** Most people become engaged in an assignment when they feel they are making a valuable contribution to a goal. Always discuss each task's objective in relation to helping achieve the department or company's bigger picture goals.

   In stating the objective, make the goal measurable and specific. Feel free to give guidance and suggestions on methodology, but don't dictate in minute detail exactly *how* the delegatee should accomplish the goal. Engage your team members' thoughts and creativity. When you don't allow people enough room to make unique contributions to the work, it's demoralizing. They feel sapped of energy and treated like automatons, and you lose out on the opportunity to tap into whatever fresh approach they may have. What's more, allowing a person to come up with his own approach to accomplishing the delegated task adds dignity to the process and gives him a chance to express himself—a great motivator.

Examples of Clear, Outcome-Oriented Direction

- "We need a two-page cover letter that is warm, clear, and personalized."
- "We need to get this issue resolved at the meeting on Friday. It will be hard to get everyone to attend, but please ensure that there is at least one decision maker there from each department."
- "Our goal is to keep the cost of supplies under $500 a month.

As you process orders, make sure we don't already have the items in stock, and that the cost per item is reasonable. Feel free to shop for vendors who can come in at more economical rates."
- "The primary goal of this research is to add credibility to our proposal. Please locate a minimum of three studies from recognizable, well-respected industry sources for inclusion."
- "Our mission is always to generate goodwill and positive word-of-mouth. In dealing with an unhappy customer, we want them to feel better after expressing their concerns to us. Please do whatever it takes to accomplish that goal."

Of course, if you want things done a particular way because you know it works, don't be afraid to spell it out.

For years, I worked from my home office and organized my files by company division in a specific way. They were color-coded and clearly labeled. When I moved my office into the Empire State Building and hired additional staff, I thought each person would want ownership over her files, so I gave them the freedom to adapt the system for their division.

Bad idea!

It was a disaster; nothing was cohesive, and I couldn't find anything. Bottom line: Most times it's wise to follow the motto, "Clear on the outcome, creative on the path," but don't hesitate to instruct line-by-line when uniformity counts. This is especially true of routine tasks—answering phones, contact management, and so on.

2. **Define the due date. Always say when.** No matter how much room you leave for creativity in the delegation process, *never be vague on the due date*. If you leave the due date vague, other priorities will usurp your delegatee's focus, or not leave you enough time to correct the work, if necessary.

   Leave enough of a cushion so that if the work doesn't come back as you'd hoped, there is enough time to correct it before the *real* deadline. It's sometimes helpful to give the person an accurate time estimate of how long you think the task should take and how long you want them to spend on it. Put a reminder in your planner to follow up on the day the task is due.

3. **Define limits of authority.** Be clear about where people can make independent decisions and where they can't. Imagine the obstacles they may face and define which problems they can solve on their own—and which problems to bring you in on

because they require your judgment. This will prevent delegatees from going too far off on their own, and perhaps astray.

If you know you will be hard to reach (traveling, in meetings), give them some authority to proceed so that they won't sit on the task waiting for you or interrupt you every five minutes with questions. By empowering them to handle such instances, you help build their decision-making skills, and make them feel you have confidence in their abilities.

4. **Define follow-up procedures.** Decide together how follow-up will occur. Do you want the person to come to you with questions as they arise, or save them to go over all at once? Who will follow up? When? What is the best mode of communication (phone, e-mail, in-person meetings)?

Suggestions for Following Up Without Taxing Your Schedule

- **Daily or weekly report.** An assistant or direct report can keep you abreast of developments, activities, and accomplishments with a daily report that outlines what got done, next steps, and any questions he has for you. This minimizes the amount of face time you have to carve out and is particularly effective in keeping abreast of progress and guiding the delegatee without having to look over his shoulder. You can even e-mail your responses back—putting your comments in ALL CAPS to make it easy for him to hop from one comment to the next.

Sample Daily Report for Software Designer

1. Researched competitor software.
2. Read through report of bugs complaints and consolidated into list of top twenty complaints.
3. Scheduled focus group session for next Tuesday.
4. Worked out kinks in booting up program.
5. Met for lunch with John, Bill, and Fran to divvy up repairs.
6. Called graphic department to request new color scheme.

- **Daily or weekly huddles.** As an alternative to the daily or weekly written report, get together on a regular basis with your direct report or assistant. In-person meetings are particularly helpful if you have materials to look over together, and to keep a sense of connection. To make sure you are prepared for the meeting, ask the delegatee to e-mail you an agenda in advance so you can have answers or solutions to her questions or problems. This also will make the delegatee feel confident that her concerns will be fully addressed.

Sample Weekly Meeting Agenda

1. Progress report on current projects
2. Questions/issues/obstacles on current projects
3. Status on deadlines
4. Upcoming issues
5. Additional help needed?

• **Benchmark appointments.** For long-term tasks, establish certain benchmarks and set appointments to review progress and answer questions to keep the delegatee from going astray, or the project from falling off your radar screen. Benchmark appointments also provide you with the opportunity to adjust the task or project's course of development if necessary.

Grab-and-Go Strategy #27
Turn It Back Around

What happens if the task you have delegated is handled imperfectly? First of all, don't be surprised; almost all the work you delegate will be handled imperfectly, at least the first time. It may come back to you needing only slight corrections, or it may require a major overhaul.

The big question is, What do you, as the delegator, do? This can be a very perilous moment for the self-reliant, who will be tempted just to fix the job themselves, figuring that's faster and more efficient. STOP! If it's a big overhaul, it goes without saying that you will drain much of your time and energy handling it yourself. But even a small adjustment that may take, say, fifteen minutes to fix is your own time spent, and if that happens four times a day, you will have given up an hour.

Also, by fixing things yourself, you are internally giving up on the delegatee and reinforcing your belief that you are the only one who can do the job. Last, you will be communicating a feeling of mistrust in the person's abilities, an enormously demoralizing statement to anyone.

Instead, figure out why the result didn't meet your expectations. Were your directions unclear? Did the delegatee focus on one part of the assignment at the expense of another? Is she inexperienced and

YES, But . . .   **It's THEM!**
What if the person just isn't up to the job?

Periodically, we give people a chance to try their hand at something and it doesn't work out because they simply lack the capacity, regardless of how much they may want to help you, or how much you need it. They still have other skills that are useful, but on one or two particular tasks, they just don't have it in them to learn quickly enough.

It's critical to recognize when you've hit that limit, for two reasons. First, to prevent sinking too much time into constantly correcting your delegatee, and second, to preserve his dignity. One of the best ways to handle this potentially uncomfortable situation is to redirect your delegatee's efforts to where they can be successful.

One of my former clients had been promoted to manager of a large bookstore. She was about two weeks into her new position when she noticed an employee who seemed to lack the finesse required to handle customers. The awkward part was that the worker had a great work ethic and was completely lacking in self-awareness on her limitation; in fact she clearly thought she was good with people. Unfortunately, she always came across harsh and brusque, and the manager was concerned about upsetting customers and losing sales.

Solution: Through a series of diplomatic conversations, my client persuaded the woman to take a position in the back room as a receiving supervisor, where if she mouthed off, it would be to the UPS delivery guys, not customers. She was able to redirect this employee's energies to another, more suitable job while preserving her dignity and self-confidence, and a self-confident worker is a productive worker.

still learning? Did you overestimate her level of skill? All are possible. Once you both know and understand what went wrong and where, turn the work back over to the delegatee and let her fix it on her own, giving her a deadline for when you will follow up again.

Point out first what the person did well, then state in a clear, simple, friendly way how you think she can improve the next time around. Don't expect instant improvement. This is a process. Your objective is to gently and firmly provide direction, while preserving her confidence. Examples:

- Making travel arrangements: "Looks good, but let's just get a backup car service number."
- Drafting a proposal: "The structure of this document makes a lot of sense, but the tone is a little off in some places. We're trying to strike the right balance between . . ."
- Running a meeting/conference call: "Next time, you might try passing out an agenda at the beginning of the meeting, just in case anybody forgot to check their e-mail; it will ensure that everyone stays on track."

Learning how to delegate will make you more productive. It might enable you to earn that promotion, or grant you higher standing with your boss. All of those outcomes are excellent, but remember, delegating is not only about getting more done faster and better; it's also one of the best ways to create a strong sense of camaraderie and respect among employees.

So take the time to spend some quality face-to-face time with your delegatees—ask how they are, how their families are, what they did last weekend, what they're interested in. You'll be surprised to find how much time you can *save* by investing small bits of time to connect with the people working on your behalf. Each little conver-

CLAIRE

Claire has grown into her skills as delegator. The biggest breakthrough for her, she said, was giving people full ownership of and accountability for their responsibilities, thereby freeing her to concentrate on her own. It clears her head of worry and distraction. Her department's synergy is growing, and the department is delivering on its promise (and her boss's expectations) of brilliant work, innovative ideas, and many pages of magazine filled.

Claire's biggest fear had been that, with *two* people reporting to her, she'd have to think of things for each person to do every day, a burden that made her head spin and her stomach churn. Instead, they are each working independently, then coming together to fuel each other's ideas, and getting vast quantities of work done in the process. Most surprisingly for Claire . . . it's fun! The sparkle is back in Claire's eyes. She's off on another adventure.

sation, even if it's only five minutes long, gives you both the opportunity to understand each other on a visceral level and build the kind of trust and rapport that makes any team nimble.

Chapter Summary
MASTER DELEGATION

Which of the grab-and-go strategies will you implement?

- Break the habit of total self-reliance.
- Always pick the best match between the person and the task.
- Create a clear division of labor.
- Delegate one skill set at a time.
- Turn it back around, if the job isn't done well.

When do you plan to implement them?

What do you think will be your biggest obstacle in applying the strategies?

How will you overcome that obstacle?

What is your motivation for mastering this competency?

WORK WELL WITH OTHERS

BRIAN

Brian, impeccably dressed, poised, and gently spoken, was in a time bind. The international director of a business development firm, he'd recently been promoted to this position after spearheading the complete turnaround of his floundering division from near bankruptcy to solid profits. Having deftly led his team through a crisis, he was now ready to guide the company toward growth and innovation.

He contacted me for advice in determining the best use of his time in his new role. During our first appointment, he expressed dismay at being bogged down in a level of detail he felt constricted by—meetings often went on too long for his taste, and his staff continued to approach him with questions he'd hoped they could now handle themselves.

Brian was proud of the people he'd hired—he had an eye for top-tier talent—and suggested that I speak with several of his direct reports to elicit their input on what the team needed to operate more smoothly and independently. His central goals were to spend less time managing others and more time on strategic planning. He wanted to increase his business-related travel, build external partnerships, and expand their product line. I asked Brian, as I do with all of my clients during an assessment, to define his workplace strengths. He described himself as being a roll-up-his-sleeves kind of guy who could make tough decisions and who was excellent with people.

Each of my meetings with his direct reports took me completely aback. One by one (and in totally separate conversations), each person I spoke with almost immediately confessed that Brian was a nightmare to work with. He had *terrible* work habits, they said, barely keeping to a schedule, was always late, and frequently canceled one-on-one meetings with his direct reports. His assistant didn't know where he was half the time, because Brian had a habit of spontaneously walking around the building checking in with staff unannounced, and then ending up lost in conversation for hours.

While everyone admired Brian for his accomplishments in turning the company around, and each described him as a charming man whom they truly liked personally, all felt that company growth hinged upon Brian being more accessible, not less so, to get the support they needed to complete their projects.

I was stunned. In over two hours describing his time-management problems, Brian had never once mentioned anything to me about lateness, reliability, or difficulty keeping to a schedule. Yet with five people offering the same complaint, I had to believe these were real issues. Bottom line, Brian had an alarmingly skewed view of his ability to work well with others!

Surprisingly, this sort of disconnect is extremely common. Nine out of every ten people I consult with cite "works well with others" as one of their greatest values on the job. Yet more often than not I get a completely contrasting picture from bosses, assistants, and coworkers.

How does that happen? How could we delude ourselves into thinking we're better at working with others than we actually are? How do we develop such misperceptions?

First, if you are difficult to work with, no one is likely to tell you. Few people feel comfortable being direct on this topic, for fear of offending, eliciting anger, or destroying a sense of comfort or trust. It's hard to give criticism (and tough to take it) on this issue—maybe because the human desire to be liked is so strong.

Second, most of us don't actually know what it means to work well with others, because we make that judgment according to what's important to us. For example, Brian abhorred bosses who yelled, and felt his soft-spoken, respectful, more agreeable style was a plus to his direct reports. It was, but his direct reports considered access to Brian the highest currency. Brian was oblivious to this because of his own easygoing, improvisational approach to contact. He'd wander, and if one person wasn't available, he'd simply check in with someone else. When we view the world through our own filters, it's easy to miss what others are truly requiring from us.

Working well with others goes far beyond likeability. If you solely focus on being liked, you risk falling into the trap of being too accommodating, working so hard at being everyone's pal that you wind up neglecting your own responsibilities. This can lead to work backlogs that make you, in fact, difficult to work with, because you hold other people up. This is not to say that being friendly and cordial isn't appreciated—just that in the bottom-line world of work, niceness can never substitute for effectiveness.

By contrast, you've probably worked with people whose flat (even wizened) personalities leave something to be desired—you'd never go out for a drink with them, for instance—but you enjoy working with them because of their talent, skill, and reliability.

Working well with others is about productivity and efficiency. It's about creating a pleasant, cooperative, energetic environment that ensures everyone gets the work done. Your ability to work well with others significantly boosts your value to your company. Employers regard your capacity to collaborate and get along as the grease in the machine, translating it directly to the bottom line: less turnover, heightened efficiency, and the ability to take charge quickly when crisis hits. Employees with strong interpersonal skills and an ability to collaborate effectively help a company get the most out of their hires. And if you're good—the Michael Jordan of your department—you elevate everyone else's game. People love working with you because your team always produces the best results, and that feels great.

Happy working relationships can make a difficult task easier, and going through tough times much more tolerable. When you are effectively cooperating and communicating, you get more done in less time and reduce the hours spent repairing miscommunications, and if you get stuck with a last-second emergency, people willingly help you out because they know you would do the same for them in a crunch.

Strained working relationships, on the other hand, make going to work each day almost unbearable, enveloping you in a sense of dread, insecurity, and worry about your job. Productivity plummets (along with your value to your company) when huge amounts of time are spent stewing, fretting, and resenting the situation as you rack your brain trying to figure out who is to blame for the conflicts: Is it me? Or is it them?

So let's take the mystery out of that burning question. Even if people won't talk to you directly about it, the good news is that in my business, they talk to me about it all the time—just like Brian's direct reports, they are hoping that somehow I can improve the person's performance, and thereby boost everyone's efficiency.

Grab-and-Go Strategy #28
Avoid the Six Gripes

No matter who's doing the talking, and whether they are expressing frustration about a boss, coworker, direct report, or customer, six common faults consistently drive people crazy about one another at work. All of the complaints I hear about workplace relationships boil down to the following six gripes.

1. **Inaccessibility.** They are rarely available to answer your questions, and slow to respond when you need their guidance, direction, or approval to complete your work.
2. **Unreliability.** They don't deliver what they promise, keep people waiting, cancel meetings at the last minute, and fail to follow through on their commitments.
3. **Rigidity.** They don't handle change well, stick rigidly to their preferred way of doing things, and don't adapt well to other people's needs, circumstances, or style.
4. **Disrespectfulness.** They come across as insulting, patronizing, condescending, and rude. Dismissive of your talents, skills, intelligence, and contribution, they also seem to have no regard for your time or boundaries.
5. **Vagueness.** It's very hard to know what they want, because their communication style is confusing. They are ambiguous, sometimes evasive, and often leave issues dangling. Or they constantly change their mind, often halfway (or more) through a project.
6. **Unfairness.** Inordinately demanding and overbearing, they take more than they give; they possess a sense of entitlement that breeds resentment in others.

That's it. Six universal gripes—they're not complicated, overdrawn, or the result of deep analysis, yet they ring true in every work relationship. We want the same courtesies from our coworkers that we want from our clients. Overworked and overwhelmed, we are all

---

REALITY CHECK

Think about one or two people you work with who drive you absolutely crazy, who frustrate you and make your life at work tremendously difficult. How many of the six gripes are they guilty of?

---

unified by the desire to get things done, done well, and in the most expedient way possible. We value the bosses, customers, coworkers, and staff who help us accomplish this goal, and we are frustrated by those who make efficiency difficult.

WHAT IT MEANS TO WORK WELL WITH OTHERS

Now, if the above characteristics define what makes working with someone difficult, it follows that the opposite traits encapsulate the qualities of an ideal working partner—someone you would enjoy working with and with whom you would find it easiest to get your own work done. Working well together comes down to the same principles, whether you consider your boss, staff, coworkers, or customers.

1. **Accessibility.** If you need them, they're available, approachable, and almost always get back to you within a reasonable amount of time.
2. **Reliability.** They do what they say, pretty close to when they say they will—and if they're going to be late, they let you know. You can count on the quality of their work.
3. **Adaptability.** They can be creative and flexible in a crunch, crisis, or emergency—and can accommodate you when needed. They have an upbeat, can-do approach to problems.
4. **Respectfulness.** They are polite and considerate of your time, admiring of your skill, knowledge, and contribution, and honor the boundaries you establish.
5. **Clarity.** You know what they want—they're not fuzzy or wishy-washy, ducky or dodgy. The measurable result they are looking for and how you are being evaluated on every task you do is clear.
6. **Fairness.** They look for win-wins in every situation, and have a good sense of what is reasonable versus what is above and be-

---

REALITY CHECK

Recall your two all-time favorite people to work with. Think beyond whether or not someone was a friend—identify people who inspire your best performance, with whom you feel the most creative, effective, and satisfying work synergy. How many of the six traits do they embody?

---

yond. They express appreciation for your extra efforts, always making sure you get something out of the deal, too.

GRADE YOURSELF

A clear and universal definition of what it means to work well with others gives you the tools to honestly assess your skills in this department, and speed the diagnosis of what's causing any strained relationship that's got you stumped.

So let's spin it back around to you. How would you grade yourself in the six qualities of working well with others? Be brutally honest. Picture yourself as you go through your day and interact with others. Think about your individual work style, the power struggles you find yourself entangled in, the practical pressures you are under. How do these things affect the way you interact with others?

Try to remember what others have either complimented you on or expressed some frustration over. Think about what's been brought to your attention in performance reviews.

Envision the majority of the encounters you have with others. What happens when someone calls or e-mails you? Do you respond within a reasonable amount of time, or do people often have to wait? How well do you follow through on your promises to deliver? How frequently do you experience miscommunications with others? Do you just have problems with one or two people, or is it with everyone? We are looking for the common trend.

"Plays well with others" was something on our report cards throughout school. Now in the working world, grade yourself in each of the six areas that define how well we work with others. Don't feel shackled by a need to be perfect—frankly, none of us are.

Grading system: A—excellent; B—good, C—average, D—needs improvement, F—failing.

Accessibility	
Reliability	
Flexibility	
Respectfulness	
Clarity	
Fairness	

Surprised by any of your answers? Where are you strongest? Which qualities do you need to most improve on? Any hunch as to why you have this particular set of strengths and weaknesses? Did you have trouble answering the questions about yourself in a general way? Did it all *depend*—on whom you're dealing with? Or on somebody's personality? Or their power over you?

Grab-and-Go Strategy #29
Watch Out for Your Relationship Traps

The six traits are all pretty straightforward, but implementing them can be a challenge. What keeps us from delivering on each quality? What gets in the way? Are we just callous and uncaring? Rarely. There are a variety of reasons we may fall short on one or several traits, often without even realizing it. Behavior can be misinterpreted as a result of work style, communication style, insecurity, unconscious power struggles, and even pragmatics.

All difficulties stem from matters of human dynamics—in the workplace, with so much happening and so many different personalities, there's an abundance of opportunity for disagreement. It's important to identify your issues so you know what's likely to set you off and can learn how to better handle workplace conflict.

As a consultant, I've observed that most of my clients have patterns influencing whom they work well with and whom they don't. Sometimes a particular personality trait or gripe sets us off, no matter who we are dealing with. There are certain things we are better equipped to handle than others. Some people let insults or disgruntlement roll right off their backs; other people prickle at the slightest hint of disrespect. Lateness and failure to deliver on time drives some people crazy, while many others are flexible and understanding, because they are overwhelmed with their own workloads. Which gripes are you particularly sensitive to?

BALANCE OF POWER

The balance of power often influences the way you behave. In some relationships, the person you are dealing with has the power to hire or fire you. In other situations, you're the one in power. With coworkers, there is more of a sense of equality, but even there, some relationships are more equal than others. With time at a premium, it's seems logical that you'd make yourself more accessible to your boss or big clients than you might to your coworkers. You're prioritizing based on people's proximity to your personal revenue line.

But many times, our behavior has less to do with pragmatics and more with our own psychology—old familial issues of authority, ego, and competitiveness that drive every interpersonal relationship. Working together brings up themes of dependency and interdependency, which in turn can bring out all kinds of old roles and behaviors that sneak up on us unawares.

Think about whether you find some kinds of work relationships easier to manage than others. Are you on your best behavior with your bosses and customers, but careless when it comes to your coworkers? Or are you buttoned down with your staff, but antagonistic with your own bosses, all of whom you find to be incompetent? Or maybe you find that you are always in conflict with your coworkers, mirroring the competitive relationship you had with your siblings. Is there a pattern to the type of person you tend to have battles with (people in positions of authority, people over whom you have authority)? Do you fight with all of your coworkers, or just a few? Do you have difficulty retaining good employees? What old hidden patterns may be driving your behavior?

For example, in grading himself on the six qualities, Brian needed two sets of scores. When it came to dealing with his boss and the board of directors, Brian received high marks—A's and B's across the board. Yet when it came to his staff, many of his grades were C's, D's, and F's. This disparity was due not so much to pragmatics, as to his insecurity as a leader. During the transition to his new role, he was much more comfortable *responding* to an authority than *being* one.

Sheila, a development assistant at a nonprofit, was just the opposite. In her interactions with her coworkers, she was a fabulous team player, getting A's across the board in all six traits. But when it came to her boss and the donors, her grades were C's, D's, and F's because she felt intimidated by them. Sheila was more comfortable with her peers than with authority figures. She also had a hard time keeping a job. To find job security, Sheila needed to deal with her fear of authority, which she could do easily, by simply aiming to deliver on each of the six traits.

The secret to successfully navigating these situations is to change your own behavior—and you can use the six traits to change the chemistry of your relationship. In the end, it's all about changing what you can control—and that is you.

In every work relationship, it's not about what the other person does, it's about how we respond. Once you've identified which of the six gripes the person is guilty of, turn the test back around on yourself. Which of the six gripes are you reacting with in response? If someone is unreliable, do you counter by being inflexible and negative to communicate your distaste? If your coworker is unfair, do you become unclear to avoid being cornered?

A small adjustment in your own reaction is usually all it takes to alter the chemistry of any relationship. Don't wait for the other person to change. People can't help some of their behaviors, and as we've learned, they are often unaware of them. In truth, everyone's a little quirky, so don't waste time being aggravated at or overanalyzing the situation.

Let's say you have a boss like Brian, whose inaccessibility drives you crazy. You're left constantly spinning your wheels, unable to progress on projects or get the answers you need. So *you* react by becoming less reliable—you "yes" your boss to his face but stop putting in full effort, because you know that whenever you proceed without his guidance, he inevitably disagrees and makes you redo it anyway. This creates a huge, unspoken tension between you and your boss, which turns into a power struggle where you're not doing your work, and he's disappointed when things aren't done. Ah, the vicious cycle begins!

In any difficult situation, instead of reacting by feeling victimized, take responsibility for solving the problem. Get your ego out of the way and focus on the common goal—getting the work done. If your boss is inaccessible, you become more accessible. If he is rigid, become more flexible. Express your desire to complete assignments accurately and on time and ask what the best way to communicate with him is when he's busy—does he prefer e-mail, phone calls, meetings?

Maybe meetings with your boss have become so rare that you've gotten into the habit of extending meetings to marathon lengths

	IF THEY ARE					
You become	INACCESSIBLE	UNRELIABLE	INFLEXIBLE	DISRESPECTFUL	UNCLEAR	UNFAIR
Accessible	X					
Reliable		X				
Flexible			X			
Respectful				X		
Clear					X	
Fair						X

whenever you do get him for a few minutes, or of writing extra-long memos. This can make you appear to be disrespectful of his time. Try changing your approach. Limit each point of contact to one or two issues, and never take more than fifteen minutes at a time. Your boss may suddenly become more accessible.

Come back to the six-trait assessment anytime you are having difficulty with someone you work with. It will help you immediately zoom in on exactly what is causing the problem, and empower you to fix it without delay. You may try to improve your performance one trait at a time, across the board, or just opt to work on an entire category of relationships in which you score very poorly. You may even decide just to accept that you're terrible in certain areas (or with certain people), play to your strengths, and try to get better at understanding why others you work with are frustrated with your behavior. The self-awareness that comes from knowing what's behind some of this behavior will help to quell workplace misunderstandings and battles.

DID YOU KNOW?

A landmark 1994 report by the Secretary of Labor's Commission on Achieving Necessary Skills revealed that 82.5 percent of employers value human relations skills higher than conceptual or technical skills.

Grab-and-Go Strategy #30
Improve Your "Works Well" Grades

This section will give you the insight and tools to find fast, pragmatic, astute solutions to improve every working relationship, including those with your boss, staff, coworkers, and customers. Below each trait is a list of some of the inadvertent causes of a lower grade; see if you can recognize your own behavior, or those of someone you work with, in any of those descriptions. Understanding what's behind the behaviors can take the mystery and anger out of the situation, and prepare you to fix the problem. Following each diagnosis are tips and strategies to change your behavior and improve your relationships.

1. BE MORE ACCESSIBLE

When taken the wrong way, your inaccessibility makes it seem as if you don't care what others are working on or thinking about. If you have trouble being accessible, what could be causing it?

- **Pragmatism.** Sometimes inaccessibility is a matter of pure logistics. If you travel frequently or keep different hours than some of the people you work with, accessibility will be a constant challenge. Are you always in a rush, never slowing down to give enough time or attention to people's questions? Given time limits, you can't be equally accessible to all people always.
- **Work style.** Are you hyperfocused? By that I mean, do you get so absorbed in the nuance and detail of your projects that you simply refuse to have your concentration interrupted? Do you keep your head down and send silent signals that you are unapproachable, unavailable, otherwise focused or distracted? I know I go "into the hole" for three to five hours at a time when I'm writing, and take interruptions from only one or two people, because when I accept any more, my creativity is derailed. When you do come up for air and review decisions made in your absence, you will inevitably have opinions and need things revised, because of that very same eye for detail and nuance. This can be frustrating to people you work with, because they may feel as though you don't respect their time or abilities.
- **Insecurity.** A confidence deficit can give rise to inaccessibility. Do you duck and dodge people, calls, issues, and meetings when you feel insecure, or aren't ready to confront them? Maybe your boss or direct report is looking for answers on a project you haven't completed, so you suddenly stop answering

the phone. Are you so wrapped up in the belief that you need to solve every single problem on your own that when unsure of a solution, instead of reaching out for help, you end up just ignoring the problem?

Tips for Becoming More Accessible

- **Give yourself a 24-hour response policy.** Even if you can't respond fully, give people some information they are looking for and plan to follow up. Giving yourself a 24-hour deadline keeps the momentum going and prevents you from getting overinvolved or overobsessed with perfection.
- **Establish and stick with daily huddles or weekly meetings with key team members.** Having a specific time every day, or week, to meet with key team members will keep you connected and assuage their lingering anxiety about not having access to you. Determine the agenda points together before each sitdown— and say no to topics that you don't have answers for. Get together for lunch every few months with people whom you can't be (or don't need to be) available to as often.
- **Let people know the most efficient way to reach you,** especially if you travel a lot or work in a different time zone. How you decide to communicate will vary according to the other person's style. You may prefer to communicate with some people via e-mail because it is available 24 hours a day, while you may find a quick phone call or in-person chat more efficient with others. Let the nature and importance of your relationship dictate your mode of communication.
- **Create open-door times** by setting up routine "open office" hours—and inviting people in. If you have an assistant, have them fill your office hours in ten- or fifteen-minute increments.

2. BE MORE RELIABLE

Some people you work with may not mind this fault, especially those who are juggling their own overwhelming workloads and deadlines. Others are not as patient. A lack of reliability does not necessarily emanate from carelessness, arrogance, or disrespect. There are several ways in which the best of intentions can backfire.

If you are less reliable than you'd like to be, what could be the reason?

- **Difficulty saying no.** The desire to make everyone happy is misguided. Typically, it produces the opposite result. If your knee-jerk response to every request from your boss, customers, coworkers, or direct reports is to drop everything and say yes, you are serving no one well. At work, where the schedules and reputations of others, as well as your own, are on the line depending upon how well you perform, delivering good results far outweighs having good intentions.

- **Poor time-estimating skills.** Lateness for meetings, in returning calls, and in meeting deadlines can emanate from an unrealistic sense of how long things take. Do you take assignments on, or volunteer to do things, thinking more about the quality of each task (i.e., you like it or you don't) rather than how long it will take? Or maybe you get caught in a tangle of denial and wishful thinking, applying pressure on yourself to be faster than you actually are. You may suffer from the shoving-one-more-thing-in syndrome, habitually trying to finish just one more thing before you leave, which *always* ends up taking much longer than expected.

- **Power struggle.** Ignoring deadlines and start times and doing things on your own timetable can be your way of asserting power, exercising the privilege of your title, or rebelling against authority in some way (your boss wants speed, you want quality). Do you keep people waiting because you believe your time is more valuable? Or attempt to preserve your self-respect and dignity by refusing to be forced to follow other people's agendas? If you only do what you want to do, when you want to do it, it is likely that your behavior is ego-driven. Unreliability may also result from a lack of self-discipline. Instead of properly preparing yourself for work every day, do you show up exhausted and moody? How do you think that affects the consistency of your performance?

- **Insecurity.** When you don't like a task, or you feel that a task is really difficult or complicated, you might end up waiting until the last minute to start working on it. If the task wasn't easy to begin with, not giving yourself enough time to wrestle with it will make it even more difficult for you to deliver the results on time and in a reliable fashion.

Tips for Becoming More Reliable

- **Watch what you promise and swear off empty/false promises.** Don't agree to do anything until you've asked yourself three critical questions: How long will this take? When will I do it? Will something have to come out of my schedule to make room for this? Pick one person to become more reliable with, and knock yourself out delivering. You'll take your promises more seriously once you see how much she appreciates your completed work and learn what it feels like to gain someone's trust.

- **Resist temptation.** Shoving one more task in before leaving for a meeting, making a phone call, or finishing a project *will* make you late!

- **Get better at saying no.** (1) *Boss.* Don't say no outright, but let her know if/when your latest assignment will be overloading your schedule, so that she can help you prioritize: "I'll do my best, but given the short lead time, if I don't get to everything, what are your priorities?" (2) *Customer.* Explain the reasoning behind your answer: "I know you'd like to skip the initial consultation, but we've found it's the best way to ensure a quality job on our part, and we're not willing to compromise our process. It wouldn't serve you or us." (3) *Coworker.* Say why you can't do something that moment: "I'd love to help you out, but my boss needs this by 4 P.M. this afternoon, and if I stop now, I'll never make his deadline." (4) *Staff.* Provide a little background: "I know you want to move this along, but I can't review your status report until after the board meeting next week."

- **Create the conditions that bring out your best performance/maximum energy.** You know yourself better than anyone else—make sure you are taking steps to help yourself succeed. If you absolutely cannot function with less than seven hours of sleep a night, make sure you get at least that much. If you know skipping breakfast makes you cranky, always eat something before you leave for work (or scarf down a PowerBar on your way in). Do you know what calms you down when you're in a bad mood? Do you need to talk a walk? Squeeze a stress ball? Listen to music? Talk to a friend? Exercise? No one is perfect—we all have our better and worse days—but if your mood swings are dramatic and affect how much you can produce at work, get them under control.

3. BE MORE ADAPTABLE

It's okay to be inflexible on some things (when you're in charge or have mastered the methods behind completing a certain task); but when your unwillingness to be flexible or embrace change has a negative effect on the productivity of others, you need to open yourself up to different options.

What could make you have trouble adapting?

- **Performance anxiety.** Rigidity often comes from a desire to do well: You know the conditions you work best under, already have them set up, and are scared to change. You fear that the loss of control in your routine will make you flop. Inflexibility can also be tied to a lack of imagination—you say to yourself, "This method has worked just fine for ten years. There *is* no better way." I once directed the reorganization of a nonprofit's loft space. The executive director warned me that one employee, the bookkeeper, was openly and extremely unreceptive to change—he was actually wary of upsetting her routines. This woman had really rooted down. Her cubicle was crammed with hanging pictures, plants, buttons, plaques, wall hangings; it looked like she'd been there for decades. So, keeping with the ED's wishes, we planned the entire reorganization around her. In fact, everyone moved *but* her! How often do people bend over backward for you because of your resistance to change?

- **Power struggle.** Some people see "adapting" as giving in to other people's needs; on some deep level, it's really a blow to their ego. You may try to be nice about it (resisting change in a passive-aggressive way, like agreeing to change, then just doing the same old thing), or you might be overtly stubborn and cop an "It's my way or the highway" attitude. Do you garner a sense of power when people yield to your schedule, instead of your going along with them? That behavior is a telltale sign of diva mentality. If it's not costing your company time and money, and not ruffling any feathers, fine. But make sure you are still providing enough value in exchange for the inflexibility you're permitted to maintain.

Tips for Becoming More Adaptable

- **Change "but" to "and."** What a difference a word makes, implying a can-do, take-charge approach to problems rather than an argument. For example, a client tells you they want to bring the budget down. Instead of saying, "*But* that's going to compromise quality," try saying, "Okay, *and* that's likely to compromise quality. Where would you be most comfortable shaving costs?" Or your boss asks you to have something on his desk in two hours. Instead of saying, "*But* then I won't be able to meet tomorrow's deadline," try, "Okay, *and* if I need to do that, what should I do about tomorrow's deadline? Can someone else finish it off?" Focus on solutions, not obstacles.

- **Experiment with a new way of doing things.** We all get stuck in ruts, and a change from your routine might actually open up your creativity, performance, thinking, and energy in ways you don't expect. We do some things out of habit, and sometimes that habit doesn't really serve any purpose anymore. For example, if you insist on holding staff meetings every Friday afternoon just because that's when you've always had them, and your entire staff moans and groans about taking two hours out of their Fridays when they're trying to finish things up before the weekend, change the day of the meeting.

- **Adopt a give-and-take attitude.** If you're willing to be flexible with other people, they're more likely to be flexible with you. You might not get something back the moment that you give it, but I guarantee, the next time you're looking for a little leeway on a deadline, or an extra afternoon off to see your kid's championship soccer game, you're far more likely to get it.

DID YOU KNOW?

Well-crafted teams help an organization be nimble and responsive amid highly volatile market conditions, customer demands, external pressures, and cost cutting. Good people skills help you as much as your employer, by boosting the quality of your work life, enriching your growth and development, and enhancing your job security.

2001 study by the Work in America Institute

4. BE MORE RESPECTFUL

Respecting someone's time, talents, ideas, and boundaries is one of the most important currencies in the world of work—in many cases people value courtesy in others more than salary. Demoralizing, patronizing behavior steals a person's sense of dignity, and for many that is the worst infraction. It's shocking to learn that people find you disrespectful, especially when you're not doing it intentionally.

How could your actions be (or perhaps be misinterpreted as) disrespectful?

- **Work style.** Do you barge in without knocking, or call people on the phone and launch into what you need without first asking if it's a good time? Often intuitive, creative types have a habit of being impulsive when an idea hits or when working under pressure, calling upon coworkers, bosses, and staff (and even customers) with a sense of urgency that they must talk *right now.* To people accustomed to structure and receiving fair warning on requests, this sort of spontaneous, sudden approach seems rude and inconsiderate. Also, if you are used to doing everything yourself and working independently, this may come across to people as an insult—that you don't value their abilities, intelligence, or contribution. Do you keep later (or earlier) hours than the people you work with? Have you been known to mindlessly dump work on people at the end of the day, as if they weren't busy doing something else? If your work ethic drives you to put in fourteen-hour days, you may find yourself annoyed by or critical of people who leave by 6 P.M. Your criticism of someone else's lifestyle—based solely on the hours they spend at the office, rather than what they produce— is disrespectful.
- **Communication style.** In the pressure of today's workplace, many people appreciate short, cut-to-the-chase, efficient points of contact in meetings, calls, and e-mails. If you need to warm up and schmooze before any discussion, people might perceive you as wasting their time. Study your conversations; observe when you've lost someone's attention (their eyes glaze over after a while; they stand up to give a signal that the meeting is over before you're done talking, or start glancing at their watches). On the other hand, a too-abrupt, cut-to-the-chase style can feel disrespectful too. If there are never any pleas-

antries offered at the beginning of your conversations—just boom, boom, boom, and you're done—people may feel you are barking orders at them and interpret you as uncaring and disrespectful, even though you may be just focused on the work.

- **Power struggle.** Do you dismiss people's ideas without listening? Do you roll your eyes and nod off in meetings when someone you think is a bore starts to talk? Are you so focused on being right, or on getting credit and attention, that you forget to thank other people or acknowledge their contributions? Do you find yourself reprimanding others in front of other people to feel more important and puff up your own ego? Or are you so overfocused on controlling every detail of every project that you hover over everyone's work, challenge every decision they make, micromanaging to a degree that squelches every ounce of their free expression?

Tips for Becoming More Respectful

- **Find something to truly admire about every person you work with.** Yes, sometimes you'll have to dig deep; but once you find it, thinking about that person with that quality in mind will change your relationship. For example, most people found Josh a pain to work with; his quirks were enough to make even the most respectful person dismiss him outright. But Josh had a passion for the work. He loved his job and believed 100 percent in his company's mission. Emphasizing that dimmed his otherwise annoying antics, and kept everyone focused on the task at hand. Try to remember that people want to do well and that everyone likes to make a contribution.
- **Use old-fashioned manners.** Ask if it's a convenient time before barging in. Don't take calls or check voice mail and text messages while you're in a meeting or on the phone with anyone. Never ignore people or be dismissive of their thoughts and opinions—they have their jobs for a reason, so listen to what they have to say. Show up on time and end meetings promptly. Set your watch: Bring work to keep yourself busy if you're kept waiting, but don't be the one to make others wait. If necessary, pick the three or four people who are the most intolerant (least flexible) and improve your performance with them.
- **Let people do their jobs.** Read Competency 7 for tips on delegating and learning to break the pattern of total self-reliance. When you allow people to do their jobs and don't hinder their work with an unprovoked lack of trust or with your crushing

tendency to micromanage, you'll be pleasantly surprised to see what they can do.

- **Limit the chitchat.** Office chatter is fine . . . within reason! If you know you're a talker, write out the bullets of what you want to say before you make a call, or go into a meeting, to keep yourself focused; or ask people to let you know if you're careening off course, so you can restrain yourself.

- **Focus less on people's hours and more on what they produce.** No one can argue with production. If someone has made arrangements to leave at a certain time every day, or to take time at lunch for a quick workout twice a week, respect those boundaries. If these people are performing at a high level, consistently delivering results, and earning their salary, it doesn't matter if they work eight or nine and a half hours a day. Maybe their strict quitting time and daily exercise is what keeps them so efficient to begin with! Isn't there some part of you that would love to do the same?

5. BE MORE CLEAR

According to an American Society for Training and Development study, communications skills are second only to job knowledge in promoting workplace success. Clarity is the essence and root of efficiency—the more clear we are in defining assignments, roles, expectations, problems, obstacles, and solutions, the more precise everyone's efforts can be. But people are not machines, and in many businesses answers are not always so clear.

What could keep you from being perceived as clear?

- **Work style.** If you're a creative thinker, you may have a strong sense of what you're looking for but have trouble articulating that vision to others. You may stay vague on purpose because you like to keep your options open, trying things out first and clarifying later. Or you may just not know what's right until you see it. Coworkers, especially more analytic thinkers, may resent expending the effort to just "try something" that you might reject once you see it. They operate more from their heads than their guts, and take pride in deciding on the destination before they start, mapping out the specific path and sticking to a plan. Understandably, it can be difficult for you and a more linear person to work together. The balance of power will guide you in who needs to adapt to whom.

- **Communication style.** If your delegatees often get things wrong, or there are frequent misunderstandings between you and your customers, boss, or coworkers, maybe you think you're being clear when you actually aren't. Are you always in a rush? Do you blurt out instructions at lightning speed, never taking the time to see if the person you're speaking with actually understands what you're saying? Do you inadvertently communicate only the aspects of a project or task that interest you, glossing over other critical pieces of information you just don't care about? For example, if you're a big-picture person, do you forget to explain the details, or vice versa? Do you have trouble remembering what you did or did not say? Are you baffled when something you "swore you asked so-and-so to do" isn't done?

- **Authority issues.** Power issues can influence one's willingness to be clear. If you are afraid to disappoint a boss or customer or anger a coworker or staffer, you may keep your comments vague enough to avoid confrontation or reprimand. Sometime a fear of being direct results from a fear of being too demanding or critical. Are you working so hard to be fair and respectful that you end up being overly polite, deferential, and unclear? Is it hard to ask for what you want because you're afraid of sounding critical? Do the people you work with express frustration about "not knowing what's going on" or feeling left in the dark? When you are vague, people fear the worst, worrying about their job security, the future of the company, and whether or not they are in trouble. Your lack of clarity may leave people feeling confused *and* anxious.

Tips for Becoming More Clear

- **When explaining any assignment, ask the person to repeat back what they heard,** so you can correct, refine, or expound on anything you may have inadvertently left out. Often, hearing the person repeat what you just said will help you get it clearer in your own mind. Writing something down before you explain it can also help you clarify your message. Keep notes about your conversations in that person's file, and refer back to them if there's a misunderstanding.

- **Explain your communication style.** If you are a more creative, intuitive thinker, help people understand the way your mind works, so they know that even shot-down ideas are helpful—

not a waste of time—because they help determine exactly what you want. Once your team understands the way you think, they will have an easier time making decisions.

- **Be honest.** Telling people what you do *and* don't know is disarming! In my experience, people are generally more understanding about things being late or incomplete than you think, and when you tell the truth—instead of dodging it—they feel respected. Once they know what's really going on, you can ask for help. If they can provide it, your problem is solved.

- **Know your audience.** Are you speaking with a big-picture person or a detail person? Some big-picture thinkers simply don't have the head for details: Their eyes glaze over at the first drop of specific information. Detail-focused people sometimes have trouble seeing beyond the next four steps in front of them, and may be confused or even scared by any big-picture talk because they don't see how it relates to them. Knowing the type of person in front of you should influence what level of conversation and communication takes place.

6. BE MORE FAIR

Next to being respectful, being fair is one of the most powerful ways to build loyalty, and fuel the productive energy with which people approach their work and one another. But it's not always easy, because every exchange is not an even tit for tat. Fairness is a fluid concern because of the fact that everyone needs to be getting something of value in the end. Fairness is usually an exchange of services for time. You spend time on various projects at work, supporting your colleagues, clients, bosses, and staffs, in exchange for something that you value: money, recognition, the opportunity to learn, experience, and so on. When people feel you are treating them in an unfair way, their productivity and commitment will wane.

What could keep you from being fair?

- **Misassumptions.** Sometimes you make a false assumption about what someone else is getting out of an assignment. You think it's the opportunity of a lifetime, but they just want the paycheck and to be home by 6 P.M. You may also misunderstand what it takes to do a job. When you are wrapped up in your own workload, you might not realize that what you're asking from someone requires a huge investment of time and effort. You figure it's no big deal—but they feel like you're asking for the world, without offering any extra form of compensation, recognition, or appreciation.

- **Sense of entitlement power struggle.** Personnel directors frequently have reported to me the arrogant sense of entitlement many people have in the workplace. If you have some belief that you deserve certain things (benefits, titles, pay, privilege, promotions), regardless of protocol, industry or company standards, or what's traditional, you may be suffering from a sense of unearned entitlement. I stress *unearned* because when you constantly ask for a special exception, there is an ego issue involved—it's some way of feeling better about yourself, feeling superior or special. You are never happy with the normal way of doing things; you want to be treated differently. If the people you work with are unwilling to grant you that special treatment, I guarantee it's because you don't deserve it, and giving in to you would be unfair.

Tips for Becoming More Fair

- **Remember that work is an even exchange.** Make sure you know what other people are getting out of the deal, whether you're asking for a favor or a long-term arrangement. And if you can't figure it out, ask them! Most people will answer quite honestly. It builds your confidence in working with them and helps you better provide what they need. (The new assistant to the president of a nonprofit political consulting firm agreed to take a pay cut and title demotion simply for the opportunity to learn and contribute to the mission of the organization. Knowing this, her boss found opportunities to bring her to board meetings and strategic planning meetings and give her

---

HOT TIP!

Rather than overwhelm yourself trying to repair your relationships with everyone at once, choose one or two key players from the group—perhaps the ones you work most closely with—and try improving your performance with each of them, one trait at a time. Changing your behavior is a hard thing to do, and by focusing your efforts you'll find it easier to monitor yourself.

additional responsibility, without having to come up with more money in the budget.)

- **Look for the win-win.** As in the art of negotiating, preserve the dignity of all concerned by finding a solution that benefits both sides of the working relationship.
- **Recognize when you are asking people to go above and beyond.** Being fair doesn't mean that you shouldn't ask people to help out in a crisis, or to accommodate you when necessary. But it does mean (a) not abusing this option; (b) checking that it's okay; and (c) acknowledging their sacrifice and showing appreciation for it. Write them a thank-you note, take them out for coffee, or offer to do a favor back. When someone feels appre-

---

BRIAN

When I met with Brian again and shared the feedback I'd gotten from his direct reports, his first reaction was complete denial. That's ridiculous, he claimed; I'm rarely late, and highly dependable. But the more we talked about it, the more he began to see that he was behaving differently with people above him than with people under him. This was less a matter of disrespect than a combination of work style and insecurity. With his bosses, he was clear on what they needed from him, and was thus able to show up on time and be extremely available.

But during this transition, Brain was unsure of his relationship to his staff—he was still trying to define his new role.

Brian was more like a jazz player than a classical musician, always in improvisational mode—he eventually confessed that he'd always had difficulty adhering to a schedule. His spontaneous approach to management worked very well during crisis-driven times but was less effective during a time of stabilization. If he was going to be out of the office more, he needed to hire a COO who could do the job Brian had always done—being on the front line, managing the day-to-day crises with the staff. This would provide Brian the flexibility he thrived on, while giving the staff the continuity they needed.

But Brian also needed to realize that showing up on time—and showing up at all—was a simple and direct courtesy that others valued highly. No matter how relaxed he might be about time, the people who worked for him regarded his punctuality and full attention as the highest expression of respect.

ciated, and the imbalance eventually gets "righted," people are usually willing to keep delivering for you.

To maintain healthy, productive relationships that benefit you and your employer, you have to rise like a phoenix above issues of personality, power, and ego and simply focus on the six "works well" traits. These six universal qualities objectify your relationships—and staying objective is the surefire way to improve any work relationship.

Even if everything else about your job is going well, one or two bad relationships with people you work with can block your productivity and happiness. Don't stand on ceremony and look to place blame. Whether it's you or whether it's them, take the full responsibility to understand what might be behind the behavior, fix the problem, and get back to the work. The better you are at the competency of working well with others, the happier and more valued a worker you will become.

Chapter Summary
WORK WELL WITH OTHERS

Which of the grab-and-go strategies will you implement?

- Avoid the six gripes.
- Watch out for your relationships.
- Improve your works-well grades.

When do you plan to implement them?

What do you think will be your biggest obstacle in applying the strategies?

How will you overcome that obstacle?

What is your motivation for mastering this competency?

Nine

LEVERAGE YOUR VALUE

CONGRATULATIONS! You are making work work.

At the beginning of this book you were drowning, overwhelmed, unhappy, and plagued by the question, Is it me, or is it them? You were working in a fog, spinning deliriously from one task to the next, wound in a knot, and consumed by the feeling that you might not be able to cut it. Your goal, more than anything, was to be happier and get a grip.

You've advanced your skills, upped your productivity, and tamed the challenges in this new world of work by learning how to work wisely. With practice, you've mastered the workplace dance and are delivering measurable results, right on the revenue line. In tune with your energy cycles, you have boosted your efficiency and are completing more critical work every day. Smarter, wiser, and more confident, you have learned in the previous eight chapters how to embrace your work/life balance, think like an entrepreneur, choose the most important tasks, get things done, control the nibblers, organize at the speed of change, delegate effectively, and work well with others.

I now challenge you to go back to the self-assessment at the beginning of the book, and rescore yourself. On the same scale of 1 to 5 (1 being never, 5 being always) rate yourself anew on the following fourteen questions:

My New Self-Assessment

1. When overloaded, are you easily able to prioritize and focus in on the most critical tasks?

1	2	3	4	5
Never	Rarely	Sometimes	Usually	Always

2. Do you turn work around quickly, rather than letting it get backed up on your desk?

1	2	3	4	5
Never	Rarely	Sometimes	Usually	Always

3. Do you have a good way of tracking your to-dos?

1	2	3	4	5
Never	Rarely	Sometimes	Usually	Always

4. Do you have a general structure to your day or week that enables you to feel in control of when you do things?

1	2	3	4	5
Never	Rarely	Sometimes	Usually	Always

5. Are you physically organized, keeping papers, computer documents, contact information, and work materials in order and at your fingertips?

1	2	3	4	5
Never	Rarely	Sometimes	Usually	Always

6. Do you have productive, efficient working relationships with your coworkers, assistant, direct reports, boss?

1	2	3	4	5
Never	Rarely	Sometimes	Usually	Always

7. Are you generally pleased with your work/life balance?

1	2	3	4	5
Never	Rarely	Sometimes	Usually	Always

8. Can you clearly identify the core responsibilities of your job?

1	2	3	4	5
Never	Rarely	Sometimes	Usually	Always

9. Are there key responsibilities you feel insecure in your abilities to perform?

1	2	3	4	5
Never	Rarely	Sometimes	Usually	Always

10. Can you easily let go of low-priority items, without guilt?

1	2	3	4	5
Never	Rarely	Sometimes	Usually	Always

11. Do you understand and believe in the mission of your company?

1	2	3	4	5
Never	Rarely	Sometimes	Usually	Always

12. Do you know what your most valuable contribution is? What makes you unique?

1	2	3	4	5
Never	Rarely	Sometimes	Usually	Always

13. Is your most valuable contribution what your employer wants?

1	2	3	4	5
Never	Rarely	Sometimes	Usually	Always

14. Do you keep yourself current in the expertise required by your job?

1	2	3	4	5
Never	Rarely	Sometimes	Usually	Always

SCORE YOURSELF

- **14–30 points:** Drowning.
- **31–50 points:** Treading water.
- **51–70 points:** Doing the breast stroke.

How does your new score compare with your old? Have you moved up a level? Gotten yourself more solidly in the middle of a tier? If you've implemented any of the eight competencies you've learned so far, there's no doubt your score should be higher. Not perfect . . . just higher. Where have you improved? Where do you still need work? Which of the competencies presents your biggest challenge? Which do you value the most? What competency, for you, is the most critical to remember? Have you learned anything about yourself that surprised you?

Take a moment, breathe deep, and pat yourself on the back. It took a lot of courage and determination to read this book, and a great effort to apply the principles; don't downplay the improvements you have already made by saying, "Gee, I'm still not there," or berating yourself for your imperfections. These skills take a lifetime to master, and if you have improved *anywhere,* this means you can improve *everywhere.* If you upped your scores even a little, it means you are ready, willing, and able. As things at work throw you off track, keep coming back to these competencies. They are your home base—a haven to which you can always return. Just flip to the necessary chapter, grab one of the strategies, and go—reenergized and focused on a more productive way of approaching the problem. Though the terrain of the working world may change, these basic skills will not, so mastery of these workplace mantras will always make you a valued employee. Remain vigilant in your study!

So far, the entire focus of this book has been on fixing you. You've learned fast, simple solutions that require nothing more than a willingness to change your thinking and shift your behavior, just the tiniest bit. A small change in thinking can dramatically alter the timbre of any situation. Consider how your work has changed since you stopped checking e-mail first thing in the morning, or shrank your container by leaving thirty minutes earlier every day, or simply started writing down all your to-dos in one place. Small changes and tiny shifts generate big results.

So now that you are dramatically improved, what if fixing yourself did not fix everything? What could still be wrong?

You may still be wrangling with four issues that definitely qualify as "It's them":

1. Workload
2. Company culture
3. Company changes
4. Compensation

These four qualify as "It's them" because someone other than you makes the decisions about them. Unless you own your own business, you cannot dictate your workload, give yourself a raise, or mandate your company's culture—all these decisions are for "them" to make.

Whether you are ambivalent or dissatisfied about where you stand on these topics, the good news is that you are in a much better place to deal with them. You have boosted your productivity, increased your value to your company, and gained the confidence to deal with these issues effectively. And you can probably take great comfort in the fact that finally, you know it *is* them, and not you.

So should you stick it out? Fight for change? Move on? Negotiate a solution? The choice is yours. With your new skills as your backbone, you can leverage your value and make these decisions from a place of confidence.

"IT'S THEM" Issue 1. **WORKLOAD**

Your job definition and daily responsibilities are the crux of your work experience. Most people crave work that is interesting, challenging, and meaningful, spanning a variety of tasks, with clear priorities and a manageable workload.

What if you are in a work situation where you are unhappy with the actual work you are doing? Perhaps, no matter how efficient you've become, your workload is more than any one human being can realistically manage. Maybe over time you've gotten pulled into tasks that don't play to your strengths or aren't what you bargained for. These days, companies tend to throw projects and tasks at any warm body, regardless of whether that person's specialty is what the task calls for. Perhaps you took your job knowing that you wouldn't love the tasks particular to your position, but you expected to be promoted to the next level fairly quickly. Instead you find yourself stagnating, denied the opportunity to prove yourself on more interesting, higher-level tasks.

Spending the majority of your time wading through tasks that don't show off your best talents can undermine your confidence and hurt your image. If every single task on your to-do list feels like a chore instead of an invigorating challenge, it's hard to enjoy going to work every day. Instead, you end up feeling drained and resentful.

What can you do about it? Do you ask for a new job description? Speak up for help? Find someone to share your workload with? On page 220 you'll read how Alex, one of my clients, leveraged his newfound confidence and skills to make the case for an additional hire.

If you are still feeling overloaded and unhappy with your workload, or are aching for a chance to do more interesting work, take a few tips from Alex:

- **Keep a results-oriented daily log.** You've heard of a results-oriented résumé—where instead of listing your duties, you describe what you actually accomplished at each job. Apply the same principle at work. Your boss may well be distracted by his or her own workload, and unable to comprehend what you do every day. Keep a daily log of what you accomplish. You don't have to detail every single step ("Left message for Bob," "Read over expense forms"), just cut to the chase and articulate what got done: "Reviewed proposal with Bob—asked for lower

——— ALEX

Alex had just landed a big promotion to become vice president of a large division at a pharmaceutical company when we started working together. Upon relocating from a satellite office in San Diego to the corporate HQ in New Jersey, he was immediately overwhelmed. Meetings filled his calendar, there were dozens of direct reports clamoring for his attention, and he could barely make a dent in his to-do list every day. His new boss kept nipping at his heels, saying, "Better, faster, more"— and Alex was trying as hard as he could—but no matter what he did, he couldn't get on top of his workload. Alex called me because he was beginning to wonder if his recent career move was a big mistake. Alex had always taken great pride and pleasure in his work, and now he was doubting his own abilities to get the job done. He was baffled by his predicament. He woke up every morning with a sinking feeling in his stomach, knowing something was terribly wrong, but not knowing whether he was the problem . . . or if it was the job.

As Alex detailed his responsibilities, it was instantly apparent to me that this job was more than one human being could possibly manage, even in a seventy-hour workweek. Alex felt a little relief knowing he wasn't crazy, but to his credit, he requested that I work with him to refine his work habits and time-management skills. He wanted to make sure he was operating at 100 percent peak efficiency before approaching his boss about the situation.

Over the next three months we worked to refine his time-management skills. Alex tracked his accomplishments and activities in a daily log, so that we could review it and make adjustments to his choices along the way. I taught him to do his most critical task first thing in the morning and to manage his energy all day long. He started to use only one planner to track all of his to-dos, and when facing conflicting priorities, he untangled the knot with the 3 Qs and 4 Ds. Alex was a man on a mission: He never dropped the ball, never procrastinated, never forgot anything; he always showed up on time and prepared, ran meetings like clockwork, and managed his employees the same way. This guy was a model of efficiency, never wasting one second of the day.

The daily logs were a testament to his productivity. They also became an invaluable tool to prove the hunch that his job description was an absolutely impossible workload. As we analyzed his log, we could see clearly that Alex spent his time only on tasks directly on the revenue line, and performed them with precision and speed. But each week there were still many critical tasks left undone—and each of those were also one and two steps from the revenue line! Together, we quantified how long each of the undone tasks would take to do, estimating this one at four hours, that one at one hour, and so on, and added it up. My gut reaction to Alex's situation was dead-on: Every single week there was an additional, extraneous sixty hours of work—all one- and two-steppers—on his to-do list, directly on the revenue line of the business. No wonder he was overwhelmed. This wasn't just him—it was a case of THEM!

Armed with this knowledge, Alex went to his boss and successfully pleaded his case for two new hires. Using these logs, he was able to (a) prove in black and white how much he was accomplishing every day and (b) make a case for how hiring another executive and a high-level administrator would help the company generate more revenue. By keeping his focus on one- and two-steppers, he could easily justify the cost of the two salaries to his boss—if the new people were effective, they'd make back their salaries fifty times over. Alex's daily logs also proved invaluable in deciding how to break up his workload, because they detailed exactly what he wasn't getting to. His boss was able to use the log information to write up job descriptions for the new people.

Six months later, with the two new hires in place, Alex began to enjoy his work again. He was working hard, but relishing the joy of completion—feeling confident and back in control again.

bid," "Completed and submitted expense forms." Recording your accomplishments will motivate you to actually complete tasks (instead of just getting started on them), and will become an in-house sales tool for your productivity. If your goal is to make the case for a new hire to help with the workload, you will have tangible evidence of why and what's needed. Keep your results log stored in a folder so the information is at your fingertips when it's time to prepare for performance reviews or ask for a promotion or raise. For example:

DAILY LOG OF ASSISTANT TO MARKETING DIRECTOR

To-dos Accomplished	Undone
• Updated and proofread slides and handouts for presentation—you're all set! • All room arrangements double-checked and confirmed. • Called/wrote to all leads from 5/17 Austin meeting. Sent Harrison a package; he's interested. Will continue to follow up. • Took care of cell phone overcharge—it will be deducted from next bill.	• Call Maribeth re: photo shoot next week. • Write thank-you notes to conference presenters. • E-mail temp agency re: received info about new hires.

- **Ask for more challenging work.** Now that you are more on top of your current workload, you can use your accomplishments to make the case for being assigned to more challenging tasks if that is your goal. But don't expect your boss to immediately trade off the tasks that bore you for more interesting work. You will probably have to do both for a while, until your abilities in the new area are proven. Even then, you'll have to make the case that if you are freed from one set of tasks (by paying someone else to do them), you can bring in more revenue for the company. At that point, perhaps you can offer to train and supervise someone to perform your old, boring tasks.

Of course, there will always be tasks your job requires you to do that you will *never* enjoy, not only because they are boring or may be hard, but because you do not consider them the best use of your talents and abilities. And in most cases you will be unsuccessful at pushing this work off your plate. My advice? Keep doing it as well, and as fast, as you can, then ask for something more interesting. Your boss may not know you detest certain tasks, and while it's not necessarily a good idea to tell her that, you can certainly express what you do like, what really gets you fired up and excited about coming to work. Your boss will probably be happy to let you strut your stuff, but you have to show you can do the other stuff first!

DAILY LOG OF FINANCIAL COMMUNICATIONS MANAGER

To-dos accomplished	Undone
• Drafted copy for direct-mail piece on IRAs. Completed and circulated for comment. • Met with designer on money market brochure artwork; will have sample 7/2. • Analyzed return rate on September mutual fund mailing—shows strong response rate of 5%.	• Meet with Diane (direct report). • Write mutual fund test copy.

"IT'S THEM" Issue 2. COMPANY CULTURE

Company culture is a mood, a tone, a style of interacting, or a way of doing business that permeates the entire company. It is established by the people at the top and filtered down through every transaction, every decision, every employee. Some companies have a formal culture, others a casual one; some are collaborative and team-based, while others are hierarchical and competitive. Some cultures are based on trusting and empowering their employees, while others are based on second-guessing everything everyone does. It's essential that you work for a company where the culture is a fit, if you are to enjoy going to work every day.

When a clash with the company culture is subtle, we can get stuck and caught. One of the biggest traps that people in this situation fall into is thinking something is wrong with them. When you are in a culture that is not a fit for you, it can be a huge assault on your self-esteem. Nothing you do is right, or accepted; you feel like the odd man out—as if everyone else understands something you don't. It is extremely hard to keep your ego intact when you are in the minority.

No matter how willing you are to stretch, grow, and adapt, it can be nearly impossible to change yourself to fit the culture without abandoning your ideals, values, and ethics. How do you adapt? One option is to simply accept the culture and stop trying to fight it—to see it for what it is and focus on the value you get.

If your company's culture is not an ideal fit, take a few tips from Brenda:

BRENDA

Brenda was an adviser at a top financial firm. A caring soul with extremely high ethics, Brenda was the antithesis of the hard-core salesperson out to make the fast buck. Revered in the business for the deep, trusting relationship she established with each client and the quiet, studied patience she used to woo new business over the long term, Brenda often found herself in conflict with her coworkers and bosses.

The culture on Wall Street was cutthroat and very bottom-line-driven. The pressure to be consistently profitable was so fierce that many of her colleagues routinely rushed clients to make a quick sale so they could meet short-term profit expectations. In Brenda's eyes they were a soulless, careless bunch, only out for themselves. She just wasn't willing to compromise her integrity by hard-selling clients; but she too was required to hit certain short-term numbers, just like her coworkers. If she didn't, her compensation, even her job security, would suffer.

During our first session, Brenda told me how she'd contemplated leaving the firm to start her own, smaller investment firm. She dreamed about a work life with less pressure to prove herself every day or risk being cut. But starting her own business presented its own challenges—and though the culture of her current employer was not ideal, Brenda knew that the resources, support, and possibilities that her global firm could provide to her clients were unmatchable in a small-scale business. By staying, she could ultimately help serve the clients she cared about better.

As much as she despised the culture, she chose to stay, devising a way to keep meeting her numbers without sacrificing the integrity her clients relied on her for. Brenda's reputation for wooing clients over the long term was well founded—she regularly took *a year or two* to land new business, while her coworkers rarely took longer than a few months. It was slow and old-fashioned, but it worked; she had secured some of the biggest accounts in the company. This kind of intense, prolonged courtship required regular lunches and conference calls, e-mails and personal notes—not tasks that fit easily into her fast-paced days.

In order to meet her short-term numbers, Brenda learned to make better use of her assistant—training and empowering her to close the smaller sales quickly, making up in volume for the short term what was required to meet the numbers. By mastering her delegation skills, Brenda was freed to concentrate her efforts on the longer-term courtships. She ended up with a very loyal team beneath her, and a slow, steady rise within the company—reaching an impressively high status through less conventional means. It took patience, diligence, and a constant inward focus to remember who she was, trust her own values, and work within the culture. Working around the culture without sacrificing her values, Brenda maintained her integrity, and even found a few others in the company who appreciated her style.

- **Earn respect and build credibility.** If you are at odds with the culture of your workplace, do the best you can to avoid it by quietly going about your work. You still may feel like the odd man out, and you may not get invited to tag along with the in-crowd for lunch; but your coworkers will respect you for the work you accomplish. You can be a team player and collaborative partner without sacrificing your core beliefs.
- **Find an advocate/buddy.** Sometimes all you need is one person at the job who believes in you, sees your value, and advocates for you. Whether it's a boss, someone in senior management, or a coworker or assistant, validating each other's beliefs, approach, or style is enormously encouraging. When you find the advocate/buddy, be warned—keep it positive. Rather than spend all your time whining and complaining about the culture, band together to share strategies for coping, adapting, and succeeding in this slightly misfit environment.
- **Focus on the positive.** A situation is never all bad or all good. Even if you are put off by the culture of your workplace, focus on what you're gaining from it, what you can learn from that culture. What are the positive aspects of the culture? Brenda recognized that the resources her firm provided were more important than the company's less-than-perfect culture. What do you value about your workplace? The paycheck? Flexibility? Challenge of day-to-day tasks? Concentrating on that can help to keep the situation positive.

"IT'S THEM" Issue 3. **COMPANY CHANGES**

Change is the only constant in the new world of work. Every day, companies merge, departments are reconfigured, bosses are rotated, coworkers vanish, and hey—you may even play musical desks! Or musical buildings! No matter how you felt about the way things were—whether you were happy in your situation or not—change is unsettling. When things change, all your systems and sense of security are up for grabs.

Change can undermine your confidence and comfort on the job. Somehow you've established a routine, and suddenly it no longer works. Or let's say a new boss is hired to lead the revitalization of your division. Suddenly your status as a top performer is leveled, and you have to prove yourself all over again. An abrupt drop in status or threat to your individuality can be humiliating, while the introduction of new rules and regimentation may erase any sense of freedom you once enjoyed. And to think all of this happens without anyone asking you first!

What if you don't like the changes? How do you cope when your once perfect model situation is suddenly imperfect? Do you dig in your heels and fight? Do you run and hide under your desk? Can you stop the change from taking place? How can you make the change easier for yourself?

When a change is imposed from the outside, for any of us, it can make us feel powerless. These changes may not be your choice, but you need to turn it around on yourself. If this is the reality, what can you do to adapt to it?

If you're feeling powerless and angry because of a change, take these tips from Lilly:

- **Don't look to the past during a time of change.** Looking to the past when everyone else is trying desperately to move forward prevents all involved from moving swiftly. You become the anchor, the weight, holding everyone, including yourself, down. It may feel like an abrupt shifting of gears—but that's precisely what you have to do. During a time of change, you can't make assumptions. The old rules don't apply. Pay attention and stop interpreting things in relation to what used to be. Don't compare. Take in the new facts so that you can respond to reality instead of your images of the good old days. Be willing to look forward and embrace new ideas.
- **Be the host, not the guest.** Change is hard on everyone. Instead of waiting for others to help you adjust, take on the job of lead-

LILLY

As long as I'd known Lilly, she had loved being a teacher—a creative, dynamic, and smart woman, she'd been fulfilled by her work her entire life. She was beginning her twenty-fifth year in the same public school system when, with no warning, along came a new administration.

Within weeks of the new administration's reign, Lilly's exuberance was replaced with despair. "Work is horrible! Just horrible!" The new administration was "teaching to the tests," altering curriculums, and forcing teachers to teach a certain way. The lack of classroom freedom and creative expression filled Lilly with rage, especially because it was what she excelled at and had prided herself on for twenty-four years. She felt as if the rug had been swiped out from under her. The new emphasis on "meeting the standards" was in direct conflict with her philosophy of education. She made minimal attempts to learn the new material, and on the occasions that she was observed in the classroom, she defiantly blended in some of her own traditional, creative methods with the new curriculum.

Lilly had always been a can-do, positive person who got along well with her coworkers and boss. Outgoing and vocal, she spoke out against the changes at several staff meetings, expecting everyone to jump in with their shared cries of protest. She was surprised when most of the other teachers stayed silent. There was a creepy feeling that they'd gone from working in an open environment, where different opinions and debate were welcomed, to a McCarthy-era state where anyone who spoke out against the new regime suddenly vanished from the system. In frequent, spontaneous conversations with her principal, Lilly often lamented about how dangerous and ridiculous the new approach seemed. That relationship was one of the few remaining in which she felt truly comfortable. You can imagine her shock during her year-end review when she learned that she'd been put on probation "for failure to conform"—by the very principal she'd confided in. It was a big, heartbreaking betrayal that seemed wholly unfair.

I asked Lilly if she was thinking of leaving. She wasn't, absolutely not. First, she loved the kids and couldn't imagine abandoning them now. What else would she do? She had twenty-five years invested in this place! That brought up the real issue: she was five years shy of retirement, and leaving now would mean sacrificing a quarter-century of investment. She wasn't willing to walk away. In fact, she was compelled to fight back.

The next year was miserable. Lilly brought her "probation" review to the teacher's union in an attempt to clear her record; she felt misled, even sabotaged, by her principal, in whom she had confided without reservation, and wanted to strike back. She did her best to avoid being in the same room as her principal, but the tension and stress was so intense during the union dispute that it made Lilly sick. She was taking antidepressants and antianxiety medication, and enduring regular panic attacks. Eventually, as Lilly realized how physically ill and mentally strained this fight was making her, she decided to look inside herself and see what she could do to improve the situation.

After two weeks of intense soul-searching, Lilly acknowledged that her principal was not initiating this change; she was simply the spokesperson assigned its implementation. And although Lilly's principal wasn't doing the greatest job helping teachers adapt to the new order of things, Lilly couldn't hold the woman solely accountable for upending her world. To improve the situation, Lilly knew she needed to do an about-face, and morph her attitude from negative and inflexible to one of positive reliability. Lilly took it upon herself to study and master the new curriculum, determined to excel at its delivery, whether she agreed with it or not.

Lilly had been so laser-focused on being the victim—so angry at what everyone else had been forcing her to do—that she'd lost her sense of control. Once she let go of that anger, the tension between her and her coworkers dissipated almost immediately, and she could see that they were all in this together.

ing the way. With a job to do, you are empowered, and take the focus off your suffering. Make the change as easy on your boss as possible. See what you can do to make everyone else comfortable. Don't demonstrate resistance or anger too freely. Be the positive one. Being willing and cooperative about change— even if you aren't thrilled about it—will make you more valuable. Take the reins and create more value for yourself. If you're stuck in a rut, a change is the perfect time to redefine your value, a chance to learn new skills or take on a new point of view. Help the company manage itself through this growth, and you are likely to grow, too. Company changes may occur without your consent, but that doesn't mean you can't capitalize on the opportunity to make a change too.

"IT'S THEM" Issue 4. **COMPENSATION**

Your compensation is a statement of the value of your work to your company. It's a deal you want to feel good about, whether you measure your compensation by the size of your paycheck, time off, benefits, bonuses, gifts, opportunities, or status. Each company has its own money culture, and we all aspire to be treated as well as is feasible within the confines of the organization we work for. If you feel dissatisfied with your compensation, you are certainly in a stronger position to negotiate for more now that you have improved your productivity and performance.

In some cases, improving your performance may simply save you from losing your job. Think long and hard about what position you really began in and where you are now. Are you now meeting expectations or exceeding them in your company's eyes? Did you pull yourself up from the bottom 20 percent into the middle 60 percent (meeting expectations)? Or have you lifted yourself from the 60 percent group into the top 20 percent (exceeding them)? In any case, it's probably wise just to sit tight for a while and demonstrate your ability to consistently deliver higher results before going in for a raise.

But no matter how much you have improved, before you start thinking that the world now owes you for improving your own job performance—stop. This is *not* a claim to entitlement. Your compensation is a reflection of the value the company places on the work itself, not on you personally. For all the psychology and emotion and personality that are wrapped up in your work, in the end it's not about what *you* are worth as a person. It's about what *it*—the product, the service, the result—is worth to the people who are paying you to make it happen.

Every encounter you have at work is an even exchange, or should be. The strength of your working relationship depends on your ability to find the balance between the value you offer (knowledge of the field, contacts, history with the company) and how you value your compensation—in salary, experience, health care, lifestyle. Where you set that balance will naturally morph over a career, as your goals change and grow. And that's normal. It's when the delicate *value equation* is upset—meaning you're getting more out of your em-

ROBERT

Robert was the solitary in-house counsel for an international nonprofit. After seven years in corporate law, taking that job had meant a pay cut, but it didn't matter. For the first time in a long time, his work felt meaningful and important. Life was good.

Five years after making the change, Robert met a woman, fell in love, and got married. He still loved his job, but his financial needs changed. He and his wife both loved the country and dreamed of owning a country home, where they could spend half their time. In Robert's former corporate law career, money would never have been the issue—he could have purchased a little country bungalow without blinking. But now, even though he made a fair and comfortable salary, he wasn't making enough to get a home, or to cut back his hours and take a further pay cut. Robert still loved his job, and though his needs were changing, he had to come up with a solution within the confines of his nonprofit, where there was a limit to the funding available for staff salaries.

Robert created a long-term five-year plan that fused his personal goals with the organization's needs. His plan was to find a way to increase his pay over the next five years, save the additional money, and then cut back his hours without cutting his pay. Here's how he did it.

A specialist in international law, he offered to take on outside clients on behalf of the nonprofit, generating increased revenue for the organization while increasing his bonus pay. This was a no-lose proposition for his company. Over the next five years he increased their client base, developed his skill set and knowledge, and built a network of loyal lawyers around the world to whom he subcontracted work to manage the increased workload. He socked the extra money away, and halfway through the fourth year, Robert and his wife purchased their country getaway; then, in the fifth year (his tenth with the organization), he made his move.

By this point, Robert knew his value. He was the only attorney in a large organization where nobody else had the skills or the knowledge to do what he did. It had taken him a long time to develop the systems he used, and he was able to work at peak efficiency, because he'd been doing his job for so long. He had become a legal powerhouse and was providing tremendous value and integrity to his organization. Coming from that place of confidence, Robert set out to eliminate some of his responsibilities, reduce his hours, and retain his salary, so he could start spending three full days each week in the country.

Robert spun off all of his nonlegal tasks to three colleagues who'd been with the organization as long as he had, spreading the work among them so that no one's workload was maxed out. We estimated that he could generate as much money through legal work alone in four days a week as he'd previously made in five. Robert's excellent work record, strong working relationships, and long-standing commitment to the health and mission of the organization made having this conversation with the executive director and board members possible. They recognized the value of Robert's contribution, no matter how many days each week he was actually working, and agreed to a three-and-a-half-day workweek.

Three years later, Robert's schedule is still working. It hasn't been totally smooth—there are times when his legal subcontractors are unavailable and he gets stuck with an extra day or two of work—but it's closer than ever to what he wanted. He consciously lets people know what he's getting done on behalf of the company (especially the naysayers, who resent his part-time schedule), and he's quick to note that the moment he can't produce the results he's promised in the four-day time frame he's allowed himself, his employers have a right to take issue with his schedule.

ployer than your employer is getting from you, or vice versa—that dissatisfaction and resentment problems at work usually begin.

If you want to improve your compensation by asking for a raise or a promotion, or by taking advantage of flex hours, take a few tips from Robert:

- **Take the long view.** Plan ahead and be patient. It's your responsibility to ask for what you want. A plan can energize you and make even the most difficult situation tolerable. Then, when you are ready, ask for what you need. Your employers are not mind readers. The likelihood of your boss calling you into his office and saying, "Well, we're giving you the opportunity to work four days a week, and, oh, here's two more weeks' vacation and a $7,000 raise," is slim to none.

- **Market yourself.** Don't be shy! It's your responsibility to make your boss and coworkers aware of the value you are providing. Letting other people know what you've accomplished is not being showy or self-centered, it's essential in a highly distracting environment where your boss and coworkers are too busy dealing with their own crises to be aware of what you're getting done. There are several ways to do this. Robert sent out a weekly memo in the form of an e-mail update to let people know what was happening. It was a concise list that simply stated his weekly victories. He found that incorporating a little humor in the body of the e-mail (jokes, funny stories, or industry references) was helpful in disarming the skeptics. He also understood the importance of face time, and he made sure he had a few quality moments with his bosses and direct reports at least once every two weeks.

- **Make a no-risk offer to your employer.** If you want to make more money, consider trying a new initiative—selling a new product, generating more repeat customers—and if your initiative is a success (you and your boss must agree on what success means), then you get that raise or bonus based on it. When you're asking for a raise, more time off, or better benefits, be sure you tell your boss how it will benefit the company. Illuminate how your employer will profit by paying for, say, graduate school. Robert's five-year ramp-up included the development of a team of support lawyers that the organization could call upon if Robert was unavailable. Eventually, he was preparing the organization for his succession. But by demonstrating his commitment to helping the company achieve its mission as well as his own, he only increased his value to the company over time. Every employer wants its employees completely devoted to its success. If you want to be more challenged at work, accompany your pitch to higher-ups with a timeline and step-by-step process, so they can see that you've thought through the added responsibility and will still be able to get your work done.

THE CHOICE IS YOURS

Work tasks, culture, change, and compensation are all big issues that are beyond your direct control and affect the quality of your work life. Regardless of what situation you're dealing with, you have two options: You can either negotiate for change by confronting the issues head-on, or let it roll off your back.

Grab-and-Go Strategy #31
Negotiate for Change

Negotiating for what you want is not easy; you're putting yourself out there with a real chance of hearing the word "no." Before confronting the situation, reinforce your confidence in your value. If you are raising the issue (whether it's compensation, workload, or whatever), your job is to enter that discussion armed with ideas for solving the problem. It's up to you to take charge and ask for exactly what you need.

Beware that even the most well-thought-out, reasonable proposals are often nixed because of external realities beyond even your boss's control.

Use the TALK formula to get your point across with clarity and respect.

> **T**ell 'em what you need
> **A**sk for their reaction
> **L**isten as much as you talk
> **K**eep it about the work

TELL 'EM WHAT YOU NEED

Be calm, clear, simple, and direct, and always come prepared with a few different ideas for solutions. No matter what issue you are confronting, adapt the same upbeat, firm, unapologetic approach. Demonstrate with your demeanor, words, and actions that you are looking to fix the problem, not create a conflict.

For example:

- "I know the company needs me to do data entry, but if I could do one creative task a day, I would feel more balanced." —*Administrative assistant*
- "Ideally, I'd like to be the front person for all clients. For now, I'd like to handle at least one client on my own, to gain the experience and show you what I can do."—*Sales associate*
- "I know that I need to do these reports, but if I could have someone help me process them, it would free me up to work with clients."—*Broker*

- "I'd like to be able to help develop the concepts, and not spend all of my time implementing the details."—*Magazine editor*

ASK FOR THEIR REACTION

Once you've made your case, ask what they think of your proposal. Is it reasonable? Does it seem fair? Do they foresee any obstacles you haven't already pointed out?

Do not make assumptions or anticipate a negative reaction from the other person. Projecting worry that they won't like your ideas or are expecting an argument is a recipe for unnecessary conflict. You have an enormous amount of influence over the tone of the discussion in the way you set it up. Most people come from a place of integrity—treat them as though they do, by granting them the opportunity to respond to your proposal. Be genuine in asking for their reaction, by demonstrating an open and positive mind-set with your voice, face, and body language. Convey that your goal is to find a win-win solution fair to both of you.

LISTEN AS MUCH AS YOU TALK

When you are nervous, it's easy to fall into the trap of talking nonstop, trying to anticipate the other person's objections before they even raise them, then convincing, cajoling, and explaining why they should see things your way in a nonstop monologue. We've all been on the receiving end of one of those monologues. It's miserable and unproductive. Listening is a great sign of respect. It also gives you the opportunity to learn how your boss thinks, understand what she needs, and grasp what her goals are. Only by listening astutely can you find the true win-win. Your goals may be different and that's okay; your job in listening is to find out where they intersect.

Obviously, your company wants to spend as little money as possible to get the most from its workers. However, if it values longevity, or the knowledge you have so that you can teach young upstarts as they come in, you can find your value increased. As you listen to their reaction, try to discern what is most important to them, then frame your solution to the problem in a light that shows the benefits to both of you. What's the win-win in each of these situations?

- After you talk to your boss about flextime, he says, "I can appreciate that you want to spend more time with your kids, but I'm afraid your direct reports will be left without enough guidance."

The win-win? Show your boss that you've thought through this issue, because you, too, thought it might be a problem. Share your solutions. Also mention that flextime will ensure you are focused 100 percent on the work while at the office— no kids' doctor's appointments or piano lessons. Those kinds of appointments would be saved for your two days at home, leaving your time in the office distraction free—a bonus to any employer.

- After you talk to your boss about your workload, she says, "I'm stumped. I just don't know who else can do what you do."

  The win-win? What is the boss really saying? It sounds like she values your contribution so much so that she doesn't think anyone else can do it. Prove it to her by showcasing your delegation skills. Assure her that someone else can do what you do (you'll train them to do it!), and ask if she is open to letting you test-run a few tasks. Also explain that you want to keep delivering on your most critical tasks, but are finding it harder and harder to concentrate as your to-do list grows. By reaching out for help, you are trying to find a way to keep producing.

- You approach your manager about helping you pay for graduate school. He says, "I don't know if we've ever done that before. How long is your program?"

  The win-win? Having your employer pay for graduate school, especially if it's not something they do regularly, is a big deal. Assure your boss of your commitment to the company— you don't want them to think that you would get your degree and run! Help them understand that this is an investment in human capital that will pay them back tenfold.

KEEP IT ABOUT THE WORK

Have you ever seen the movie *Dragnet*? You know, Officer Joe Friday and Sgt. Frank Smith—"Just the facts, ma'am, just the facts"? Emotions have a way of clouding our judgment and making it difficult to stay focused. When you're having a conversation as intense as one like this can be, the surest, fastest way to get yourself stuck and angry is to permit yourself an emotional response. Stay calm. Remember— in most cases, the most straightforward interpretation is the right one. Focus on what is being said, not how it's being communicated.

For example:

You've worked up the nerve to discuss your overwhelming workload with your boss and request a shift in some of your tasks. The conversation seems to go well, but at the end, your boss says, "Let me sleep on this one."

Possible emotional responses:

- Oh, great. I have *no* power. Nothing I do to improve my performance will ever make him value me as much as everyone else. He doesn't care that I'm burned out and practically drag myself to the office every day.
- Ha! I knew even attempting this conversation was pointless. I bet he'll use the fact that I brought this concern up in the first place to block my promotion next year. He probably thinks I'm a crybaby who wants special treatment.
- Oh, sure. He's going to "sleep on it." I'll bet he's just avoiding saying no right away—he'll probably never get back to me on this.

Possible neutral responses:

- Wow—he didn't give me an immediate no. It seems like he's willing to figure out a way to make it work.
- I suppose this whole idea was a lot to throw at him all at once. It makes sense that he would need a little time to think it through.
- He may want to run it by his boss, to make sure that my ideas won't cause too many other waves in the department.

Bringing up any situation you're unhappy about is not for the fainthearted. Having these conversations is a hard thing to do well. The most difficult part, though, is that initiating any negotiation places the responsibility squarely on your shoulders. If you bring it up, you are the one who needs to be able to articulate the problem and suggest a fair solution, all while approaching the topic in a way that minimizes conflict (even though you may be unhappy, or even angry with the situation) and establishes common ground.

Bringing an issue to your boss in the right way can be advantageous—you make your voice heard, gain respect from higher-ups, and maybe even get what you want. But before you dive headlong into negotiations, make sure you've really thought through the situation, and are prepared to handle outcomes good *and* bad.

HOT TIPS!

1. **Always ask for an appointment.** Broaching important topics impulsively, on the spur of the moment, will catch your boss off guard, make her defensive, and put you at an immediate disadvantage. Try to set your appointment for a time when there are no immediate deadlines or extra pressures on your boss—during lunch or right after work are usually two safe bets.

2. **Pick the right location.** Your comfort, and your boss's, are important when having a negotiation conversation. Consider whether your office (where you're most comfortable) or your boss's office (most formal) would be most appropriate and conducive to an upbeat, open conversation. Or try for a neutral location off-site, so no one's at a power advantage.

3. **Limit the time . . . and topics.** Thirty minutes keeps the pressure off and the conversation concise and controlled. Even if you have a whole laundry list of issues, never attempt to resolve more than three problems at a time.

4. **Write it down.** Nothing focuses your thoughts better than writing them down. A bulleted list will keep you on point and curb repetition.

5. **Acknowledge your boss's reality.** Build rapport and reduce defensiveness by demonstrating your genuine understanding of your boss's situation. Recognize the pressures and limitations unique to the company and your boss, as well as appreciating what they have done for you. Entering a conversation rooted in this basic human understanding builds confidence, reduces defensiveness, and engenders receptivity to solutions ("I know you are . . ."; "I appreciate the way you . . .").

Grab-and-Go Strategy #32
Let It Roll off Your Back

In handling the big four "It's them" issues, another option is to just let things roll off your back. This choice is not about apathy, or being wimpy—it's often about having the wisdom to recognize that some things don't matter, or are not worth the battle; it's about managing your *reaction* to the things you don't like, rather than trying to change the source of your displeasure. Allowing things to roll off your back is a key to stress management. It's about releasing things you cannot control.

Now, I'm not much of a sports fan, but a sports analogy comes to mind. Star athletes are geniuses on the field because they perfect everything that's within their power—speed, strength, and power of concentration. Then they acknowledge the "uncontrollables"—the referee, the opposing team, the weather, the condition of the field. They don't waste energy complaining about these uncontrollables, or fighting against them; they overcome them. And they still come out making the shot. In tennis, compare Vitas Gerulaitis with John McEnroe. McEnroe was legendary for his temper tantrums on the court—challenging decisions by the judges, railing against the uncontrollables. Ultimately, his crusades didn't influence the judges; like Gerulaitis, he had to adjust his game to the unfair calls. Both were champs, but one was a cool, calm pro, and the other had a red face and high blood pressure. Which would you rather be?

Often the ability to let things roll off your back is a matter of putting things in perspective. So you may not have a corner desk, but your company has enormous respect for your ideas and you have a lot of creative expression. Okay, the culture isn't ideal, but there are opportunities to make excellent contacts for future employment. Sure, this merger is miserable and tense, but it's a chance to develop a tough skin and work on your people-management skills.

Grab-and-Go Strategy #33
Develop Selective Vision

Letting something roll off your back is easier if you develop selective vision. Compartmentalize your thoughts, paying attention to the positive elements of your job and tuning out the points of dissatisfaction. Focus on why you are choosing to stay in this job—what are you getting out of it. For as long as you choose to stay at your job, recognize that it is your own *choice* that puts you back in a position of power.

How do you know when to fight for something and when to let it roll off your back? If your timing is off (a crisis at work happens, your boss is fired, the culmination of a year's worth of work is two weeks away), let it go for now. It's always better to study the situation before you make your move. Then look around. Use your powers of observation. Has your boss made changes in the past when asked? What is the industry standard—and how reasonable does it seem to ask for an exception to that standard for yourself? Have accommodations been made for others in your organization? How important is the matter, really? Is it about ego or the work? Stay away from issues that are about ego and pride; you'll likely never win. Never bother with issues that are merely an annoyance but not a direct affront to your success. But if the situation is jeopardizing your job security or your ability to accomplish your critical responsibilites, then it's worth a fight.

Keep in mind that all jobs have their ups and downs. As one wise friend said to me, "Whether you like it or whether you hate it, don't get comfortable, because things are bound to change." This new world of work will keep throwing you off your game, raising the bar of mastery, requiring you to continually work to perfect your skills.

No matter what frustrations and difficulties you face at work, remember that the solution always lies inside you. Whether it's you or it's them, keep turning the focus back on yourself. Stop looking outside yourself for the change; turn your attention inward and do what you can to take control. Go back over the competencies, improve your performance, change your reaction, focus on the work, do your job. It takes constant attention to keep these competencies sharp. When you're having trouble, flip back to a relevant chapter and see what you can glean from it that time around. Take your temperature. Remember, one small change in your own behavior can have a huge impact.

Grab-and-Go Strategy #34
When You're Thrown Off Track,
Always Go Back to Competency 1

No matter how what's going on with your job, on the days when you feel like you are losing your grip, when you don't get what you want, when your to-do list is a mile long, when you have a disagreement with your boss—and all of these things will happen—it's important to remember to let go and regrab, to leave work behind for a moment to regain your perspective and get you back in step. Keep coming back to the first competency—embracing your work/life balance.

In fact, go reskim that chapter before putting this book back up on the shelf. It is too easy for all us high achievers in the world to be swept up by our careers. There will always be more that we can do to be better, faster, smarter, more competitive, less vulnerable, and further ahead of the pack.

The people who keep landing on their feet, continuing their success over the long term, are those who cultivate sources of self-esteem and recognition outside work—who know how to let go and regrab. No matter what calamity happens in the office, they are always able to draw new strength and energy from the inside out. They have the energy to try new things, win big, lose big, and always recover. They are resilient.

The competencies in this book will guide you throughout your career, in any job, in any situation.

No matter where your travels lead you, in the business that is you, here's to your power in making work work.

Chapter Summary
LEVERAGE YOUR VALUE

Which grab-and-go strategies do you plan to use?

- Negotiate for change.
- Let it roll off your back.
- Develop selective vision.
- Always go back to competency one.

When do you plan to implement them?

What do you think will be your biggest obstacle in applying the strategies?

How will you overcome that obstacle?

What is your motivation for mastering this competency?

Index

About the Author

Julie Morgenstern is the founder and owner of Task Masters, an organizing and time management consulting service for individuals and corporations. Her corporate clients have included American Express, Microsoft, IKEA, and the Miami Heat.

She is the author of the *New York Times* bestseller *Organizing from the Inside Out* and *Time Management from the Inside Out*. Julie and her teenage daughter Jessi coauthored *Organizing from the Inside Out for Teens*.

Julie is a monthly columnist for *O, The Oprah Magazine*. She has also been a guest on many national television and radio programs, including *The Oprah Winfrey Show, Today,* and NPR's *Fresh Air*.

A speaker, media expert, and corporate spokesperson, she lives in New York City.